Next Generation Ireland

Edited by

ED BURKE AND RONAN LYONS

BLACKHALL
Publishing

Published by Blackhall Publishing
Lonsdale House
Avoca Avenue
Blackrock
Co. Dublin
Ireland

e-mail: info@blackhallpublishing.com
www.blackhallpublishing.com

ISBN: 978-1-84218-211-6

A catalogue record for this book is available from the British Library.

Printed and bound in Great Britain by MPG Books Ltd., Cornwall.

To my mother and in memory of my father
– Ronan Lyons

Foreword

Shane Ross

Do we need to start again?

Ireland is on its back, but this book is not about past sins. Neither does it pander to the palpable anger of the Irish nation against the sinners. It recognises the nation's near-death experience and plots the road to resurrection. No less.

Such ambition, expressed here by the youth of a country at rock bottom, reflects the attitudes of young Ireland. The authors are from the 'can-do' generation. All contributors are under the age of forty. All share a common determination: to fix a politically and economically dysfunctional state. Thank God we still have them among us. Some of the authors have temporarily left our shores, but with the determination to return to Ireland.

As 2010 closed, Ireland was in a state of quasi-despair. We had lost our economic sovereignty to external forces. The IMF was no longer at the door; it was squatting in Government Buildings in Merrion Street. Students were marching, negative equity was growing and so was unemployment. A punitive December Budget had crippled an already concussed nation. A general election was looming, promising the same old tribal politics. The banks were bust. And so, people thought, was the nation. Perhaps, just perhaps, there was something terminally wrong with Ireland?

The ideas in this book will lift readers' spirits high enough to convince them that the disease is not terminal, and its contents might just persuade us that those who have created Ireland's mayhem are not the ideal people to lift us out of it. There is an army of untainted youth brimming with ideas, waiting in the wings.

This book is radical. It is hopeful. And it is realistic. It addresses the political system that has allowed the crisis to climax. It tackles the economic catastrophe and questions our foreign policy. It refuses to allow the next generation to accept the incarceration of thought that has captured its predecessors. That is the beauty of the work inside.

The book does not provide all the answers, but it carries a subliminal message: there is a future for Ireland. Gloom may be today's prevailing sentiment but let us turn our back on the old official Ireland of banking oligarchs, social partnership, mighty mandarins and state monopolies. That model is horribly broken. Today's leaders, whether politicians or officials, offer few fresh solutions. They have readily accepted a future path dictated to them by powerful insiders in cahoots with global bankers. It is time to question the old guard's ways and to discard their ideas. The year 2011 could mark a watershed in Irish history.

The political crisis is well addressed in this book. Reform is advocated. Think of the Cabinet of 2010. The Taoiseach Brian Cowen, his Tánaiste Mary Coughlan and his Finance Minister Brian Lenihan all sprang from powerful political dynasties. Each one has pedigrees that virtually dictated their career paths. Similarly, Enda Kenny's father was a prominent Fine Gael TD. Loyalty to tribe often took precedence over loyalty to country. Cronyism, the inevitable consequence of such a system, became embedded.

Cronyism has run riot in Ireland. State companies and agencies have been corrupted by party loyalties, while boards were stuffed with friends and relations of the ruling class. Good governance suffered. Greed flourished. Similarly, the banking industry was characterised by a clique of middle-aged men (and nearly all men) massaging each other's interests within an inner circle of Irish oligarchs. The oligarchy included developers, civil servants, politicians and regulators.

The economic crisis, while joined at the hip to the banking debacle, reflects the recklessness of the same elite circle with the finances of the nation. They borrowed, they spent, they won elections and many lined their own pockets while impoverishing the citizens.

The next generation has been forced to pick up the tab. Instead, in this book, it has picked up the gauntlet. It explores the options through the eyes of the generation that will be cursed – or blessed – with the task of implementing the changes needed.

Surprisingly, the authors do not yield to the temptation to fulminate against the waste and cronyism of their predecessors. Nor do they wail

– as well they might – over the weight of debt bequeathed to them. They seize the problem by the scruff of the neck, take the challenges head-on and tackle them fearlessly.

The thorniest of problems – the public service – is forensically examined. The tough choices that will decide the future of the environment are not ducked, while the sensitivities and evasion that characterise the debate over immigration are radically addressed, along with the future direction of foreign policy.

This is not a familiar book, covering the ground of the ancient battles of the Roman Catholic ethos, the liberal agenda or social partnership. It is neither a narrative of the economic crisis, nor a long moan about the banking catastrophe or our deep indebtedness. It is a roadmap for a bright future for Ireland. It is a reminder of all that is hopeful.

Take a walk down Dublin's Barrow Street and pass the European headquarters of Google. Head for the Sandyford Business Park on the outskirts of the capital and enter the premises of Microsoft. Hewlett Packard and Facebook have followed suit with investments to demonstrate that others from far-off lands have voted confidence in the Irish economy. It is a vote of confidence in young Ireland, who form the bulk of their employees.

That generation, the generation of this book, is better educated, more confident and less inhibited by past taboos than any previous one. It carries neither an inferiority complex about the 'old enemy' nor any fears of the new competition. It has tangible results to show for its energy and abilities, not least in the stock of foreign direct investment in Ireland. Total investment by US firms in Ireland now stands at €130 billion, more than the combined US investment into Brazil, Russia, India and China. This investment generates spending of €15 billion a year in Ireland.

It is clear that the rest of the world is not giving up on Ireland. They acknowledge our business environment, our skills, our European Union membership and our entrepreneurial culture. The message is clear: Ireland has both advantage and opportunity on our side, we must not write ourselves off.

No, we do not need to start again. We need to weed out the excesses and the culture of old Ireland, to put in place a new system and to encourage the young entrepreneurs and thinkers who will lead the recovery.

Over to the under-forties.

Acknowledgements

Putting together a volume like this is easy, once you have the right friends! The editors would particularly like to thank Shane Ross, who has always listened to and encouraged voices from a new generation. Long the scourge of the cronyism that has brought Ireland so low, he is also keen to recognise the strength of new ideas. His vote of confidence in the idea behind this book – and the ideas in this book – means a lot to us.

Much gratitude is due also to Blackhall Publishing, who backed this project from the beginning, including Ailbhe O'Reilly, Elizabeth Brennan and especially Eileen O'Brien, who worked tirelessly and with great patience to smoothen the edges of this book.

Each of the contributors took time from more profitable ventures to tackle critical and complex challenges to Irish policy. Asking people to develop a strategy completely reforming an area of Irish policy in language accessible to the non-expert is no average request, and yet they met that challenge head-on. The contributors have poured hundreds of hours into thinking and writing about their country's future for this book. The experience of working with such a varied and exceptional group of people has been a welcome tonic to the lethargic pessimism that has gripped much of the national discourse.

A constructive debate of ideas is at the root of the motivation behind this book. Thanks to all, from policy-makers and diplomats to academics and journalists, who took the time to discuss the writing of the individual chapters of this book with its authors. We hope the finished product offers some reward.

Finally, the editors would like to thank their families and friends in Ireland, the UK and Afghanistan who put up with anti-social absences and long policy monologues during the gestation of this book.

Ed Burke and Ronan Lyons
Cork/Kabul and Dublin/Oxford
February 2011

Contents

List of Abbreviations

American Ireland Funds	AIF
Bord Gáis Éireann	BGE
Border, Midland and Western Regional Assembly	BMW Regional Assembly
Brazil, Russia, India and China	BRIC
British–Irish Council	BIC
British–Irish Intergovernmental Conference	BIIC
British–Irish Parliamentary Assembly	BIPA
building energy rating	BER
Capital Acquisitions Tax	CAT
Capital Gains Tax	CGT
carbon dioxide	CO_2
carbon dioxide equivalent	CO_2-eq
Central Statistics Office	CSO
Commission for Energy Regulation	CER
Committee for Civilian Aspects of Crisis Management	CIVCOM
Common Agricultural Policy	CAP
Common Foreign and Security Policy	CFSP
Common Security and Defence Policy	CSDP
Competiveness Effects of Environmental Tax Reform	COMETR
Córas Iompair Éireann	CIE
Danish Energy Agency	DEA
Democratic Unionist Party	DUP
Department of Foreign Affairs	DFA
Economic and Financial Council	ECOFIN
Economic and Monetary Union	EMU
Economic and Social Research Institute	ESRI
Economic Research Institute of Northern Ireland	ERINI

Education System Development Plans	ESDPs
electric vehicle	EV
Electricity Supply Board	ESB
Emissions Trading Scheme	ETS
Environmental Protection Agency	EPA
Environmental Resources Management	ERM
erasable programmable memory chip	EPROM
European Economic Community	EEC
European External Action Service	EEAS
European Union Police Mission in Bosnia	EUPM
foreign direct investment	FDI
Foundation for International Relations	FRIDE
Foyle, Carlingford and Irish Lights Commission	FCILC
Gaelic Athletic Association	GAA
General Agreement on Tariffs and Trade	GATT
Global Irish Network	GIN
global positioning system	GPS
Government Economic Service	GES
greenhouse gas	GHG
gross domestic product	GDP
gross national income	GNI
gross national product	GNP
Gross Value Added	GVA
human resources	HR
Independent Commission for the Location of Victims' Remains	ICLVR
Industrial Development Agency	IDA Ireland
information and communications technology	ICT
information technology	IT
Institute for Management Development	IMD
Institute of International and European Affairs	IIEA
Intergovernmental Agreement	IGA
Intergovernmental Panel on Climate Change	IPCC
International Atomic Energy Agency	IAEA
International Data Corporation	IDC
International Energy Agency	IEA
International Security Assistance Force	ISAF
Irish Business and Employers' Confederation	IBEC
Irish Farmers' Association	IFA
Irish Innovation Centre	IIC
Irish Republican Army	IRA
Irish Technology Leadership Group	ITLG
Judicial Arbitration and Mediation Service	JAMS
liquefied natural gas	LNG

megawatt	MW
Migrant Integration Policy Index	MIPEX
Millennium Development Goals	MDGs
National Asset Management Agency	NAMA
National Climate Change Strategy	NCCS
National Competitiveness Council	NCC
National Council for Business and Public Sector Costs	NCBPSC
National Council for Curriculum and Assessment	NCCA
National Institute for Regional and Spatial Analysis	NIRSA
National Treasury Management Agency	NTMA
nomenclature of territorial units for statistics	NUTS
non-resident Indians	NRIs
North Atlantic Treaty Organisation	NATO
North/South Ministerial Council	NSMC
Northern Ireland Council for Voluntary Action	NICVA
Nuclear Non-Proliferation Treaty	NPT
Nuclear Suppliers' Group	NSG
Organisation for Economic Co-Operation and Development	OECD
Organisation for Economic Co-Operation and Development – Development Assistance Committee	OECD-DAC
Organisation for Security and Cooperation in Europe	OSCE
Organization of Petroleum Exporting Countries	OPEC
overseas citizenship of India	OCIs
Overseas Development Assistance	ODA
people of Indian origin	PIOs
Performance Management Development System	PMDS
Permanent Structured Cooperation in Defence	PSCD
Police Service of Northern Ireland	PSNI
Programme for International Student Assessment	PISA
Promoting Ireland Abroad Division	PIAD
property-assessed clean energy	PACE
Proportional Representation by Single Transferable Vote	PR-STV
Provisional Irish Republican Army	PIRA
purchasing power parity	PPP
Real Irish Republican Army	RIRA
research and development	R&D
Secretary General	SG
Services, Industrial, Professional and Technical Union	SIPTU
Social, Democratic and Labour Party	SDLP
South African Network of Skills Abroad	SANSA

Special European Union Programmes Body	SEUPB
Sustainable Energy Authority of Ireland	SEAI
Terrorism and Situation Trend Report	TE-SAT
Ulster Unionist Party	UUP
United Arab Emirates	UAE
United Nations	UN
United Nations Operation in Somalia II	UNOSOM II
United Nations Relief and Works Agency	UNRWA
vehicle registration tax	VRT
World Economic Forum	WEF
World Trade Organization	WTO

About the Contributors

Ed Burke is a senior liaison officer at the International Police Coordination Board Secretariat in Kabul, Afghanistan. Ed is on sabbatical from his position as a political and security analyst with the Foundation for International Relations (FRIDE), a European think tank based in Madrid and Brussels. Ed's research is primarily within the context of Europe's Common Foreign and Security Policy (CFSP). He has contributed to a number of books, most recently a chapter on EU–Iraq relations published by Johns Hopkins University Press. Ed has also written for a wide range of international media, including opinion pieces for the *Irish Times*, *The Guardian* and *El Pais*. He is a native of Rosscarbery in west Cork.

Ronan Lyons is an economist with experience in national competitiveness, real estate markets and economic development. He has worked for the Irish government, as an economist for Ireland's National Competitiveness Council, and in the private sector, with the IBM Global Centre for Economic Development. He runs one of Ireland's most widely cited economic reports, the *Daft.ie Report*, which presents the latest trends in Ireland's residential sales and lettings markets. He has an award-winning blog, www.ronanlyons.com, which publishes weekly analysis on Ireland's economy, government finances and the property market, and which has been cited widely nationally and internationally, including in the *Financial Times*, Reuters, the *International Herald Tribune*, the *Sunday Times*, and the *New York Times*. He is currently pursuing his doctorate in urban economics in Balliol College, Oxford.

Eoin O'Malley lectures in political science at the School of Law and Government, Dublin City University. His main research interests are in prime ministerial power and power within parliamentary executives. His research has been published in a variety of international scholarly journals, including the *International Political Science Review*, the *European Journal of Political Science*, *West European Politics* and *Government and Opposition*. Eoin is also the co-editor of *Irish Political Studies* and a co-editor of the blog www.politicalreform.ie.

Michael Courtney is an IRCHSS government of Ireland Ph.D. scholar in the Department of Political Science, Trinity College Dublin. Michael's research examines the extent to which social background factors shape the political attitudes of members of European parliaments, with a particular interest in the growing number of MPs of an immigrant origin. He is also the postgraduate representative to the committee of the Political Studies Association of Ireland. Michael is based in the Institute of International Integration Studies at Trinity College and has a B.A. in Economics, Politics and Law from Dublin City University.

Stephen Kinsella is a lecturer in Economics at the Kemmy Business School, University of Limerick. He is the author of *Ireland in 2050: How We Will Be Living* and co-editor of *Understanding Ireland's Economic Crisis: Prospects for Recovery*, as well as the author of a number of refereed journal articles and book chapters. His first Ph.D. is from the National University of Ireland, Galway and his second Ph.D. is from the New School for Social Research in New York; both are in economics. His primary research area is Irish public policy and macroeconomics. He currently supervises five Ph.D. students.

Michael King is a senior research officer at the Institute for International Integration Studies, Trinity College Dublin and he lectures in the Department of Economics, Trinity College Dublin. Michael's research interests include access to finance in developing countries, development policy – in particular policy coherence for development and impact measurement – and national competitiveness. He has previously worked as an economist with Forfás and the National Competitiveness Council in Dublin and is the founder and former chief executive officer of the Dublin-based international development agency Suas Educational Development. Michael holds a Masters in Economics and International Development (MPA/ID) from Harvard University and a B.A. in Economics from Trinity College Dublin. Before joining Trinity fulltime in 2007, Michael was awarded the O'Reilly Foundation Scholarship (2003), the Fulbright Scholarship (2004) and the John F. Kennedy Scholarship (2004).

Joseph Curtin is senior researcher at the Institute of International and European Affairs with responsibility for energy and climate change policy. Joe is currently working with the OECD as a contractor evaluating climate policy implementation in several OECD countries, and on a project related to the political economy of the implementation of the Copenhagen emissions pledge. He has written extensively on building energy efficiency policy and advised government on policy development in this area. He is a guest lecturer on EU climate change and energy policy on M.Sc. courses at National University of Ireland, Maynooth and Dublin Institute of Technology and is also currently working on a project related to reform of the Irish political institutions, www.reformcard.com.

He has written on climate change and energy policy for publications including the *Irish Times*, *Open Democracy* and *Business & Finance*, and regularly contributes expert comment for national and international press.

Aoibhín de Búrca is an Ad Astra research scholar with UCD's John Hume Institute for Global Irish Studies, and the School of Politics and International Relations. Aoibhín's research focuses on political violence, ethno-nationalist conflicts and the targeting of civilians by militant groups, especially in the contexts of Northern Ireland and the Middle East. She also lectures part-time on Middle East Politics in UCD's School of Politics and International Relations, and has conducted fieldwork in the West Bank and Israel. She previously worked as a researcher and producer with Newstalk, on both international and domestic news and current affairs programmes.

Neil Sands is a management consultant based in Silicon Valley, California. Having previously graduated from National University of Ireland, Maynooth, he conducted postgraduate studies in the US and most recently received an MBA from the Smurfit Graduate School of Business, University College Dublin. Neil worked for several years in Canadian banking, holding positions in anti-fraud and web 2.0 strategy. In 2010, Neil co-authored a report on next generation diaspora engagement for The Ireland Funds, and is a regular contributor on new media and internet technology. With initial support from Accenture Management Consulting, Neil is developing an online diaspora toolkit for the US State Department's Global Diaspora Conference to be hosted by Hillary Clinton in April 2011.

Nicola White LL.B., LL.M. (Dub), Attorney (NY), is a consultant on diaspora strategies with The Ireland Funds. She was an author of the report on diaspora strategies for Ireland which was published for the Global Economic Forum held at Farmleigh in 2009. She is currently working on the publication of a global diaspora strategies toolkit with The Ireland Funds which will be launched by Hillary Clinton at the US State Department's Global Diaspora Forum in April 2011. Nicola is also a leading expert on dispute resolution and she has published two reports with the Law Reform Commission on this area. She was awarded the Weinstein International Fellowship in Dispute Resolution by the Judicial Arbitration and Mediation Service (JAMS) in 2011 and was a visiting researcher at the Gould Center for Mediation at Stanford University Law School. Nicola lectures at Independent Colleges and has been a guest speaker at conferences, both in Ireland and internationally, on the area of dispute resolution.

1

Introduction: Ireland, Punch-Drunk at the Crossroads

Ronan Lyons and Ed Burke

Ireland in the 2010s: Crisis and Opportunity

Just as in the late 1980s, and before that in the late 1950s, Ireland in the early 2010s stands at a crossroads. The country has been transformed dramatically in so many ways over the last generation. Many of these changes have been for the better. However, most of the changes since 2007 have been painful ones, with a sharp contraction in employment, incomes and expectations compounded by a staggering increase in the national debt. Future generations will no doubt do a double take when they see that government borrowings for 2010 alone were one-third of the size of the entire economy.

But the crises facing Ireland have not just been confined to the economy. Ireland is mired in self-doubt and bitter recrimination over the failure of a wide range of institutions affecting Irish life, from political and regulatory bodies to the Catholic Church. There is a sense of entrenchment taking hold, as seen in a lack of confidence in Ireland's membership of the EU after the difficult negotiations over the national debt in late 2010. Ireland is digging in to nurse its wounds and recount its grievances.

This feeling of betrayal, of waking up bleary-eyed to the awful destruction caused by a party to which some, but by no means all, were invited, must now be set aside. Almost three-quarters of TDs in 2010 were over the age of 50; for how long more will the 'Google generation' fail to grasp the importance of policy and policy-making to their lives? As the bank recapitalisations have shown, indifference is expensive.

This book does not set out to contribute to a counterproductive cycle of recrimination. While past sins may need to be punished, more importantly, the energy of a younger generation must now be channelled into rebuilding the country. For all the challenges facing Ireland, the phrase 'standing at a crossroads' is not a backward-looking one. It is a phrase about the future, about opportunity.

No generation has been so well-equipped with education and skills to change Ireland from what it was to what it should be. This is the same generation that, through its skill sets and ideas, continues to attract rates of foreign direct investment that are among the highest in the world. As Ireland's *annus horribilis* came to an end in 2010 and many were worrying about the minutiae of a golf game two years previously between Taoiseach Brian Cowen and former Anglo Irish Bank Chairman Sean FitzPatrick, it was announced that further expansion and new investments from companies such as Google, Facebook and Hewlett Packard had created over 11,000 new jobs during a year when many in the country thought Ireland had gone bust.

The aim of this book is to respond to the general loss of direction and the oft-repeated question: 'What should we do now?' This is not a book for specialists – its intended reader is a member of the general public who is interested in how Ireland can reorganise itself for the coming decade and the coming generation. Its focus is on government policy, not every last aspect of Irish life. Therefore, the more specific question this book hopes to answer is: 'What broad principles should guide government policy to help it build the best possible future for Ireland?'

Who can answer this question? We don't believe that one single person has all the answers. We also believe that sustainable solutions to Ireland's current challenges must involve the ideas of the generation that is emerging. It would be foolish to think that the generation that took the country to where it is in 2011 can continue to lead it into the 2020s and 2030s. The focus must turn to a new generation, Irish people born between 1970 and 1990, who will form the backbone of Irish society during the next 25 years. Therefore, in this book, you will find contributions from a collection of people under the age of 40 who are establishing themselves as researchers in their fields.

Books in which different chapters are written by different authors can sometimes be little more than loose collections of papers. To ensure a sense of consistency throughout the book, readers will notice a similar structure across the different chapters. Each chapter deals with a specific area of policy and has four main sections. The first is an introductory one that sets the scene. In the second, there is a brief analysis of policy in the particular area of focus over the past generation, showing the reader how Ireland came to be where it is today. This second section also highlights why carrying on as normal is not an option and why new directions are needed. The main section is the third section. This contains the core principles – typically between three and five – that should guide decision making into the future. The focus is on pointing out the shift in thinking required for policy to deliver success for Ireland over the coming generation. The fourth and final section provides a conclusion.

Themes across the Book

A book that is written by many different people does have a huge advantage over single author works: if a theme emerges again and again across very different policy areas, the reader can take that as a strong signal about its importance. In editing this book, we have seen three key themes emerge. These are the importance of learning from others, re-organising decision-making structures, and information and interconnection.

Learning from Others

Whether it is Denmark's decision in the 1970s to move away from dependence on imported energy (Chapter 7) or Korea's decision in the 1980s to develop a multifaceted strategy for leadership in technology (Chapter 6), there are concrete examples that Ireland can learn from of countries making a strategic decision and delivering results over the course of a generation.

Ireland can also learn from the mistakes of others. As is discussed in Chapter 4, the experience of countries such as France and the UK has shown the limitations of certain approaches to integration, lessons Ireland can apply as it deals with its 'New Irish'. As Chapter 9 discusses, our strategy on engaging Ireland's diaspora can be informed by the successes and failures of similar strategies elsewhere in the world, from Israel and India to Taiwan and Chile.

Re-organising Decision Making

A company with the wrong decision-making structures will ultimately fail. The same holds true for countries, where out-of-date systems can lead to stagnation. Ireland has much to change in its decision-making structures over coming years. In some areas, the reorganisation needed is about streamlining and greater efficiency. As Chapters 7 and 8 show, for example, a lack of clarity about responsibilities has undermined a coherent approach to policies on climate change and Northern Ireland, while Chapter 2 discusses the advantages of a vastly reduced Cabinet.

Much of the reform required, however, is in the greater decentralisation of decision making. The EU has as one of its core principles the notion of subsidiarity. Essentially, this means that decisions are taken as closely as possible to the affected citizen. Subsidiarity is meant as a check on the growth of bloated, distant and inflexible bureaucracies. No similar principle exists within Ireland. The centralisation of power in Ireland, as we now know, greatly increases the risk of everything going wrong if one person gets it wrong. The advantages of more collective decision making are discussed in Chapter 2, including strengthening the Oireachtas to incentivise better policy-making, while Chapters 3 and 5 show how putting regional authorities and organisations in the public service in charge of their resources, both human and financial, is much more likely to lead to sustainable public services.

Information and Interconnection

There has been a revolution in the way the private sector works over the past generation, particularly in relation to interconnection and information, following the changes brought about by information and communication technology. Businesses operate across boundaries like never before in the 'project economy'; as production processes become fragmented, the greatest 'value added' now comes from activities that turn streams of new data into information and insight. In comparison, how government works has remained largely the same, with the notable exception of EU-facilitated interconnection.

Over the coming generation, interconnection and information must take centre stage when designing Irish policy. Interconnection is not just important in energy markets (Chapter 7), but also when one thinks of policy structures across the UK and Ireland (Chapter 8), engaging Ireland's diaspora (Chapter 9) or how Ireland works with the new EU diplomatic service (Chapter 10). On a related theme, Chapter 3 discusses how the public service should adapt to the 'project economy'. We will require new sources of data, measuring concrete targets, to ensure the effectiveness of future policy decisions. These can range from measuring Ireland's services economy, its competitiveness or its true economic geography (Chapters 5 and 6), to ensuring policy targets, for example in relation to integration, are met (Chapters 2, 3 and 4).

This argument for interconnection applies to the system of decision making itself. The need for decentralisation is not an excuse to avoid implementing a more cohesive, 'whole of government' approach to key national priorities. Indeed, decentralisation is how resources at the top level can be freed up to drive that approach. This cuts across all major issues facing Ireland, including the economy, energy policy, Northern Ireland and the EU. To deliver coherence on our most vital interests, Ireland needs not only the Department of the Taoiseach in a strong coordinating role but also more oversight from the Oireachtas and greater autonomy for regional authorities and other organisations in the public service.

Chapter-by-Chapter Outline

The nine remaining chapters of the book are broken down into three sections: politics and society; the economy and the environment; and Ireland and the world. Below, the principal ideas of each chapter are explored.

Politics and Society

In Chapter 2, Eoin O'Malley discusses the changes that Ireland's political system needs. In reviewing the system as it stands, he points out that the easy scapegoats – such as the whip system or the PR-STV electoral system – may not be the right ones. In fact, the type of voting system that Ireland has may be much less to blame than the nature of the executive and legislative branches of government. His principal recommendation is that the system must be changed to enable more powerful mechanisms for members of the Oireachtas to question and oppose legislation, so that the decisions made are more robust. This would more than likely involve a better separation between the Cabinet and the Oireachtas, and give the Dáil a new focus, for example by empowering committees to more proactively review and propose legislation. Eoin also suggests a significantly smaller Cabinet and the creation of a Department of the Opposition, to strengthen decision making, and a changed role for the Ceann Comhairle to ensure that parliamentary procedure is strengthened to foster debate and accountability.

In Chapter 3, Ronan Lyons contrasts the enormous changes in society and the economy over the past century with a public service that would be familiar in design to someone from the nineteenth century. He shows that almost two decades of incremental reform have not tackled the root problems facing the public service, and argues that transformation rather than reform is needed. Ronan stresses the importance of turning the state into a twenty-first-century employer, something that will not only put it on a sustainable financial footing but enable it to attract the talent it needs. He also suggests dramatically reforming the structure of the public service, by changing from a pyramid structure to a pooled one and by decentralising decision making so that individual public service organisations have to match their budgets to the benefits they deliver for society.

In Chapter 4, Michael Courtney examines integration and migration policy in Ireland. The fact that Ireland has been presented with its own integration challenge up to fifty years after its Western European neighbours gives Ireland a unique opportunity to learn from the successes and mistakes of others. Michael advocates an integrationist policy, as distinct from a multicultural or assimilationist approach. He also stresses the importance of evidence-based integration and migration policy-making, not traditionally an area the Irish system is used to measuring. Lessons from other countries include that Ireland needs to act ahead of time on contentious issues and to avoid falling into the trap of talking to 'community leaders'. Any future strategy for integration will require reform in relation to residency status and migrants' political integration. However, equally important are linguistic integration and the roles of the community, voluntary and sporting sectors.

The Economy and the Environment

In Chapter 5, Stephen Kinsella and Ronan Lyons issue an important reminder that the last generation brought economic successes as well as failures. Addressing those failures means recognising the vital importance of fiscal policy in a small open region of the Eurozone economy – and thus putting in place annual spending targets that would be Ireland's equivalent of interest rate announcements. It also means that the economy's most important sectors, such as building and banking, need to be managed. Looking to the next generation, the authors recommend putting data at the centre of economic policy. Among other things, this would enable taxes to become, in effect, prices for services that are provided by the state. Ireland is also not in a position to defy the rules of economic geography, and regional policy must reflect that the island of Ireland can be home to, at most, four or five economic centres.

In Chapter 6, Michael King outlines the foundations for Ireland's international competitiveness. This has waxed and waned over the last generation, although IDA Ireland's record remains an enviable one. To secure future export-led growth, the traditional 'Competitiveness Pyramid' needs to be modified to reflect the importance of knowledge and skills as supports, and exports and productivity as measures of success. This means developing a capabilities approach to education that goes far beyond bonus points for maths and prepares schoolchildren with the skills they need to thrive in the twenty-first century. Two other key factors that Michael highlights are digital infrastructure, an area in which Ireland can learn from the multifaceted strategies of countries like Korea, and cost competitiveness, where introducing a Costs Council could highlight areas of concern.

In Chapter 7, Joseph Curtin discusses the future of Ireland's policy in relation to energy and climate change, comprehensively outlining how the status quo is simply no longer viable. He highlights the fact that Ireland's recent conversion to sound environmental commitments can't hide the shortcomings of Irish policy since the early 1970s, a piecemeal approach that stands in stark contrast to that of countries such as Denmark. Joseph points out that, in order to ensure energy security and to meet Ireland's emission reduction targets by 2020, future governments have little choice but to revolutionise three key emitting sectors at the heart of Irish life: agriculture, transport and housing. In addition, we will need changes to our institutions and to our energy markets, interconnecting Ireland more deeply with our European neighbours.

Ireland and the World

In Chapter 8, Aoibhín de Búrca provides a sobering analysis of the state of policy in relation to Northern Ireland. Although relations between Dublin and London have never been better, fond memories of historic days of peacemaking overshadow the demonstrable failure to deliver on all aspects of the Good Friday Agreement. In many areas, North/South cooperation remains symbolic rather than effective and the Northern Ireland power-sharing Executive has at times been simply dysfunctional, lurching from one crisis to another. Opportunities exist for greatly advanced economic cooperation and to secure a hard-won peace. Seizing them requires addressing the failure to prioritise a cross-departmental focus on strengthening North/South cooperation, and Aoibhín proposes the establishment of a Minister of State portfolio in the Department of the Taoiseach to provide a much-needed focus and authority on North/South cooperation, as prescribed by the Good Friday Agreement. As the rise of dissident Republican activity makes clear, complacency on Northern Ireland for the next generation is not option.

In Chapter 9, Neil Sands and Nicola White discuss the importance of a comprehensive strategy for engaging with Ireland's diaspora. They review the numerous disparate elements that are currently in place, such as the

Irish Leadership Technology Group and Gateway Ireland, and concretely outline what a comprehensive strategy might look like, which would include both 'inch-deep, mile-wide' policies open to all seventy million people connected to Ireland, and policies that target potentially high-impact members of Ireland's diaspora. The most recent wave of diaspora leaders, often skilled and working in some of the most innovative commercial locations in the world, need to be re-connected with Ireland. Neil and Nicola's golden rule is that Ireland must not forget that the relationship is two-way – the diaspora cannot just be a cash cow; rather, any diaspora policies must present opportunities for mutual benefit.

In the final chapter, Ed Burke reviews Ireland's foreign policy, in particular membership of the EU and the UN, the two cornerstones of Ireland's foreign policy over the past fifty years. Ed describes how Ireland's commitment to the EU has been reactive, obsessed with gaining short-term tactical advantage at the expense of committing to deeper integration and strengthening Europe's weight and coherence. A more multipolar world, centred on countries with which Ireland does not have any advantage of language or ancestry, spells increasing irrelevance for Ireland on the world stage, unless we act collectively through the EU to advance our interests and values. Although Ireland likes to consider itself as 'punching above its weight' in the UN, in reality the Irish commitment to international security is decidedly modest, with little coherence between tools of diplomacy, defence and development assistance. By adopting a strategic, coherent and constructive foreign policy, Ireland can leverage significant opportunities and meet the challenges of conducting international relations in a globalised world.

2

Permanent Revolution:
A Political System Capable of Renewal

Eoin O'Malley

Introduction: What Old Cars Tell Us About Our Political System

In December 2009, the Irish government was running a budget deficit of (depending on what you included) between 10 and 20 per cent. On the latter figure, this was the highest deficit in the Eurozone, and possibly the world. So €4 billion was cut in Budget 2010, and mainly so that more money could be put into a bank that had little strategic importance, and had up to the previous year nothing to do with the state. Yet despite these straitened times, the Irish government announced a new policy that was estimated to cost about €10 million and introduced a car scrappage scheme. It was regarded as 'mad' by a respected economist, being compared to a 'Prada handbag scrappage scheme'.[1]

Under this scheme, people with cars over ten years old could get a reduction of €1,500 on the vehicle registration tax (VRT) for a new car if their old car was scrapped. At such a time, one would have thought that a subsidy to the cash rich was the last thing that the state would have engaged in. Had there been a debate on the issue then, the Minister for Finance may have said that it was a green measure in that it took older cars off the road and replaced them with newer, presumably cleaner, cars. But there was no requirement that the new cars were on any lower emission limit. And the idea that scrapping functioning older cars to be replaced by newly manufactured ones is bizarre if one considers that the amount of energy and materials that goes into manufacturing new cars is high compared to what cars use over their lifetime. Nor was there a requirement that the old cars would be recycled for parts or materials – in fact this is explicitly prohibited. In any case, a scheme for the promotion of cleaner cars was already in place. The Department of Finance might also have argued that it would in fact be revenue raising, so the increased cars sales would mean that extra VAT and VRT income would be raised. But we don't know how many cars would have been sold anyway, and so it is difficult to work this out. What it did say was that this was a measure to protect jobs in the motor industry. Of course Ireland does not have a motor industry; it imports and sells cars and a small number of people in the country get very rich through this trade. So this measure was a subsidy for the export of large amounts of money in return for commodities with little long-term or productive value.

This small number of people lobbied government hard and one of its members, who also happened to be a government minister, informally made the proposal to government. Despite opposition to the scheme from the members of the Green Party, the scheme made it into the Budget announced in December 2009 and the Finance Bill in February 2010. In all, there was no debate on the issue in the Dáil. A Freedom of Information request reveals that the Department was aware of the potential for deadweight loss and that it did not really know what it would cost or raise.[2] It privately set out some of the disadvantages to the scheme and even claimed to quantify these (in fact it didn't). The advice took into account some of the objections and notes that the likelihood that it would break even was unlikely on reasonable assumptions. It thought the scheme would cost between €8 million and €10 million in 2010 and up to €30 million in 2011. In all, two pages were given to the decision, much of which admitted the shaky ground the measure was based on.[3]

Most of the public debate consisted of the car sales lobby groups' press releases about the number of jobs it would save and the money it would raise reprinted as fact in the national newspapers.[4] Fewer than 1,000 words were exchanged on the issue in Oireachtas debates and most of them were calls for its introduction or extension.

What this shows is the limited amount of thought or debate that goes into many measures. This was a small, inexpensive measure, but many more expensive and equally ill-thought-out policies are passed without sufficient analysis. The Finance Bill, one of the most important pieces of legislation, receives virtually no informed debate as opposition spokespersons are forced to react on the hoof to policies announced that are virtually certain to be rubber-stamped later. Finance Bills are sometimes used wholly inappropriately to introduce policies that have little to do with the state's Budget. The decentralisation scheme was introduced and passed this way with virtually no debate. According to some accounts, it was sprung on the Cabinet as much as on the rest of the Dáil. This policy, which had merits in principle, was poorly thought through and could have benefitted from debate and some expert intervention. Instead, it became a short-term electoral tool that has practically collapsed because of its poor initial design.

There is an assumption in Ireland that our political system has failed us, that it is a failure and must be radically reformed. This probably goes too far. Our political system has delivered remarkable stability and should not be blamed for all Ireland's ills. That said, it is the political system from which public policies emerge and if we have poor policies it is reasonable to say that the political system caused these policy failures. But when we think about the political system, what political system do we mean? Or rather, what aspect is the problem? We tend to hone in on those features that are most available or most visible to us; so we see the electoral system, the empty Dáil chamber, and TDs working in their constituencies as much as, if not more than, in the Dáil. We assume that these are the problems and these need to be fixed in some way.

In this chapter, I will argue that we should be willing and expect to constantly change our political procedures and systems – a modern-day permanent revolution – in order to ensure that they serve us well. But I will show that some of the prominent features of the electoral system that come in for most blame are not in fact problematic. I will attempt to identify the problems in the political system that may have led us to where we are now, and suggest changes that could be made. These include empowering the opposition with a Department for the Opposition, separating government and parliament through the use of ministers who are not TDs, electing the Ceann Comhairle in a different way and improving the committee system. These are not magic bullets – there is no best political system – but these should improve the political system so that it produces better policy.

The Dangers of Blaming It on PR-STV

When we look at the collapse in the Irish economy since 2007 there is a natural desire to search for the cause and apportion blame. We run the risk, though, of mis-apportioning blame to *prominent* factors rather than the actual factors. Just as we might attribute some success to a policy, we might attribute failure to a policy even though it may have had no real impact. An example of this is the impact of penalty points on driving deaths. In 2001, there had been some debate about the number of road deaths in Ireland being among the highest in the EU15. The number of deaths was persistently over 400 per year. Partly in reaction to a moral panic on this issue, a penalty points system was introduced, whereby if drivers accumulated enough points they might lose their driving licence. In the immediate aftermath of the introduction of this system there was a decline in driving deaths, falling below 400 per year for the first time since the 1980s, which the then Minister for Transport claimed was due to the new penalty points system. However, not long after this the number rose again. In fact, things were not as bad as all that, as, when one looked at the number of deaths controlling for the number of vehicles on the road (which was surging at the time), there was a long-term downward trend, which the penalty points system did not seem to accelerate. The policy probably had no impact. Laws such as that on penalty points tend to be introduced in reaction to a 'crisis', such as an increase in road deaths. And there is a natural regression to the mean, i.e. things go back to normal by themselves.

This 'attribution error' is common, as politicians usually claim their intervention was crucial when something goes right. It is natural for us to attribute blame for the economic collapse to the political system. It is not unreasonable to claim that many of the policy failures seen in Ireland can be put down to the political system. Just as the political decision to liberalise the economy and society with attendant economic growth was a result of the political system, we must acknowledge that the policy failures evident in the last ten years were also due to the political system.

The *Irish Times*' 'Renewing the Republic' series was instructive as to how many figures in the Irish establishment regarded the political system as the source of all Ireland's problems.[5] Most focused on the electoral system and the nature of the Dáil. This is unsurprising; these are the two most prominent political institutions in Ireland. To summarise the arguments made in the series, it is asserted that the Dáil does not do its job because the people in it are sheep who are too easily whipped and not of the intellectual calibre to hold the government to account. Furthermore, even capable TDs spend much of their time making representations on behalf of their constituents. Most of these problems could be solved by changing the Proportional Representation by Single Transferable Vote (PR-STV) electoral system that makes TDs compete with others from within their own party, so that they spend their days filling out passport application forms for their constituents or other such unparliamentarily behaviour. Furthermore, this electoral system is of peculiarly malign origin (British!) and not used anywhere else worth speaking of.

The tendency to attribute blame for the current economic crisis in Ireland on the assumed deficiencies in the electoral system is a fallacy. Electoral systems have big effects, and political scientists know more about the effects of electoral systems than they do about the effects of most other institutions. The arguments that the electoral system is to blame for the country's ills and must be changed have been dealt with extensively by Michael Gallagher and David Farrell.[6] It is worth mentioning some of their points here.

Firstly, Ireland's system is not that unusual. As Gallagher points out, while different systems have many different names, they have a smaller number of relevant characteristics. One is proportionality and the other is openness. On each of these, Ireland is quite close to many of the electoral systems in northern Europe where voters can choose between candidates. So, although PR-STV is rarely used, the features that affect how politicians behave are not that unusual.

Another argument is that PR-STV forces TDs to spend most of their time in the constituency, because they are always under threat from a constituency rival, frequently a party rival. It is true that TDs spend a lot of time in their constituency, though some voters may actually want that. It is also true that TDs are often more at risk of losing their seat to a party colleague than to a rival from another party. But the assumption that the electoral system is the cause of their avid attention to constituency details is misplaced. MPs in the other country in Europe that uses this system, Malta, do not spend large amounts of their time on constituency work. And the alternatives that we might find acceptable would not reduce the incentives for TDs to 'nurse' their constituency. We can see in the US, where there are no party colleagues to compete with, members of Congress make delivery of constituency 'pork' high on their list of priorities.

The argument that TDs who must compete with party colleagues end up competing on the delivery of constituency services to voters is based on the fact that they cannot compete on policy, because they share the same priorities. Firstly, if this were true then we should expect that TDs for parties without multiple candidates in a constituency would not be under such pressures and thus should do less constituency work. There is no evidence that this happens. Secondly, there is no reason inherent in the electoral system why TDs or candidates who compete with party colleagues cannot compete on some other feature. Some voters presumably faced with two candidates from the same party could choose that candidate more likely to make useful Dáil contributions or produce better policy papers.

But there's the rub. It is difficult to make incisive Dáil contributions and thankless to produce policy papers. The Dáil is structured in such a way that the government has an inbuilt advantage. It controls the two most useful resources – time and information. TDs will find it difficult to bring up issues of national importance if the government does not want them raised. Even major pieces of legislation, such as that on the National Asset Management Agency (NAMA), are subject to guillotine, limiting the time that could be spent debating this issue. Even if there is a limitless amount of time, a second problem hinders those who wished to debate the issue. Labour finance spokeswoman Joan Burton pointed out that there was a huge information deficit that prevented real debate about NAMA and the earlier bank guarantee scheme. If the Minister for Finance controls all the information, and the timing and nature of its release, it's difficult for opposition parties to set the agenda. Most of what we were told about the Bank Guarantee Scheme in September 2008 now seems hopelessly optimistic or irrelevant. How can the opposition do its job if the information it receives is misleading or inaccurate?

...And the Dangers of Blaming It on the Party Whips

The other feature of the Irish political system that people point to as a problem is the whip system, where TDs vote along party lines in the Dáil. The fact that some TDs have at times spoken one way but then voted another way highlights the apparent oddity of the whip system. The whip system is often linked to the electoral system, where people think that the electoral system tends to elect a particularly stupid cohort of individuals incapable of independent thought or action. In fact, the Irish electoral system would seem ideally suited to independent-minded TDs who could ignore their party. Yet Irish TDs are no more rebellious than their counterparts across Europe.[7] Though many wish to see a fully independent Dáil in which TDs vote only on the basis of good arguments and unsullied by base transactions or party whips, in truth it would be the only parliamentary democracy in Western Europe to operate that way.

Even so, is the whip system really that bad? Gallagher has written on this topic and points out that it would be virtually impossible to get a Budget through without the whip system.[8] The whip system allows politicians to get what they want more of the time and over a longer period. If they have to endure voting against something distasteful at times, this is a price for getting what they want more of the time. If one did not have a whip system, TDs would have to think about the issues before voting rather than follow their colleagues. Though this would appear attractive, where would they get the information from? Interest groups. At the moment, TDs can reasonably say to interest groups trying to get their support that they have to vote with the party. If the whip system did not exist it would be much easier for interest groups to capture individual TDs. Another problem of politics without the whip system would be the almost inevitable instability. Governments are more likely to lose crucial votes and resign. Is this really what those who blame the whip system really want?

One factor that people rarely point to when discussing why TDs spend a lot of time filling out forms or pursuing cases with the administration is problems with bureaucracy. Despite the Irish public service's penchant for producing reports praising itself, there are reasons why ordinary citizens approach TDs to speed up their passport application form or advance their social welfare claim – because it works. (The topic of public service reform is taken up in Chapter 3.) TDs have 'hotlines' to departments, which means that people's queries get answered with a speed that would never happen ordinarily. TDs can jump queues, so it is perfectly rational for voters to contact TDs to jump queues on their behalf. This is the demand-side force that pulls TDs to behave as they do.

Another is a supply-side reason. TDs and Senators have little or no power. Why would an average TD spend a great deal of time on national policy issues? These debates ignore a fundamental aspect of Irish politics – that *policy is made in government, not the Dáil*. Therefore we need to think about reforming government and measures that would make government more effective. That does not mean we should ignore the Dáil, but we should not expect to see more policy-making power in the Dáil; rather, we want to see more policy oversight.

The dismal nature of Dáil oversight can be seen in that way the Dáil Public Accounts Committee, one of the more powerful of the committees, dealt with the Secretary General (SG) of the Department of Finance in July 2010 when it called him to answer questions on the Bank Guarantee Scheme decision. Most members, with some exceptions, did not actually ask questions of him or try to discover what caused the Minister to choose one option over another. Rather they fulminated against Anglo Irish Bank, the Financial Regulator, the Department and the Minister (unless they were on the government side). Most left when they had asked their questions, apparently uninterested in hearing what the SG had to say to their colleagues.

It is hard to blame them. The committees in the Oireachtas have virtually no power. Many committees produce reports, but the majority of
the time they lie on shelves to gather dust. For instance there have been
countless reports on the status of the Seanad, many on the Constitution
and, in 2010, a pretty sensible report on the electoral system and voting
reform. But in their hearts, the committee members must know that it
will make little difference.

What Is the Problem?

The Irish political system is durable and has served us reasonably well in
the last 90 years. It has delivered stability, which was something many
contemporaries in Europe did not have. But in the post-war period it
became obvious that Ireland was an economic and social laggard. Yet still
in the 1960s, there was a political impetus to modernise Ireland which
largely achieved its goal (if it did not sustain it). However, in the 1980s
the political system appeared incapable of fixing the economic problems
and Ireland reverted to basket-case status. Again the political system
responded and Ireland appeared to be moving in the right direction from
the 1990s.

Now if the same political system existed when we were brought great
wealth and then brought to economic ruin, one might reasonably wonder
is the political system relevant. I think it is. If we do nothing to our political system, I suspect the world will not end, and, in fact, by delivering an
able political leader, it might facilitate the delivery of a solution to the
problems we now face. But there is no guarantee that we will not then lull
ourselves into a false sense of security and once again face problems, be
they economic or social, on a colossal scale.

So what are the problems with the system of government we have? On
paper the Cabinet system is a good one. Proposals are made by ministers,
usually on the basis of a point in the programme from government, in
turn based on inter- and intra-party negotiations and subject to scrutiny
by the media and maybe even the electorate. In theory, the elite of a country's political system then subject the proposal to rigorous scrutiny and,
from their different perspectives, poke at and punch holes in the argument, until bad proposals get rejected and acceptable ones are improved.

The problem is that this doesn't seem to happen. Why not? One problem is ministerial overload. Ministers are busy with their own departments
and don't have time to start thinking deeply about other ministers' responsibilities. If you are the Minister for Housing, you don't have time to think

about the fiscal situation – all you care about is the housing budget. It is there that your name will be made.

There is also log-rolling, whereby a minister who wants to get her proposal through Cabinet will refrain from questioning another minister's proposal so he will return the favour and support her proposal. The Minister for Housing is not going to argue against the Minister for Children's proposal for fear that she might return the compliment.

The size of the Cabinet probably prevents it from being a real decision-making body, or even an effective forum for policy discussion. The meetings now consist of fifteen Cabinet members, a super junior minister, the chief whip, the Attorney General and the Secretary General to the government. Anyone familiar with decision-making bodies of any type will know that nineteen people is too many for constructive discussion. This is acknowledged by the Cabinet system, which has moved to increase the importance of Cabinet committees and decreased the amount of time Cabinet meets.

Another problem is the type of ministers. In juries we think that if twelve people's opinions converge, they're likely to converge on the truth. The same assumption can be made of Cabinet government. But for jurors and Cabinet ministers to converge on the right answer, as opposed to just any answer, then their opinions should be independent of each other. In statistical theory, two events are said to be independent if the occurrence of one event does not affect the probability that the other will occur. So if I toss a coin and get heads, this does not make heads or tails any more or less likely in the next toss. We may assume that Cabinet ministers (and jurors) are independent. But we'd be wrong. Most ministers (like jurors) follow what goes around the table. So if a minister's proposal appears to be gaining acceptance, sceptical ministers might remain silent – what in public opinion theory is known as the 'spiral of silence'.

And why would they be independent when the political system throws up a remarkably homogenous lot? The Cabinet in 2010 included six school teachers, a couple of lawyers, but not much else; no scientists, social scientists or people with much experience of business. They are all full-time career politicians who have been in the Dáil for a long time and have almost never had a significant career outside politics. All of these people live in a strange world around Kildare Street and, while hardly cocooned from the real world, view the real world through an unusual lens and crucially almost all have the same lens. So instead of having fifteen different points of view, government is centralised into one or two particular points of view.

That these policy failures could happen is in part because there is not enough expertise or diversity of views in government. Ireland has generalist ministers who are career politicians, but the current system marries generalist ministers with generalist career civil servants (see Chapter 3 for a discussion of the future of the generalist civil service). Those civil servants are trained within the civil service and tend not to challenge the hierarchical culture there. The hierarchical culture and the complete deference given to ministers is a problem. For good specialists to work well in a department, they need to work in an environment where they can speak freely to their seniors, including ministers. While different secretaries general have differing styles, at the moment it seems ministers rarely interact with civil servants without the SG being present.[9] This probably hinders a free flow of information where those experts may not easily get heard if they wish to voice dissent with the departmental view. One of the greatest dangers in any political system (or country or organisation) is that consensus is so great that dissenting voices are rarely heard or when heard not considered.

Governments, particularly ones in power for a long time, get lazy. When opposition parties have few resources to challenge government research and few mechanisms to challenge government in a timely and effective manner, government can get a bit too comfortable. But government should not be a comfortable place to be, and if we are to reform our political system it should be with this in mind. People work best if they know everything they do can be observed and is open to scrutiny. In 2010, the Ombudsman, Emily O'Reilly, criticised the government for refusing to accept her report into the 'Lost at Sea' scheme or even allow the Dáil to debate it.[10] Where government can effectively bury criticism like this, government will be less thoughtful in how it behaves.

Most generally, Ireland needs to institutionalise a system where dissenting views are argued and debated, where policy gets poked and pulled at until good policies remain and poor ones get thrown out. The question is how do we achieve such a situation?

Fostering Dissent: Some Possible Solutions

If we want to reform the political system we need to **rebalance power within the political system**. We need to enable greater scrutiny of government, to allow the opposition and backbenchers do their job. The public should have greater access to independent information, not information spun by government departments. As is discussed in Chapter 5, quantifiable metrics are the cornerstone of good government. Therefore, government statistics should be generated by independent agencies and government policy could be independently analysed and tested against stated objectives in the same way the Central Statistics Office (CSO) independently collects statistics. The Dáil procedures should be changed to allow Cabinet ministers be subjected to better oversight. At present ministers can dodge questions. Journalists such as Vincent Browne can ask ministers the same question until they answer it or have made clear to the public that they are dodging it. TDs can't do this. A minister can answer another question and then the Ceann Comhairle will move them on. Replies to parliamentary questions should not be written to protect the minister but to enable the proper accountability of the minister to the Dáil. In short, we should enable the opposition to subject the government to greater scrutiny.

Empowering the Opposition

The role of opposition might be threefold: observing, interrogating and proposing alternatives. So it should first, because we have better things to do with our time, keep an eye on government for us. The opposition should tell us what the government is doing, thus reducing government's temptation to tell lies. As well as observe and report, secondly, the opposition should also challenge and question government. It should poke about at government, generally making being in government less comfortable than it otherwise would have been. If the government proposes something, the opposition's job is to ensure that poor proposals are exposed and an embarrassed government withdraws or amends them (or better still, doesn't propose poor or self-serving policies in anticipation of being embarrassed). Government should be able to defend and justify its decisions and the opposition's job is to make sure that we hear these justifications. Finally, the opposition is meant to provide an alternative government. So it should come up with proposals as to what it would do in government and also appear competent enough to be a credible alternative.

Another significant advantage government has is the huge mismatch in resources between government and opposition. Each minister has a small army of civil servants working for him or her. They can come up with well-costed, credible proposals. Opposition spokespeople, on the other hand, are more or less on their own. Opposition parties are now better funded than they were, and now have their own research officers and policy officers. But much of the research they engage in is market research. Party leaders have a leader's allowance to fund activities, but in the past these have included the purchase of handmade shirts, and now are more likely to fund opinion polls. Each TD now has, as well as a secretary, a parliamentary assistant. But most of these are engaged in constituency service. Opposition TDs also have access to a library and research service, but it is small and frontbenchers have to compete with backbenchers (including government party backbenchers) and Oireachtas committees for its services. Opposition spokespeople are battling virtually alone against the impressive armoury a minister can bring to bear. It's no wonder opposition parties can appear inept.

One way to even up the contest, without threatening the government's ability and reasonable expectation that it can manage and push through its legislative agenda, is to set up a Department for the Opposition. This could be a civil service department with small units that would match the government departments. Each opposition spokesperson might be able to draw on up to, say, ten civil servants who could do research work, and they might also be allowed appoint a non-civil-service policy adviser. They would then be able to direct and manage this team in order to observe and interrogate government as well as develop and offer alternative policies that could be introduced when it is in government.

A Department of the Opposition may seem like a strange idea, and to civil servants especially. Civil servants after all serve the government of the day and it is the control of these that allows one to govern. But there already are some civil servants who are not civil servants to the government but civil servants to the state. These include those who work for the president, a position that serves no useful function.

By giving over the use of some civil servants to opposition spokespeople, they will ensure that there are greater resources at the disposal of the opposition. As well as evening up the gap in skills and knowledge between government and opposition, it will mean opposition will have some experience managing a small section and the leader of the opposition will have skills honed in managing a department that has to oversee the work of a large number of individuals. I suspect most taoisigh would have welcomed this type of challenge before taking over the complete apparatus of government. Especially at a time when policy issues are increasingly complex and sometimes highly technical, the opportunity to manage such a department and draw on civil service expertise would increase the professionalism of the opposition, enabling it present itself as a credible alternative government.

It would mean that when a new government takes office it spends less time finding its way around the system and will arrive with a more or less workable policy agenda. Currently, new ministers have to come into their jobs with little training or experience and are surrounded by completely unfamiliar faces. While civil servants strive to make ministers' lives comfortable, this might be at the expense of ministerial control. If opposition spokespeople (or shadow ministers as we might call them) could reasonably expect to go into government with a familiar team around them, this should decrease the possibility, whether real or imagined, that ministers become 'captured' by their new department.

There are other benefits to this. It might be a useful place to put former secretaries general, who are currently effectively forced to retire after seven years. This could give opposition parties access to some of the better brains in the civil service and would weaken the 'us versus them' attitude prevalent in the civil service with regard to the opposition. If a civil servant suspects he or she may soon be serving the opposition, he or she may well adopt a friendlier attitude to opposition when serving the government. An important aspect of democracy for Aristotle was that the ruler could become the ruled – this is not something the civil service need worry about and it is possibly evident in their attitude in drafting answers to parliamentary questions.

By having a Department for the Opposition one increases the effectiveness of the opposition to oppose without giving it the right to block. So there can be some checks and balances on government activity without the destabilising effect that a veto might have on the government, perhaps leading to deadlock.

Of course problems with this proposal exist. On a practical level, does control of the department go to the leader of the main party of opposition or would one allow smaller opposition parties access to it? It could be difficult to manage if it had to be shared with other parties, though it might be good practice for coalition. It might lead to a politicisation of the civil service, where some senior civil servants go in and out of government with the party they have become attached to. It is already the case that ministers grow attached to civil servants, who follow them around from department to department, but equally good civil servants have gone from being seen as close to a minister from one party to being close to a minister from another because ministers recommend them.

Separate Government and Parliament

As it is currently structured, TDs, particularly government TDs (which is more than half of them), have neither the opportunity nor the motive to provide robust oversight of government legislation. The political career path for most TDs leads to the Cabinet at its summit. We can reinvigorate our democracy by (metaphorically) opening the doors of government.

By giving the Dáil access to more and better information from government and opening government to people from different backgrounds and expertise, we can in the future avoid the type of policy failures that brought us to the political and economic crisis we find ourselves in.

One of the first ways we can increase the motive of the Dáil to oversee the activities of government is to separate them properly. Though there is a formal separation of powers in the Irish system, it does not really exist. How could it? All ministers, bar a tiny number of exceptions, are TDs. They spend time together and experience the same problems of re-election. Ministers are the leaders of backbench TDs' parties. There is a symbiotic relationship where ministers rely on TDs for parliamentary support, and in return ministers try to deliver electoral success, which may come in the form of popular policies or through the delivery of political goods, such as services to constituents and their areas.

Ireland is unusual in having all ministers coming from parliament. In many countries, such as Sweden and Belgium, there is a requirement that ministers resign their seats, if they have one, on their appointment as minister. This makes MPs much less likely to view ministerial office as a career, as taking a ministry risks the potential longevity of life as a parliamentarian. It also means that MPs treat their job as a parliamentarian seriously. This would create a parliamentary class of TDs who see their career within parliament rather than aspiring to ministerial office.

The idea that people who are good parliamentarians will make good ministers is silly. The jobs are quite different. One requires one to be a good interrogator, whereas the other also needs the ability to bring people along with you. Michael McDowell's aggressiveness probably made him an outstanding TD but this also made him a poor minister. His seemingly deliberate attempts to upset people made a relatively uncontroversial measure such as the citizenship referendum much more problematic that it could have been. Conversely, Batt O'Keefe, never noted as a parliamentarian, turned out to be a competent minister.

Separating the government and the Dáil will mean that the village atmosphere that exists there will be weakened and a culture where even government backbenchers feel able to question their own party's ministers will ensue. It will strengthen the motive for the Dáil to be a proper overseeing body. If it were possible for ministers to come from other walks of life, we might see ministers with different points of view and because they would not all be career politicians, ministers would be more willing to resign for bad performance or unsuitability for office.

One of the advantages of having ministers who are full-time career politicians is that they have a greater understanding of politics and the political process. It is not the case that people who are successful in one walk of life will automatically succeed in another. For instance, Lech Wałęsa was an inspiring leader of a resistance movement but struggled in government. So Michael O'Leary of Ryanair may not make an effective minister, even if one could give him a job. In many European countries, academics are seen as notoriously poor ministers. But even successful ministers sometimes find they do not succeed in a different set of circumstances. And there is no single 'right' type for a political leader. The problems faced by political leaders sometimes are best suited to certain types of personality. So Winston Churchill, regarded by many as washed up, became stunningly successful in the context of war, but then went on to become a poor peacetime prime minister. What made Bertie Ahern invaluable in Northern Ireland (that is, his desire to keep everyone happy) may have also been what caused his government to mismanage the Irish economy. Many complain about the apparent intellectual inability of some ministers, but Garret FitzGerald's intellectual curiosity may have made him an ineffectual Taoiseach. Perhaps the system we should aspire to have is one with a small number of strong personalities with a diverse set of skills and interests.

A More Focused Cabinet

A Cabinet should have a smaller number of ministers, because large bodies make effective decision making difficult. A smaller Cabinet with, say, eight ministers, including the Taoiseach, would make it a more effective body. If many of these are not from parliament or powerful within their party, but are chosen by and owe their position to the Taoiseach, this will reduce the ability of these ministers to stand up to the other members of the Cabinet. For that reason, it might be a preferable if all eight ministers were elected politicians as a minimum guarantee that these are powerful in their own right. Otherwise, there could be a presidentialisation of the system. The smaller Cabinet should mean that there will be no drift towards cliques or 'sofa politics', which probably necessarily occurs when the decision-making body is too large and unwieldy.

The smaller Cabinet will mean that ministers have much broader portfolios, so it might reduce the types of turf warfare we see in politics. The smaller group should be more cohesive and there could be a better sense that the Cabinet was working together for a shared goal rather than against each other. To support these eight ministers each could be given up to three junior ministers, most of whom would not be elected politicians. For these people, to whom smaller areas of policy could be devolved, the Taoiseach and ministers could use outside experts or people with different experience. These people could be brought into Cabinet for the decisions on those aspects related to their briefs. It would mean that Cabinet was exposed to a plurality of advice from people much less likely to accept civil service advice unquestioningly.

A Ceann Comhairle for the Dáil

If these changes to the cabinet system should create a more effective decision-making body, which the Dáil feels sufficient distance from to question willingly, then the Dáil also needs to have the opportunity to oversee the government. Changes are needed to the way the Dáil operates. The government currently decides the time allocated to the Dáil and sets limits on what can or cannot be debated. Questioning of government is difficult when ministers are protected by the Ceann Comhairle, even when not answering questions. Because of the separation of powers, the courts have been and presumably will remain unwilling to enforce the duties of ministers as regards the Dáil. The Standing Orders can be changed reasonably easily to a form which might allow good parliamentarians to shine.

However, the relationship between the Ceann Comhairle and the government must also change. At the moment it is a position in the gift of the government. It should become a position which is the protector of the Dáil's interests. If the position were elected by secret ballot and if Cabinet ministers were barred from voting, then one would ensure that the government would lose its right to choose and candidates for the job of Ceann Comhairle would have to pitch to backbenchers for why they want the job. The post of Ceann Comhairle is paid a salary that would indicate that it matters. Maybe it is time that the position rose to meet those high rewards. The Ceann Comhairle could be made a genuinely powerful political figure if parliament had a small number of 'parliamentary principles' to guide it instead of detailed rules that are strictly observed.

These guiding principles should then form the basis for the more intricate parliamentary rules, but, importantly, the rules could not contravene the principles. So rules that made it difficult for a TD to question a minister could be revoked and over-ruled.

Making the Dáil Work

We should also rethink what the purpose of the Dáil is. According to some outdated constitutional theory, parliaments are meant to be legislative bodies. We could admit that parliaments do not make laws and instead enable them to improve and oversee the making of laws. One way to improve how laws are made is to remove the overly partisan nature of legislative debates. As outlined in the introduction, much of our legislation goes through the Oireachtas without proper scrutiny. One of the reasons is that it arrives in the Dáil as agreed government policy. Government parties are then much less likely to (publicly) question the policy and opposition parties are less likely to engage in the constructive improvement of policies. The tone of the debate is partisan and the quality of the debate suffers.

One solution to this problem is if committees can study legislation at a much earlier stage. In some countries there is pre-legislative scrutiny of policy proposals, which still allows the government to set the agenda but gives more time for real scrutiny *before* mistakes are made. If we assume that rushed legislation tends to be flawed legislation, under this system one will see that legislation is more considered and government is more willing to accept improvements. A pre-legislative scrutiny committee could ask expert witnesses to comment on the legislation, thus ensuring more points of view are considered. Critics of this approach say that it takes away the agenda-setting role of parliamentary committees. But this role does not really exist. How many times have the Oireachtas committees produced worthy proposals which have never been delivered?

Conclusion: Politics that Works

The changes outlined are not the limit of what Ireland should look at in renewing its political system. The different proposals made here also have flaws. But the guiding principle, that the political system could be redesigned to encourage and manage dissent, is the correct approach. If it is to ensure that there are a plurality of views in politics and it is difficult for a single point of view to become accepted without serious challenge, information needs to flow freely between government and the public. The proposals I outline do this. But we could add that a strengthened Freedom of Information Act is important. Nor is it advisable that policy debates rely on information that the government has a hand in preparing, so economic forecasting could be taken away from the Department of Finance. Policy proposals should also state more explicitly the purpose of the policy, what problem it is designed to solve and what it expects to achieve, so that we can then measure the effectiveness of government policy. The hierarchical nature of the senior civil service should be 'flattened' to allow more open discussion of policy and better access for ministers to different points of view.

The changes outlined are quite radical, but they are focused on the real problems in the political system, not what appear to be the problems in the popular press. Some of the proposals made here would be difficult to implement. Some would need a constitutional amendment, for instance to limit the number of ministers to eight – though it is unlikely to be a proposal that would be defeated in a popular vote. Fixing other aspects of the relationship between the Ceann Comhairle and the Dáil probably only requires changes to the standing orders, but it might be useful to have parliamentary principles in the Constitution, to ensure that a simple majority could not revert to the old mechanism for selecting a Ceann Comhairle. The proposal for a Department of the Opposition would probably be resisted by the civil service. But the advantage is that it might introduce more competition within the service, and could be a good training ground for senior civil servants taken from outside the service.

Conservatives will point to the likelihood of unforeseen consequences. But the problems within government are so serious that risks should be taken. In any case, while it changes the power distribution within the political system, it maintains the basic structure of the political system. Any society, country, company or institution that aspires to success in the long term needs to be willing to adapt and change constantly. Ireland found a successful economic formula in foreign direct investment, but rested on its laurels and didn't try to move beyond this strategy. It is as if Apple, having developed the iPod, decided that product was enough for it to ensure the company's viability. Our political system is like anything else, it gets rusty and worn out. It can't handle new pressures put on it. If it doesn't adapt, it will die.

3

From Reform to Transform: Rebuilding Ireland's Public Service

Ronan Lyons

Introduction: Comparing Experiences in the Public and Private Sectors

Personal experiences are hugely important in understanding the world. So it has been for me. After my studies, I worked first in the public sector and then in the private sector. Despite the difference in sector, there were many similarities in the two jobs, not least the nature of work: conducting economic analysis and then communicating findings. In both, I was part of an organisation with more than 350,000 workers, which meant that there were a significant number of other teams and departments whose work was often related to our team's. Finding these, however, could be tough and clearly informal networks were a natural starting point.

Finding these stakeholders also highlighted the differences between the two sectors. In the private sector organisation, ensuring you reached all relevant stakeholders was facilitated by a further tool, an online professional network, where formal structures sat side-by-side with an individual's expertise, current areas of work and informal connections with other employees. This enabled people working on a project to put together groups of stakeholders easily and find a path to each, through formal or informal channels. In the public service, I had no equivalent tool. If working on, say, Irish policy matters relating to global trade and the World Trade Organization (WTO), it would be a lengthy task to find out who was also working on these and related issues across the Departments of An Taoiseach, Foreign Affairs, Agriculture, Enterprise Trade and Innovation, Justice, and Finance, let alone other public servants in agencies such as Irish Aid, Teagasc, the National Economic and Social Development Office, Forfás, the Industrial Development Agency (IDA Ireland) and Enterprise Ireland.[1]

The presence of that extra tool in the private sector strikes at the heart of the difference between the public and private sectors as they currently stand. The private sector organisation put in place that online system because it had an incentive to do so: the system would pay for itself by boosting efficiency and reducing wasteful time spent finding out who did what. There is no incentive currently in the public service to do the same for its shareholder and customer, the taxpayer. Ultimately, the transformation of our public service has to be built around fixing that problem. What is the incentive for government departments to save money? And how can we reward public servants who change how they do their work, to deliver efficiencies for the taxpayer and to give a better service to the citizen?

After decades of little activity, public service reform in Ireland has, since the 1990s, almost become its own industry. Every year, new initiatives are launched, using fashionable jargon, such as 'citizen-centric', 'integrated service delivery' and 'best-in-class'. It is not the intention of this chapter to contribute to this. Instead, it aims to outline a series of high-level principles that can guide the transformation of Ireland's public service into one where workers are always looking for ways to improve the service they give, a service that is focused on citizens as customers, rather than one focused on processes and compliance.

After this introduction, there is a brief overview of the history of public service reform in Ireland, with particular attention paid to the growth of the 'industry' of public service reform since the mid-1990s. The second section also reviews the weaknesses in the public service highlighted in the 2008 Organisation for Economic Co-Operation and Development (OECD) review.[2] The third section then highlights three key principles to guide public service reform over the coming generation. Firstly, the public service needs to be transformed into a twenty-first-century employer. By changing its attitude to contracts, performance reviews and pensions, the public service can find the skills it needs and use them for as long as it needs them. Secondly, as the balance of specialists and generalists evolves, the public service will need to change from a pyramid-based organisation into a flexible pool of talent. Finally, each organisation in the public service will need to understand the outcomes it delivers and match its budget to those outcomes.

Before proceeding, though, it is worth making two points. The first is outlining what exactly is included in 'the public service'. The 360,000 people employed in Ireland's public service in 2009 were broken down into five main groups. The first – about 38,000 workers – is the core civil service, which includes the permanent staff of the fifteen government departments and other 'core' agencies such as the Central Statistics Office and the Revenue Commissioners. The second is organisations involved in the delivery of public services, three key strands of which are health (hospitals, about 110,000 workers), education (schools, institutes of technology and universities – 97,000 workers), and security and defence (an Garda Síochána, prisons, the Defence Forces – about 30,000 workers). The third category is state-sponsored agencies, such as IDA Ireland or the Health and Safety Authority, which are connected to particular departments, and employ about 10,000 people. The fourth category, comprising 37,000 workers, is the local authorities, of which there are 34, and the 8 regional authorities. The final category of the public service comprises commercial state-sponsored bodies, which employ 42,000 people, for example, CIE (Córas Iompair Éireann, Ireland's semi-state transport body, in charge of the national and local bus and train services), the Electricity Supply Board (ESB) and Bord na Móna. The focus in this chapter is on the first four elements.

Secondly, should we say Ireland's 'public services' or its 'public service'? This is more than semantics. Is Ireland's public sector a collection of organisations and agencies, linked only by how they are funded? Or is it akin to one large corporation with different divisions that have complementary capabilities, all ultimately contributing to the same shared set of goals? It should be clear that Ireland's public service must think of itself as the latter – not a loose confederation of taxpayer-funded specialist organisations, but a large collection of teams and workers, creating huge benefits for Irish citizens by delivering some of the most important services in the state. Throughout this chapter, reference will be made to a singular public service, in recognition of the fact that all those employed by the state in public service are working towards the shared goals of society.

From Stasis to the Industry of Public Service Reform

Public service reform fits the generational scope of this volume well, as its history on these islands has, until recently, been of reform to last a generation or longer. The earliest major review of Ireland's civil service took place in the 1850s, when Ireland was part of the UK, with the landmark *Northcote–Trevelyan Report*. The reforms that followed put in place a permanent, unified and politically neutral civil service, which is essentially the system that remains in the UK and in Ireland today.

Since then, attempts to reform have – until recently – been sparing. When Ireland was still part of the UK, there were further reforms in 1874, 1886 and again in 1914 with the *MacDonnell Report*. Upon the formation of the Irish Free State, almost all civil servants working in Ireland availed of the option to transfer and work under the government of the Irish Free State. In the 90 years since independence, there has been no equivalent to the Northcote–Trevelyan reforms, and the way Ireland's public service works would look very familiar to someone from the 1890s.

1922–1994: A Largely Unchanged Public Service

The lack of large-scale reform of Ireland's public service is not due to a lack of reviews or even ideas. The first fifty years of independence saw two main reviews of the public service. The *Brennan Commission Report* of 1932 reported that the civil service system was, after substantial reforms in the previous eighty years, still working well and therefore not in need of major reform. A further review of the public service took place in the late 1960s, known as the *Devlin Report*. As with the *Fulton Report*, its contemporaneous UK counterpart, it found that major reforms were, by then, necessary. Chief among its recommendations was the separation of policy formulation, in a central departmental core, and service delivery, in the wider department. In some departments, this was done, and in the 1970s a Department of the Civil Service was established, but in general the *Devlin Report* was not implemented.

A similar fate befell the 1985 *Serving the Country Better* review, apart from its impact on how top civil servants were appointed. Indeed, the Department of Civil Service was disbanded shortly afterwards, and its functions remain with the Department of Finance to this day. This review, though, did establish an important change regarding who the reforms were about. Whereas reform from the 1850s until the 1960s had been about public service workers and processes, *Serving the Country Better* was about public service customers, i.e. citizens, and how public services could be made better for the citizen.

1994–2008: The Rise of the Public Service Reform Industry

The modern history of Irish public service reform dates from 1994 and the *Strategic Management Initiative*, the first major review of the public service since independence to have the backing of senior politicians and public servants. Its aim was to make the public service more effective at meeting the needs of citizens and, as its name suggests, it made government departments and other public service bodies write down their strategic objectives for the first time. This was quickly followed by the *Delivering Better Government* review of 1996, which focused on the civil service and outlined areas of change needed to deliver the goals of the *Strategic Management Initiative*.

The priorities outlined in *Delivering Better Government* included greater openness and flexibility, a high quality of service, partnership across the public service and effective human resource (HR) management. These are largely the challenges that still face the public service in the 2010s. This is despite a plethora of subsequent reform initiatives over the past fifteen years, and a quick recap of the main initiatives will not only give a flavour of the growing industry that is public service reform, but also make the point that marginal changes to how the public service works often have limited success.

In customer service, there has been the Quality Customer Service Initiative (1997, revised in 2000), the Customer Service Action Plans (1997), replaced in 2002 by the Customer Service Charter Initiative, and the Public Service Excellence Awards (started in 2004). There have also been initiatives in relation to e-government, which (for some reason) fall outside the *Strategic Management Initiative*, but which have implications not just for customer service but for processes and structures also. However, progress in this area has been limited. As countries from Malta to Malaysia develop integrated portals for citizens to access public services in an easy-to-use way, Ireland's 'Public Service Broker' project remains stalled. In a 2007 study for the European Commission, Ireland's government came thirteenth out of the EU15 for 'online sophistication maturity'.[3]

In the area of HR and management of workers, the principal initiative has been the Performance Management Development System (PMDS), based on 'role profile forms' for each worker that are reviewed by line managers (launched in 2000). In relation to financial accounting, there was the Expenditure Review Initiative (1997), which was re-launched as the Value for Money and Policy Reviews in 2006, as well as the Management Information Framework (launched in 2000), and, more recently, departmental Output Statements (a requirement from 2006).

In the area of regulation and legislation, the government established the High Level Group to Promote Better Regulation in 2002, which led to the establishment of Regulatory Impact Analyses, mandatory since 2005 for all primary legislation.

Lastly, there is local government. There have been numerous reports on the reform of local government in Ireland, from *The Financing of Local Government in Ireland* and *Better Local Government – A Programme for Change* under the Rainbow Coalition in the mid-1990s to Indecon's 2005 *Review of Local Government Financing* and the 2008 *Green Paper on Local Government Reform*. The most recent major report was one published in July 2010, by the Local Government Efficiency Review Group. It identified about €500 million in waste annually from inefficient local authority structures and recommended the merger of 20 local authorities and the reduction of the number of county managers from 34 to 24. In adopting a tone closer to transformation than incremental reform, the report was welcome. However, it is by no means the first review group to suggest, for example, the abolition of town councils and yet they continue to exist. Therefore, the ability of the current public service to implement the recommendations is far from clear.

This long list of initiatives, programmes and reports gives a flavour of the major initiatives that have been announced as the industry of public service reform has grown and grown since the mid-1990s. And yet, fifteen years on from *Delivering Better Government*, the key challenges identified then still remain.

'Agencification' and 'Decentralisation'

Two further developments over the past fifteen years have potentially significant on-going consequences for Ireland's public service. The first, what the OECD calls 'agencification', has been largely by accident, while the second, what the Irish government calls 'decentralisation', has been by design.

'Agencification' refers to the process of a greater number of public service functions being carried out by agencies funded by core departments rather than by those core departments themselves. Much agencification has occurred due to recruitment bans put in place by the Department of Finance. While this has often allowed the public service to expand and take on new responsibilities, the way in which agencification has occurred in Ireland has led to greater fragmentation and reduced transparency across the public service as a whole. It has also complicated career prospects for generalist public servants, as they work in increasingly smaller organisations.

A major public service change introduced in the 2000s was decentralisation. As decentralisation typically refers to the transfer of powers away from central government to subnational authorities, rather than just the relocation of public servants, the OECD 2008 review of Ireland's public sector referred to the policy as 'administrative relocation'. This was an ambitious plan announced in 2003, the aim of which was to relocate 14,000 public servants to 55 locations across 25 counties. With turnover as high as 90 per cent in some departments affected by administrative relocation, the plan has been hugely problematic.

In addition to HR issues, there are major concerns about the efficiency and coherence of work undertaken by a single central government public service spread across more than 50 locations largely for reasons of political expediency as opposed to service delivery. As the OECD review says, so-called decentralisation 'may further contribute to fragmentation ... [and] poses significant challenges to modernisation and the ability to achieve an integrated cohesive Public Service'.[4] In short, decentralisation is proving a spectacular failure and has no place in a public service focused on the needs of its customers – the citizens of the country.

Key Issues for Ireland's Public Service

As the on-going repeated attempts at reform show, it is clear that business-as-usual is not an option for Ireland's public service. This would be the case, even if Ireland's public service was not living significantly beyond its means. As is discussed in Chapter 5 on economic policy, however, in 2009, the amount spent by Ireland's public service exceeded the amount taken in as revenue by €20 billion. This highlights the urgency with which Ireland's public service needs not just reform, but transformation.

Leaving aside budgetary issues, there are significant further issues facing the public service. OECD reviews in 2001 (*Regulatory Reform in Ireland*) and 2008 (*Ireland: Towards an Integrated Public Service*) have highlighted – in suitably diplomatic language – persistent shortcomings in relation to Ireland's public service and its reform agenda. The 2008 review outlined four key weaknesses of Ireland's public service, which are discussed below.

Ensuring Capacity

The public service currently has huge capacity issues and is not able to move around skills to ensure they are allocated where they are needed. Public service organisations have very little freedom in HR management:

the Department of Finance has an effective veto on core employment numbers, while the trade unions and the Department of An Taoiseach have control on pay scales, via social partnership. This limits the management of public service organisations to respond to changing conditions. Bizarrely, given the generalist nature of the public service, there is also very restricted mobility across the service.

Motivating Performance

The OECD review highlighted the need for a total change of culture in Ireland's public service so that the focus is on value for money and performance, rather than compliance. Much of what is there now is monitoring of inputs, creating a disconnect between information generated in, say, the Management Information Framework and the information needed for a department's annual Output Statement. Also, the legacy of waves of initiatives on the administrative burden facing workers and managers has created 'reform fatigue' among many in the public service.

Moving Towards a Citizen-Centred Approach

Despite a generation of attempts to transform the public service to be focused on the citizen, rather than worker-focused, the OECD still found that the system is not focused on the needs of citizens. In particular, it highlighted the need for a unified front for delivering the full range of public services to citizens in an integrated way. Ireland has isolated e-government successes, for example, but citizens still suffer from the lack of a unified strategy across the public service.

Strengthening Governance

Lastly, the OECD believes that the structures of governance and accountability in the public service – particularly given the agencification that has occurred since the 1990s – need to be overhauled. Despite social partnership agreements, there remains a deficiency in service-wide long-term objectives. The priority for the two core departments, Finance and An Taoiseach, seems to be direct control, rather than establishing frameworks and objectives.

There is widespread agreement among all stakeholders, including public service workers, about the scale of the issues pervading the public service. This is seen, for example, in the remit of the Croke Park Agreement of 2010, which – at a time of unprecedented stress on public finances

– gave equal billing alongside pay issues to building an integrated public service 'focused more on the needs of the citizen'. Clearly, though, with a range of issues facing Ireland's public sector, there is a need for more than just reform of the existing system. Instead, it is time that Ireland considered transformation on the scale of the Northcote–Trevelyan reforms of the 1850s – a redefinition of the principles underlying the public service.

Transforming Ireland's Public Service over the Next Generation

If the public service is to be based on a new set of principles, what should those principles be? This section highlights three principles that a modern public service should look to enshrine. To actually turn the public service into an organisation that is focused on its customers, firstly, the public service needs to first become a twenty-first-century employer, which has implications for contract length, performance reviews and pension provision. This will enable the transformation, secondly, of the public service from a pyramid organisation into a pool organisation, one that can act with flexibility and expertise in the coming 'project economy'. Lastly, in order to serve its customers better, the public service needs to understand what value it provides to them. This means not only transforming prices into taxes, as is discussed in Chapter 5, but giving public service organisations – in particular local government – greater financial responsibility.

The State as a Twenty-First-Century Employer

Review after review of the public service discusses the need to ensure that it is focused on citizens, rather than processes or workers. Nonetheless, to transform the public service into one that is actually focused on its customers will require a complete overhaul of how the state employs its workers. It is almost beyond argument that the current model is unsustainable. Three aspects – firstly, permanent employment until retirement, secondly, the absence of meaningful on-going performance reviews and thirdly, a defined benefit pension after retirement – are not only outdated but threaten the sustainability of the public service.

The existence of 'bank days' – where civil servants get time off to lodge and cash cheques – in a world with electronic banking highlights how outdated some aspects of public service employment have become. **Permanent contracts** are a relic of employment conditions over a century ago, when there were concerns that changes of government would result in similar and sudden changes in public servants, with the resulting loss of expertise for the system and security for the worker. In a modern society that is a member of the EU, which has some of the strictest employment standards in the world, it is inconceivable that a political party now would try to replace out-of-favour public servants, let alone that it would be successful in so doing, given the labour relations apparatus available to the public servants affected.

The public service as a whole can no longer guarantee that there will be demand for a particular set of skills in twenty or forty years. Indeed, with the requirements and priorities on the public service changing over time, tethering future taxpayers to spending commitments by today's public service can hamstring a public service in its reaction to new challenges. It would make much more sense for the public service to have as the norm, rather than the exception, a series of one-year to five-year contracts, which, for a proven service need, can be made permanent after a certain minimum length of service.

This would assist in the introduction of meaningful **performance reviews**, a second key feature of the public service in the future. Until recently, there was no systematic evaluation of performance across the public sector. Since the introduction of the Performance Management Development System (PMDS) described above, there is at least now a service-wide framework for measuring and understanding performance at the individual level. In theory, it is also possible for pay increments to be withheld if performance is unsatisfactory. However, in a practical sense, pay increments are practically guaranteed to all staff and unions have reacted angrily to departments that have attempted to follow the underlying spirit of meaningful performance reviews.[5]

The public service will need to turn the PMDS framework into a meaningful tool for performance, one that rewards outstanding performance and punishes unsatisfactory work. This will require greater skills of people management throughout the public service, as the on-going relationship between worker and manager is the most important one for performance review. The average worker will have, by definition, an average performance. For obvious reasons of fairness, an average performance should not be rewarded with the same increase in salary as an outstanding performance.

Not having such a system has significant detrimental effects on the public service. At the time of the *First Benchmarking Report*, a Goldsmith Fitzgerald survey of those leaving the public service found that their main reason for leaving was nothing to do with private sector pay levels; rather, they left because they felt a lack of recognition and reward for personal effort.[6] This is not just about pay. Two generations of research in psychology and behavioural economics have taught us that directly linking performance to pay can have unintended adverse consequences when the task involved is a complex one; thus, performance-related pay should only be one strand of a meaningful system of recognition and reward. The public service must – in a comprehensive sense of the word – reward individual effort.

Lastly, in relation to **pensions**, there is no free money any more. Defined benefit pensions, where the worker knows before retirement the scale of benefits, have proved to be completely unsustainable and are now being phased out in the private sector. A 2010 report in the UK, which has a similar scheme to Ireland, estimated that the pensions for new entrants to the public sector are worth over 40 per cent of salary, about twice the combined employer and employee contribution of 20 per cent.[7]

The pensions system has only lasted as long as it has in the public service because of inertia, because the population was growing and because there was traditionally a short life expectancy on retirement. International trends suggest that Ireland cannot depend on its population growing substantially in the future. Much more importantly, people are enjoying long and healthy lives after retirement. Lastly, there are huge issues in relation to equity across sectors, with private sector workers who have no pension paying taxes to pay guaranteed pay-linked pensions for public sector workers. Therefore, there is no future in the public service for defined benefit pensions, which essentially make large promises far into the future, based on a gamble.

Out-of-date employment conditions may be related to an out-of-date dialogue between the state as an employer and its workers. Modern companies are shaped around the belief that workers, be they managers or not, are working together to give a service to customers, and in so doing creating benefits for themselves and for shareholders. Relations between managers and workers in the public service still seem to be confrontational in nature, something that strikes those outside the public service as more nineteenth century than twenty-first century. And yet the scope for potential partnership in the public service is huge: four out of five workers in public administration and defence were members of a union in 2009, compared to just one of out five in the rest of the economy.

In 2008, a government minister described much of the employment of entry-level clerical officers in Ireland as 'disguised unemployment', i.e. the public service employing people who would not otherwise find work. This is not the role of the public service and no public service can be expected to perform well under such circumstances. Instead, the public service needs to become a twenty-first-century employer. By moving to fixed-term contracts, the public service will be able to acquire the skills it needs for as long as it needs them. By putting in place meaningful performance reviews, it can reward performance and keep its best workers. And by putting in place modern pension provisions, the public service will make a significant contribution to its financial sustainability.

From Pyramid to Pool: The Public Service in the Project Economy

Currently there are numerous barriers within and around the labour market in the public service. These are legacies of the pyramid structure of the public service put in place in the nineteenth century, where a secretary general is in charge of a number of assistants, each of whom has responsibility for a number of principal officers, and so the organisation expands under the secretary general. Over the coming generation, these barriers will need to be removed, and the pyramid system radically overhauled, if the public service is going to be able to access the skills it needs when it needs them.

The most obvious barrier is between public and private sectors. Perhaps in the near future, it will be illegal for an Irish (or EU) citizen to be prevented from applying for *any* post in the public service, as seems reasonable given the philosophy behind EU anti-discrimination laws. Currently, however, there is very little opportunity for entering the public service above junior roles. This prevents any entry of meaningful private sector experience into the public service, itself a significant drawback for Ireland's public services, and has clear consequences for the willingness of public servants to gain useful experience in other sectors. Coupled with the lack of private sector experience in political circles, as discussed in Chapter 2, it is very difficult to see where the expertise comes from in a system with generalist politicians and generalist public servants. An argument could be made, also, that this sort of environment attracts a disproportionate number of workers who are averse to risk, relative to society as a whole.

An open labour market across public and private sectors would put an end to the allocation of staff based on considerations other than return to society and would prevent the need for expensive benchmarking procedures. The first benchmarking exercise, carried out by the Public Service Benchmarking Body in 2002, added significantly to public sector pay costs at the time and that cost has increased exponentially over time, as it is multiplied in with increments and national wage agreements. This would not be an issue if the increases were necessary. However, there does not appear to have been any research underpinning the findings of the *First Benchmarking Report*, and subsequent research has revealed that the public sector enjoyed a substantial wage premium in 2001.[8] This serious failing of the Irish policy-making system has cost the taxpayer billions over the last decade. This exercise would have been completely unnecessary had public service jobs been open to private sector workers.

As highlighted in the OECD 2008 review, there are also numerous barriers existing within the public service. This is of particular frustration given the explicit preference in Ireland's public service for generalists over specialists. Many of these barriers have come about due to agencification, which fragments the public service into smaller and smaller units. Other barriers are due to legacies of older divisions, such as the paucity of opportunities to switch between local and national levels of the public service. The creation of a central careers planning service, as is common in most public services and large employers, would help significantly, as existing barriers would be highlighted and steps could be taken to remove them.

However, a more fundamental problem remains, namely, the balance between generalists and specialists. Ireland's public service has its origins in a generalist culture. Now, however, different parts of the public service have different roles, each of which has requirements for very different skills: some are funders and some service providers, some work with partner organisations in the private or community and voluntary sectors, while others are regulators and others still policy-makers. The complexity of the public service means that a flexible approach is required: witness, for example, the complexity of policy challenges presented by climate change or swine flu. Meanwhile, information technology (IT) is transforming the more routine aspects of service delivery, as online services such as MotorTax.ie and Revenue.ie have shown. The result is that the core skill requirements for the public service now are very different to what they were a generation ago. There is a growing share of activity in the public service that is project-based, rather than indefinite, while indefinite activities require particular skills, e.g. IT maintenance. This is true in the wider economy also. Deutsche Bank's think tank, DB Research, describes the growth of for-purpose teams working on finite collaborative projects as the 'project economy', with team membership varying flexibly over the life of the project, as needs dictate.[9]

Having a pool of generalists with project management skills has significant implications for organisational structure. Rather than a set pyramid, the public service can be thought of instead as a pool of skills, with individual workers belonging to a particular division – based on their home region or key skill – but undertaking their core work by participating in different teams. Having over 350,000 employees presents a huge opportunity for the public service. Breaking down the barriers and uncovering the full range of skills that workers have will significantly boost productivity. This looser organisational structure – combined with more modern work contracts – also prevents unnecessary fixed costs from arising and prevents the phenomenon of one department having to manage legacy staff from an out-of-date programme.

A looser structure will also make it easier for the public service to develop core teams of specialists that different parts of the public service can access when required. A relatively formal example of this model is the UK's Government Economic Service (GES), which employs 1,500 economists who can be accessed by over 40 different departments and agencies in the UK public service. The GES dates from the 1960s, when the UK's *Fulton Report* highlighted the limitations of a public service staffed entirely by generalists. The OECD refers to this as a network-based approach, or an integrated public service. Another way of viewing this – and a test to see if it has happened in a generation – is the language used: departments or teams? The current public service is a pyramid organisation and thinks in terms of departments, while a project-based organisation with a flexible pool of labour thinks in terms of teams.

Matching Budgets to Outcomes

As mentioned above, the public service faces a huge challenge in the 2010s in relation to living within its means. Chapter 5 explores ways of moving away from the reckless fiscal policy of the 2000s and recommends the principle of turning taxes into prices. This involves estimating the value that a public service gives and pricing accordingly (and progressively, so that the better off pay more). It also involves a total transformation of the financial organisation of the public service. Currently, the public service works primarily off central revenues distributed by the Department of Finance. Revenues are rarely ring-fenced, with some exceptions. The result is a complete disconnection between the value that a particular public service brings and the expenditure its delivery causes.

This disconnect is seen most clearly in the need for 'An Bord Snip Nua' in 2009. The reaction of most interest groups to announcements in the *Bord Snip Nua Report* of cuts in their area was to state that focusing on costs is only one half of the equation and that while money might be saved, the country would be worse off without the service in question. This shows an understanding of both costs and benefits, ultimately what economics is all about and what the public service should be about. But an Bord Snip Nua was not an economic exercise, it was an accounting one.

It could only ever be an accounting exercise because the public service has no idea of the scale of benefits it gives to society.

Over the coming generation, the public service must switch from an accounting approach to an economic approach. In addition to, as outlined above, giving greater autonomy to public service organisations to hire who they need for as long as they need, public service organisations must also be given greater responsibility to manage their financial affairs. The *Devlin Report* from the late 1960s noted, 'central Departments engage in such strict control that the responsibility and initiative of local bodies and, thus, their adaptability to change has been diminished.' The same holds true now, with the OECD 2008 review recommending that the two central departments – Finance and An Taoiseach – move from their current paradigm of direct control to a new model, where their responsibility is to set the framework.

What Ireland's public service actually needs, however, is greater devolution of financial responsibility. This means that when excesses happen, they happen on a much smaller scale than Ireland has just witnessed. One could think of this as similar to credit unions versus banks in the financial crisis of 2008–2010. With such a small number of banks, there is a much greater risk of the entire banking system collapsing. With a far greater number of credit unions, while one or two may overstretch themselves, it is incredibly unlikely that every last credit union would collapse. As with financial institutions, so too with public service organisations.

Devolution of financial responsibility means an end to the culture of allowing departmental or agency budgets to drift upwards by some percentage year on year, based on arguments about wage inflation. Instead, public service organisations must be incentivised – and required, if budgetary conditions dictate – to deliver productivity improvements each year. Put another way, for a given set of core programmes, the budget should shrink by a certain percentage each year, to reflect efficiency improvements.

The full extension of the principle of matching budgets to outcomes, however, means devolution of revenue-raising powers where appropriate. Nowhere is this more necessary for Ireland's public service than in local government. Currently, the structure of local government expenditure is an oddity among developed countries. In Ireland, local government spends almost as much as central government: 44 per cent of total government revenues, according to OECD figures for 2004. This money is spent in areas such as environmental protection, waste management, road transportation and safety, and water supply and sewerage. But local authorities in Ireland raise almost no revenues, compared to what they spend. They may account for almost half of all public expenditure, but they raise less than 5 per cent of revenues.[10] Ireland's local authorities are almost entirely bereft of fiscal autonomy.

As discussed in Chapter 5, part of this is because Ireland is almost unique in not having an annual residential property tax. The introduction of a property tax in Ireland should be done as part of an overhaul of local governance in Ireland, an overhaul that places local authorities as masters of their financial affairs. The reorganisation of Ireland into a manageable number of economic regions (see Chapter 5) would mean a very different implementation, one that could tap into economies of scale while still promoting regional financial management.

The logical end-point of establishing the value of public services and of giving public service organisations greater financial independence is giving them the ability to issue their own debt to finance particular projects of value. This is, in some sense, a return to the past. Consider the idea of municipal bonds, where a city issues debt on global capital markets. While such an idea may sound radical, it was well-established practice for cities around the world to issue their own debt in the 1800s. In any given issue of the *Investor's Monthly Manual* from the 1880s, the international bond market listings had bonds for cities such as Dublin, Liverpool and Nottingham alongside UK bonds, and Buenos Aires bonds competed with Argentinian national bonds for buyers.

The guiding principle, that budgets match outcomes, requires that all parts of the public service understand the value of the outcomes they deliver. This will require ingenuity on the part of those providing particular services. In some cases, this may prove easy: local authorities will avail of valuation research, which estimates how much private households value public transportation or education services. Often, however, this will prove much more challenging. In all cases, it will require the generation of information, and of data in particular, in far greater volumes, and in a far more timely manner, than is currently the case, a theme taken up in Chapter 5. The recently launched Output Statements are just the first step in a long journey.

Consider education, for example. It is no longer enough to use the amount of money spent on education as a success metric. In a logical flow from inputs through process and outputs to outcomes, money spent is an input. The focus should ideally be on outcomes, or at the very least outputs. Public examination results may be regarded as outputs, at least for secondary education. Outcomes need to be broader. Education can learn from other industries, particularly those other services that have to deal with nebulous results. Teachers are responsible not for getting every student to an A1 standard, but for improving the performance of each student so that they achieve their potential. To know if this is happening, an evaluation needs to be made about the expectations for each student, each year. (See also Chapter 6 for a discussion on improving Ireland's education system.) Student-level indicators may sound either radical or overly bureaucratic, given the current systems used in the education system. However, anything other than a thorough knowledge by a teacher about the prospective performance of each student is an abdication of responsibilities. More often than not, such a system would merely formalise what good teachers do already.

Ultimately, matching budgets to outcomes requires changing how public services are funded, so that the value they add is understood and financial responsibility is devolved to those responsible for managing the service. This requires a fundamental change in how the Department of Finance works, as well as putting huge emphasis on outcomes, not inputs or expenditure, for all publicly provided services.

Conclusion: Escaping the Old Ideas

John Maynard Keynes wrote in the 1930s: 'The difficulty lies, not in the new ideas, but in escaping from the old ones, which ramify, for those brought up as most of us have been, into every corner of our minds.'[11]

It would be reassuring, particularly given the challenges Ireland currently faces, to be able to say that Ireland's public service has come a long way since independence and that change along similar lines will be needed over the coming generation. In truth, however, what is startling is that Ireland's public service would be so recognisable now to someone who worked in public administration a century ago. The lack of contrast is made starker by the huge transformations that private sector organisations have undergone in the same period. The challenge for the public service is, as Keynes put it, to escape the old ideas.

Starting in the 1850s, the civil service underwent a transformation and the result is the permanent, unified and politically neutral public service that still exists today. It is now time for a similar scale of transformation. It is time, because of the huge challenges Ireland's public service faces today. Perhaps the most urgent is the huge discrepancy between what the public service costs and what it raises in revenue. However, it is by no means the only challenge. As the OECD review of 2008 highlighted, the public service is currently unable to ensure it has the skills or flexibility required to meet its customers' needs. There is no motivation of performance, rather a culture of compliance that does not foster efficiency, let alone excellence. Despite the efforts of the past fifteen years, the public service is still not focused on its customer, the citizen. Lastly, the governance structures need to be overhauled, and the two central departments – Finance and An Taoiseach – need to move from direct control to setting a framework for public service organisations.

On what principles might a transformation of Ireland's public service be based? Three broad principles have been outlined. The first is transforming the state into a twenty-first-century employer. This will mean an end to permanent posts, as these restrict the ability of the public service to use the skills it needs when they are needed. It would mean the introduction of meaningful performance reviews, where outstanding work is recognised and rewarded, enhancing the performance of the public service and its ability to attract the best workers. And it would mean an end to open-liability pensions that rely on demographics that Ireland no longer has.

The second is adapting the public service for the project economy. This will only be done when the default unit in the public service is not, as it currently stands, the permanent department, rather it is the finite team. By doing this, the public service will free up the skills of its workers so they can be used where they are needed most. This will involve the abolition of all barriers to worker mobility within the public service and between it and the rest of the economy.

The third principle is that of matching budgets to outcomes. Budgets in the public service are primarily set currently by inputs, not outcomes. By matching budgets to outcomes, this will mean that public service organisations will think in terms of the impact they have, and organise their work and teams around that impact, rather than the other way around. Measurement of the impact of public services will require ingenuity, particularly for some services, but it is the only way of ensuring that the public service is sustainably engaging in the activities that society needs it to be providing.

Each of these three principles has significant implications for how Ireland's public service operates and each would require a decade-long transition phase. But difficulty is not an excuse for avoiding a task. Understanding how our public service will work in the 2030s means we can work back from there and start making changes straight away, to build the future we want.

After decades of inactivity, there has been a surge of public sector reform initiatives since 1995. Some have been a failure, such as benchmarking and decentralisation. Others have been well-intentioned adjustments to the current system that have merely added to a worker's administrative burden. The endless stream of announcements, initiatives and new requirements has caused 'reform fatigue' in many parts of the public service. But the problems persist. Ireland's public service does not need more reform, it needs to transform.

Ireland, But Not As We Knew It:
Migration, Identity and Citizenship

Michael Courtney

Lessons from Cork

In 2009, a Cork taxi driver, Lama Niankone, crossed a picket being staged by the Cork Taximen's Association and continued with his job. He had been refused entry to the association on the grounds that the union was not currently accepting black taxi drivers, due to their inexperience and indeterminate legality to operate as taxi drivers. This story received national attention and it became clear that the union was operating discriminatory practices against black taxi drivers. In the context of a large increase in the overall number of taxi drivers, migrant drivers were predictably singled out in the resulting backlash, with unique vitriol being reserved for black or 'Nigerian' drivers. The leader of the Cork Taximen's Association, Derry Coughlan, attempted to justify the exclusion of the black drivers on the grounds that 'they are too new to our shores', claiming that 'our union is not racist because we have members from India, Chile, Poland, Pakistan, Albania, Bangladesh, England, Scotland and Tunisia.' Some union members went so far as to allege that African drivers were more likely to rape customers.[1]

What is perhaps most shocking about the racism evident in refusing union membership to black taxi drivers in Ireland is the deafening silence from senior government ministers in response to such incidents. Junior Minister for Labour Affairs Billy Kelleher did state at the time that any individual who wished to join a representative trade union should be allowed to do so. However, for an incident as serious as that in Cork, at the very least the Minister for Integration and the Minister for Enterprise, if not the Taoiseach, should have made a statement to condemn this overt racism. The fact that they did not do so lends legitimacy to the taxi drivers' actions, leaving others who may hold similar views less afraid to express them publicly. The experience of other countries shows that political neglect of the issue of integration can in the long term cause serious social problems such as race riots, ghettos and extreme right-wing parties.

Despite the severe economic recession that followed the Celtic Tiger period, the number of non-national people resident in Ireland is unlikely to ever again recede to pre-2000 levels. It would therefore be irresponsible to plan the next generation of Ireland's development without giving considerable thought to how the state can adapt to large-scale migration to our shores. This chapter discusses how Ireland can learn from the experiences of others and manage the integration of the 'new Irish' and their children into Irish society over the coming generation. The next section outlines national and international experiences of identity and migration during the twentieth century. The cultural and economic integration of diverse immigrants has been a policy challenge for many countries, such as Germany, France and the UK, in the post-war era. Ireland has the almost unique advantage in the Western world of being able to draw on decades of experience from neighbouring countries in dealing with a challenge that in Ireland has only emerged relatively recently.

The following section outlines what integration requires, in particular the promotion of intercultural engagement and understanding. It outlines policy proposals based on quantifiable goals that can be measured at ten-year intervals for the next thirty years. Three areas are of particular importance: Firstly, the rights available to immigrants, including voting rights, access to language training and awareness of statutory rights. Secondly, the use of social and cultural activities, for example sport and the voluntary sector, to assist in the integration process. Thirdly, ensuring respect for diversity by developing channels of communication that go beyond religion.

A Tale of Two Irelands

The 2006 census provides an illustration of Ireland's cultural make-up at the height of the country's prosperity. Although there was a significant influx of half a million people into the state up to the census date, migration tended to be predominantly from a handful of countries, namely the UK, Poland, Lithuania, China, Germany and Nigeria.[2]

The onset of the recession in 2007 has tested immigrants' commitment to Ireland in terms of the extent to which they choose to remain despite the scarcity of jobs or wage reduction. It is estimated that over 100,000 people have left Ireland as a result of the economic downturn, with this number evenly split between emigrating Irish and immigrants returning home. Therefore, of the half a million people who identified themselves as 'non-Irish' in the 2006 census, and even discounting those who identified themselves as UK citizens, upwards of 300,000 remain resident in the state. One can only conclude that these individuals have a long-term commitment to a life in Ireland, despite the country's economic woes.

Moreover, given the size of the migrant population in Ireland, it would be irresponsible of any government to ignore the potential problems of culturally integrating those who have chosen Ireland as their new home. Ireland's history contains reasons for both pessimism and optimism, but it is perhaps the experience of other countries, such as France and the UK, that will provide the most instructive lessons for twenty-first-century Ireland. Figure 4.1 displays the immigration flow over the past several

Figure 4.1: Foreigners as a Percentage of the Total Population, Selected Countries, 2000 and 2009

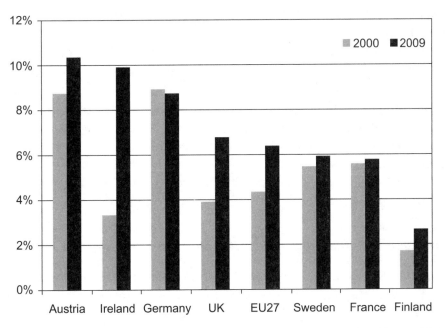

Source: Calculations by Michael Courtney and Ronan Lyons, based on Eurostat data.

years. The commitment of certain migrant groups is striking, given the recession, and shows that there was more to the allure of Ireland than mere short-term economic gain over the past ten years.

Ireland in the Twentieth Century – Closed Shop or Open House?

Ireland in the twentieth century was a tale of two countries. One Ireland was a culturally homogenous society ultimately ruled by the Catholic Church with an almost autarkic attitude to international relations. The second Ireland was one which, by necessity, spread its people all over the globe, to the extent that the number of those who claim some sort of Irish ancestry is, at seventy million, almost twenty times Ireland's current population.[3] Coupled with experiencing only temporary holiday visitors and very few migrant workers, Ireland has generally been perceived internationally as an open, friendly and welcoming society.

The first Ireland is one that might be expected to show a hostile reaction to large-scale migration from widely divergent cultures. By contrast, the second offers hope that Ireland, with its extensive diaspora and long history of migration, would in turn be a more welcoming place for international migrants to settle. As a result of the culture of emigration, other aspects of our culture, such as St Patrick's Day, are celebrated with a degree of international fanfare enjoyed by no other nation on the planet. Its closest rivals are major Christian and Islamic holidays, which really belong to no one country.

The welcoming reputation of the Irish is largely predicated on our relationship with tourists, and is one which economic rationale dictates that we court assiduously. It remains to be seen whether the reputation will survive into the future given the sudden and large influx of immigrants observed over the past decade. So far, Ireland is not doing too badly at all; in 2008, *Foreign Affairs* magazine ranked Ireland first in a list of the best countries to be an immigrant.[4] The challenge for Irish society in the coming decades is to retain that title. In doing so, it is critical that we learn from the experiences of other European countries.

Assimilation, Multiculturalism, Integration and the Dangers Therein

Upon abandoning their imperial ambitions, the British and the French faced the challenge of constructing a post-colonial identity that included not only their own indigenous citizens (the autochthonous, as they are academically referred to), but also many citizens of their former colonies who had migrated to the 'motherland' and set down roots.[5] Germany, too, brought this challenge on itself by opening its borders to Turkish guest workers in order to fill the labour shortages of the 1960s. The common lack of foresight evident in all of these cases was the assumption that the migrants would just pack up and leave when colonial ties were severed or labour requirements met. Such a belief in the logic of voluntary repatriation was merely wishful thinking. The opportunities available to migrants in their host countries, not only in terms of economics but also the liberties enjoyed by Western societies with respect to freedom of expression and equality before the law, were enough to ensure that significant populations remained, and others were continually attracted.

From a public policy perspective, the methods of incorporating immigrants into these European countries can be identified within three broad categories: assimilation, multiculturalism and integration.[6] The first of these, assimilation, is embodied in the French approach. Immigrants are required to renounce their identity as, for example, Algerians, and become 'French' in every practical way. The underlying reasoning here is that by eliminating cultural difference, the prospect of interethnic conflict will be diminished. This approach does not sufficiently appreciate or accommodate two overt measures of difference and the possible bases of social exclusion, namely, skin colour and religion. Regardless of the normative assessment of such an approach, the policy has largely succeeded in its aim of ensuring that immigrants, particularly immigrant children, identify themselves as French rather than Algerian.

A further successful aspect of this policy is that immigrant children have been shown to perform on a par with autochthonous children of similar socio-economic circumstances in school. However, secularisation is a slower process, with many migrants resisting the French state's general indifference towards accommodating religious traditions and difference. This tension, coupled with the ghettoisation of migrants – evidenced particularly in the Paris suburbs where the 2005 race riots took place – illustrate the fact that assimilation is not a sustainable policy. Nevertheless, the July 2010 336–1 vote by the National Assembly to ban (indirectly but most conspicuously) Islamic dress in certain public places demonstrates French policy-makers' commitment to this approach, regardless of the cultural tensions it produces.[7]

By contrast, Britain adopted the equally undesirable policy of laissez-faire multiculturalism. Here, the state simply allows migrants to form their own communities, with little effort on the part of the state to integrate these communities into the wider socio-political realm. The advantage of this, proponents argue, is that concentration of ethnic minorities in such a way allows them to achieve descriptive political representation.

This means that 'their own' can win office and advocate on behalf of their community. The objective of this approach is to minimise racial tensions, which it succeeds in doing in the short term but with significant drawbacks in terms of integrating second- or third-generation migrants. Autochthonous representatives are less inclined to respond to or advocate for these communities, particularly in terms of broad social policy at the national level, as they see that issue as being taken care of by 'multicultural' representatives with whom they liaise from time to time, including for support during electoral campaigns.

A trend of the government working with self-anointed or state-appointed 'community leaders' undermines the incentive for migrants to engage with conventional elected institutions or, if they stand for elected office, to reach out to other communities in their locality. Moreover, the tendency of the British government to engage with religious leaders (from, for example the British Pakistani community) on political issues risks undermining more secular migrant leaders and focuses on the 'differences' between Britain's communities rather than their common interests. This has exacerbated a trend whereby a significant proportion of migrants and ethnic minorities do not fully identify themselves as British, despite living most of their lives in the country. This policy has recently borne some questionable outcomes such as the increasing deference of some British policy-makers to the demands of Islamic groups for a 'parallel' *Sharia* legal system.[8]

The alternative to the assimilationist approach of France and the multiculturalist approach of the UK is an 'integrationist' approach. The goal of an integrationist approach is to fully incorporate migrants into the host society without forcing them to make unreasonable compromises in respect of their cultural identity and origins. This must be balanced by the migrant's willingness to accept the fundamental values of their chosen destination. This is embodied in the Canadian experience.[9] Here, the state recognises that a successful integration process is dependent on the active participation of all members of society. One practical embodiment of this policy is that children of immigrants are encouraged to learn their parents' mother tongue in school as well as English or French, leaving them with the opportunity and the choice of how much of their own country-of-origin identity they wish to incorporate into their new Canadian identity. Most importantly, in this case there are none of the undesirable side effects of integration policy, such as ghettos and race riots. The problem with looking to Canada for policy proposals is that the success of this process is due as much to the cultural attitudes of Canadian society as it is to active policy processes. A critical distinction from Ireland is that Canadians accept that theirs is a country of immigrants. Canadian society will thrive or sink as a result of its divergent component parts. Indifferent attitudes and populist rhetoric on the part of the host society are not an option.

Ireland's Immigration Experience: The Attitudes of 'Us' and 'Them', and the Danger of Complacency

In 2008, *Foreign Policy* ran an article listing the best place in the world to be an immigrant. Of particular importance in their assessment of Ireland was the fact that no nationalist far-right party had emerged in reaction to the immigration experience, as had been the norm in many European countries. Many policy-makers have correctly pointed out that Ireland has undergone twelve years of large-scale immigration without the emergence of overtly racist political movements in the style of Jean-Marie Le Pen's *Front National* in France or Geert Wilders' *Partij voor de Vrijheid* (Party for Freedom) in the Netherlands.

The most organised attempt at establishing such a party in Ireland came from a group called the Immigration Control Platform. It ran candidates in the 2007 general election and the 2009 local election. Although being in existence since 1998, it was prohibited from registering as a political party as the result of a law passed that required political parties to have a minimum number of dues-paying members. Their candidates officially ran as independents. They managed a meagre 1,329 votes in the 2007 general election between three candidates.

The absence of any successful politicisation of the immigration issue in Ireland, the citizenship referendum of 2004 notwithstanding, is profoundly welcome. However, this phenomenon may be partly explained by the fact that large-scale immigration to Ireland coincided with high levels of economic growth and abundant jobs here. In a scenario where immigrants are not perceived to be displacing the autochthonous, and where the media narrative of the current crisis focuses the blame for the country's woes on the banking and political elite, anti-immigrant sentiment has yet to find a coherent political expression. This is unlikely to last indefinitely.

The establishment of a Ministerial Council on Integration, consisting of four regional fora where the Minister of State for Integration can engage directly with migrants, is a welcome step.[10] Each regional forum is set to meet up to three times a year, and to include up to twenty migrant representatives. However, the limits on eligibility for participation in this forum are actually more restrictive than those for voting and running in local elections, as migrants must be legally resident in the state for two years. Given the small size of the forum, it would be better to allow a percentage of migrants to apply who do not meet such criteria. Moreover, a more effective way to encourage integration is to include Irish citizens in the forum also, not least political representatives, as these are the people with whom the migrants must integrate and become interdependent. By holding broader fora like this, a better understanding of each other's needs will be fostered.

In terms of standing as political candidates, migrants have only engaged with formal politics to a minimal extent. The perceived wisdom prior to the 2007 election was that the political parties would seek to capitalise on any potential political payoffs from a growing migrant population.[11] It seems that, in the end, little effort was made to pursue any potential votes among naturalised migrants. When quizzed about the lack of migrant candidates, the political parties claimed to be committed to running more migrants at the next election. Of course anything can be done at the *next* election.

Members of the Oireachtas are currently not incentivised to pay much heed to migrants, given their inability to vote in general elections. However, it is too easy to paint an overly pessimistic portrait of the inability of naturalised citizens to break into Irish politics. Nonetheless, there are important exceptions. In a rural constituency of culturally homogeneous Ireland, Labour candidate, Muslim and pro-divorce activist Dr Moosajee Bhamjee was elected for one term in the 1992 general election, in which Labour doubled its vote share from 10 per cent to 20 per cent and won 33 seats. More recently, in 2007, the town of Portlaoise elected Rotimi Adebari, a Nigerian immigrant, as its mayor, having elected him to the town council in 2004. So, although diversity in the political system has been slow, it has in some instances been highly significant.

What makes the above developments more interesting is the strong tendency of many Irish voters to vote for the person rather than the party, usually because they have multiple options within each party. This emphasis on the individual would intuitively lead one to conclude that the electoral prospects of candidates from diverse social backgrounds and dissimilar experiences to most of the electorate are diminished in such a system. But the alternative argument would be that the purpose of voters focusing on the individual candidate is not to ensure congruence of social background, but to support the candidate who will have the greatest commitment to advocate on their behalf.[12] This is a race-blind hypothesis and one that is widely accepted in the study of Irish politics. In Ireland, there is certainly evidence at hand to conclude that hard constituency work pays and that racial background may not be such a critical factor.[13]

The reasons for the absence of negative politicisation of the immigration issue are many, including, on the one hand, the fact that the mainstream parties have not adopted an anti-immigrant populist stance.[14] To the credit of Irish society, the fact remains that immigrants have had more success in Irish politics than anti-immigrant parties. However, much of the kudos for this development must be awarded to the individuals who chose and fought to run as candidates than to the established parties. It was presumed by the political parties that the 2009 local elections would be a 'tipping point' for the involvement of migrants in electoral politics.[15] Out of the 1,635 candidates across the town, local and county competitions, 41 were migrants and only 2 were elected: Katarzyna Gaborec (Fianna Fáil) was elected to Mullingar Town Council and Rotimi Adebari (Independent) was re-elected to Portlaoise Town Council and simultaneously elected to Laois County Council for the Portlaoise ward. Taiwo Matthew lost his seat on Ennis Town Council, having been elected in 2004. Migrant candidates' countries of origin were principally Poland and Nigeria, but candidates from Bangladesh, Colombia, Russia, the Netherlands, Pakistan, Latvia, the US, India, Lithuania, Moldova and Zimbabwe also participated.

Every party except Sinn Féin ran a migrant candidate in the 2009 local elections. However, more candidates were independents (11) than ran for any one party. The argument could be made that this demonstrates an eagerness to participate by the migrant community that was not being catered for or sufficiently encouraged by the parties. However, a natural conservatism among mainstream parties in selecting candidates they view as newcomers to an area, and therefore without the same intrinsic knowledge of local issues as long-term residents, is perhaps to be expected. Moreover, adding any more candidates to the ticket could dilute the party vote and eventually cost seats.

On the migrants' side, non-national candidates were urged by their supporters not to run for the parties as they felt they would then be constrained by their party of choice in the degree of flexibility they had to raise issues which concerned them. Moreover, migrant candidates resisted the term 'immigrant representatives' as it implied that they only sought to represent the migrant community.[16] They preferred if people saw them as candidates who happened to be migrants, stressing the fact that they represented the entire electorate, not merely the migrant community or any Irish people who happened to vote for them.[17]

If Irish government policy could be criticised for being laissez-faire with regard to the integration of migrants, the redeeming feature of Irish society is that the public's mind on the immigrant issue has not yet been made up with regards to integration strategy. However, the opportunity for policy-makers to take a firm lead is narrowing. Ireland faces its most severe economic downturn in a generation, ripening conditions for an upturn in populist sentiment. There is still sufficient scope for policy-makers to lead public opinion rather than desperately following it, like their counterparts in France. French public opinion is almost steadfastly assimilationist and there are no votes to be gained in trying to change the status quo. Indeed, the almost immediate entry of the term 'new Irish' into the national conversation since the mass arrival of immigrants in 2004 signals a willingness on the part of the host society (us) to do its (our) fair share from the outset to promote cultural integration. If Ireland is to successfully pursue a strategy of integration, rather than assimilation or multiculturalism, the first steps must be to understand where the Irish system is currently strong and weak.

From 'New Irish' to 'Full Irish': Integrating Migrants

The business-as-usual lip service that is paid to integration, without quantifiable goals and fixed dates for their achievement, is insufficient to deal with the altered state of Irish society. Lack of substantive action could lead to, at best, a significant proportion of society being alienated from political discourse and, at worst, ghettos, riots and the polarisation of identity between the 'old' and 'new' Irish. In that regard, policy-making requires information about the current state of Ireland's policies in relation to migration and integration.

Ireland already has an objective analysis of its relative position with regard to the integration of migrants, against which current government policy can be measured in the extent of its vision, and from which further reforms can be suggested. The Migrant Integration Policy Index (MIPEX)[18] measures policies to integrate migrants in 28 European countries. The index covers policy areas such as labour market access, family reunion, long-term residence, political participation, access to nationality (citizenship) and anti-discrimination, and creates an overall ranking of countries.

On this scale, Ireland comes in at around the halfway point with an integration score of 53, with the worst practice country being Latvia with a score of 30 and the best practice country being Sweden with a score of 88. Of these policy areas, Ireland scores best on political participation rights (59 per cent) and worst on long-term residency rights (39 per cent), with all the other indicators scoring at least halfway to best practice. With the threat of anti-immigrant sentiment heightened due to economic pressures, an initial step in addressing how Irish society can ensure cultural cohesiveness into the future is to consider some of the areas where MIPEX indicates that reforms should be made.

Residency Status: Migrant Limbo

Ireland has no formal long-term residency status for migrants. This is probably due to an expectation that after five years of residency migrants should either establish themselves on the path to citizenship or return to their home countries. This is an inadequate approach in an ever-globalising world, particularly when the Irish state has lobbied for favourable treatment towards its own citizens residing illegally in the US.

What this lack of status means is that there is little or no flexibility in migrants' work status. Changing jobs is not the seamless task (in the event that a new job can be found) that Irish citizens take for granted. Non-EU migrants must technically seek the Minister of Justice's permission to change their employer, giving the Minister an opportunity to review their status entirely. This also gives the employer a dominant position over their migrant employee and distorts the natural equilibrium in labour market conditions achieved through the ability to change jobs. A competitive labour market diminishes the opportunity for employers to impose overly onerous working conditions. One need only consider the experience of migrant workers in the widely publicised cases of Irish Ferries and Gama Construction, to observe the extent to which employers will try to exploit those who have little knowledge of their rights and grievance mechanisms.[19]

Although the stated aim of the Immigration, Residence and Protection Bill 2010 is to address these issues by introducing a more automatic right to remain after ten years of employment (having been granted five years' long-term residency after five years of employment, subject to an application to the Office of the Minister for Justice), a more detailed reading of the Bill reveals that its emphasis is on monitoring migratory flows. The Minister remains extremely influential in the immigration process, with the resulting potential for political subjectivity trumping a candidate passing objective criteria. This could be problematic if in the future the public conversation on the immigrant issue turns negative, as the Minister could refuse applications for short-term populist gain. If a migrant has observably contributed to society, not being involved in criminality nor excessively dependent on welfare throughout their initial residence period, there should be some degree of automatic renewal of residency permissions.

The potential impact of leaving people in such limbo is that it hinders the social integration process of these migrants. Those who contribute to a society for such a period as five years should have formal recognition of their efforts and status. The government should act to create a long-term residency regime that recognises the contribution of the migrant to the Irish Exchequer and to society, and, as such, offers them certain legal guarantees and protections.

Integrating Immigrants into Politics

The quantitative evaluation by MIPEX of migrants' political rights masks a critical fact. The extension of the right to vote and stand for election to all legal residents is on paper an impressive feature of the Irish political system, and indeed Ireland is ranked highly by MIPEX for it. However, the fact that local government has relatively few powers (as highlighted by Eoin O'Malley in Chapter 2 of this volume), and what power it does possess lies to a great extent in the hands of the unelected county managers, makes this provision qualitatively weak. From a public policy perspective, the solution here is a complete overhaul of local government, which would include reforming the relationship between the local and national level. Therefore, in the process of incorporating the 'new Irish' into political life and in keeping with the theme of synergy, efforts should be made to re-ignite the democratic tendencies of all citizens.

If one were looking to go beyond even MIPEX's best practice recommendations, an argument could be made for giving long-term residents the right to vote in national elections. This is a highly sensitive issue as such rights go to the heart of a nation's sovereignty and what it means to be a citizen. Despite this, it would have two distinct benefits. The first is that it would offer migrants greater acceptance into their host society, encouraging greater and broader civic participation. The second is that national politicians would have a real incentive to respond to all the political preferences within society, as opposed to the two-tier system that is currently in place, where politicians respond primarily to their voting base and then to anyone else if they have political capital to spare.

This proposal could be justified using the old adage 'No taxation without representation.' It seems very unjust that people can make such a significant contribution to the national finances yet have no say in how these finances are re-distributed. However, this is not to advocate that non-citizens should be permitted to run in national elections; the essential right of the Irish citizenry to legislate for the state should be preserved. The situation would then be analogous to that of the relationship between young people and the presidency, where those under 35 may vote in the contest, but are not permitted to run themselves. The policy is a bold one but would engender a greater commitment to Irish society among those legal residents who have been in gainful employment for a period of more than five years.

The Importance of Language

In terms of cultural compatibility, Ireland has been fortunate in its immigration experience. The majority of immigrants in the Celtic Tiger wave were white, Catholic Poles. Many UK citizens, who make up the majority of immigrants, had been here for a long time already. The result is that immigrants are not as distinctively 'visible' in terms of ethnic and cultural difference as they might have been had all 500,000 come from Africa and Asia.

In an interview with the author, Artur Banaszkiewicz of the Polish Embassy in Dublin outlined the experience of the Polish community in Ireland. Racist incidents were generally not that common, despite the horrific double murder of two Polish men by teenagers in Drimnagh in 2008. Polish people are generally regarded as hardworking and this impression has stood to their advantage in the current recession. Moreover, changing jobs has a lesser psychological effect on Polish immigrants than it may have on the Irish. Mr Banaszkiewicz attributed this to his sense that if one is prepared to change countries in search of better opportunities, switching jobs becomes much less of a daunting task and Polish people are generally flexible in the job market. Social cohesion is enabled by the fact that Poland and Ireland are both members of the EU. This gives Polish people a sense of a psychological connection to Ireland that they would not have otherwise. However, he stopped short of saying that Polish people feel some sort of European identity superseding their Polish identity. Ultimately, though, this is an insufficient condition for a successful integration process in itself. Polish adults are generally averse to integrating with the Irish and succumb to the natural urge to stick to their own group.

The children of Polish immigrants, on the other hand, integrate very well in school. In Mr Banaszkiewicz's view, the most positive integration measure that policy-makers could adopt is, if possible, to establish a language requirement for residency and employment regardless of whether language proficiency is required for a job. In his opinion, if Poles had a real incentive to learn the local language, they would do it and it would significantly improve the integration process. Although enforcing a language constraint upon EU citizens is obviously impossible, there is nothing to stop the state imposing this requirement on non-EU migrants. Shared language and effective communication go a long way to ensuring social harmony in the long term. Similarly, the government should promote greater cultural exchange between Poland and Ireland, providing opportunities for cooperation in social sciences and the arts, not least in terms of Polish language classes.

Preemptive Policy-Making: Disarming Contentious Differences

As Ireland knows all too well, religion is frequently the ultimate expression of cultural difference and a cause of many of the undesirable outcomes of migration across Europe, such as ghettoisation and the emergence of extremist political parties. The Office of the Minister for Integration's policy statement on integration strategy and diversity management merely states in this regard that migrants and Irish citizens should respect each other's cultural differences without going into any greater detail. The document does not foresee any problem arising from Islamic extremism or misconceptions arising as to the true nature of mainstream Islam. Be that as it may, a policy statement that clearly sets out a government position on the more contentious issues of integration would be a useful measure. Any such policy should be grounded in the principle of tolerance. An interesting way to illustrate this approach is to consider the debate surrounding religious clothing, in particular Islamic dress, which has taken place throughout Europe, and how we might deal with this issue to avoid it being politicised to the same extent in Ireland.

A widely held view within European societies is that the requirements of Islam for women to 'dress modestly' has occasionally been taken to extremes and used as a tool to oppress women by requiring them, in an extreme minority of instances, to cover all parts of their bodies but their hands and eyes (*al-niqab*). Conversely, many Islamic women argue that wearing any sort of veil, whether it covers the face or not, is their own personal choice and they do not feel pressurised into doing so.[20]

Despite the Integration Office's predictions, Islamic dress has begun to become an issue in the Irish context. The subject arose when the *Irish Times* printed correspondence between the Department of Education and the principal of a school which concerned a lack of national policy on the wearing of forms of Islamic dress within state schools.[21] As media attention increased, the government issued a response in which it categorically stated that 'The issue of a school uniform is one for school authorities to design a policy on, following local consultations with the various members of the local community.'[22] In particular, the Minister for Integration at the time, Conor Lenihan, referenced the Education Act of 1998, which clarified the management role for school authorities as one of 'respect for the diversity of values, beliefs, traditions, languages and ways of life in society'. Referencing outdated legislation combined with vague aspirational rhetoric is far from the type of leadership required at this critical juncture. The government should show leadership rather than issuing opaque statements and delegating decision-making authority on this important issue to local school boards.

As a public policy measure, the state should take the view that cultural norms should be respected, to the extent that they do not infringe on any other individual's personal choice and do not contradict existing legislation. If there is a line to be drawn at which the state should not compromise it should be to resist the establishment of parallel and independent legal entities based on *Sharia* or any other law, as the sovereignty of the state may be undermined and individual rights cannot be guaranteed. Such a move would be typical of the multicultural approach to integration discussed above. That is not to say that some principles of foreign jurisprudence cannot be incorporated into Irish law by an Act of the Oireachtas. Indeed, aspects of *Sharia* have been accommodated by an Act of the Oireachtas in the 2010 Finance Bill in order to attract Islamic business.[23] Provided justice is administered in public, based on laws enacted on behalf of the Irish people and enforced by individuals accountable to the state, it is unproblematic to incorporate some foreign legal principles into Irish law.[24] Ultimately, the state should not fudge or evade this issue any longer. Instead it should provide clear legislation on the parameters of religious expression and civic responsibility. Legal obligations to respect religious tolerance and civil liberties should override the autonomy of local organisations like school boards.

Taking Matters into our own Hands: The Role of Non-Governmental Organisations and Civil Society

There are limits to the extent that a government can (or should be expected to) mastermind a successful integration process. The role of non-governmental organisations and wider civil society will be crucial. Ireland has strong foundations upon which to build; according to the Central Statistics Office, two-thirds of Irish adults are involved in over 25,000 community and voluntary groups.

Given the weight and importance attached to such organisations, it is vital that entities such as trade unions and sports organisations, including the Gaelic Athletic Association (GAA), realise that they have a responsibility to positively contribute to the integration process. The trade unions have been proactive in this area; this development is unsurprising given the high numbers of migrants employed in the economy over the last decade. SIPTU (the Services, Industrial, Professional and Technical Union) has Polish officers to aid its engagement with the Polish cohort of members and possibly to demonstrate to Polish non-members that the union is open to them, and advocates for them as equally as it does for any other members. Moreover, a search of the SIPTU website highlights policy documents and news about protest marches that emphasise migrant issues, such as the government curtailing work permits. Many of these policy documents and news pieces are relatively recent at the time of writing (late 2010).[25] These developments show that the unions realise that cultural diversity is now a permanent feature of Irish society and their membership will increasingly come to reflect this new reality.

On the sporting side, the GAA and the Football Association of Ireland are publicly committed to encouraging integration and the involvement of migrants in their activities.[26] The GAA has demonstrated leadership on this issue by stressing that it is not about *who* plays Gaelic sports, but that they *play* Gaelic sports. Their integration strategy is a six-year plan (2009–2015) to develop diverse interest in the GAA from school programmes to recruiting 'new Irish' players and coaches. Although these developments come at a relatively late stage in the migration experience, they are decidedly welcome.

It is comparable to the political dimension in that the real test of the GAA's commitment to integration will be whether it successfully recruits the 'new Irish' at senior level, given the competition for participation. The most likely scenario will be that children learning the sport in schools today will make a significant impact on the make-up of senior teams within ten to fifteen years. It is unlikely, given adult migrants' hesitation to integrate and the complexities of learning GAA sports, that any significant progress will be made with this generation. The focus should be on children; as the GAA aduits itself, if it does not focus on children it risks losing large swathes of the population to other sports such as rugby and soccer. It would be a poor reflection on our national sport for it not to reflect Ireland's more diverse population. The GAA should, however, set numerical benchmarks for the inclusion of 'new Irish' in the country's traditional sports, going beyond rhetoric towards concretely evaluating the progressive realisation of its commitments.

Conclusion: Accentuating the Positive

Opportunities are naturally occurring phenomena. Motivated citizens recognise this and do not wait for government to create them. So, what organisations are being proactive as a result of the migration experience, and what is their current role and possible future role in the integration process?

The Centre for Creative Practices on Lower Pembroke Street in Dublin is an example of migrants leading the integration process. Established in 2009 by Monika Sapielak, this organisation brings together all styles of artists from a variety of cultural backgrounds. An organisation like the Centre for Creative Practices is indicative of the type of innovative drive and commitment throughout society to enable a successful integration process. Many integration policies and procedures are fuelled by questions of cultural difference rather than similarity: How do we respect religious difference? How do we integrate people who speak a different first language? How do we relate to people with different cultural attitudes? The lesson from the Centre for Creative Practices for integrated social life in Ireland is that if Irish citizens and migrants focus on our fundamental similarities and shared interests, the differences will take care of themselves.

There is also a role for the national broadcaster and independent media to aid the integration process. Several survey respondents independently indicated that this would benefit intercultural dialogue and understanding.[27] Broadcasters should be encouraged to develop programmes that look at daily life and culture in other countries from which we have received significant numbers of migrants and from which we may do so in the future, such as Poland, Turkey and Nigeria.

Allowing integration to be decided on an ad hoc basis at a local level without a clear overarching policy framework is, very possibly, a recipe for disaster. Merely because there has not been a significant backlash against immigrants to date, necessitating direct government intervention, does not mean that preemptive action should be ruled out. Currently in Ireland there is an opportunity for a more rational public debate that may be conducted on the integration issue than would be possible if the government had to react quickly to a sensationalist story or tragic event with ill-considered emergency legislation or in an attempt to stave off an electoral threat from a far-right nationalist party. An open-minded citizenry and a wealth of evidence with regard to policy options from other countries offer a tangible opportunity and conditions for getting integration policies right the first time. This will ensure Ireland is as harmonious a society in 2040 as it was homogeneous in 1940.

Immigration poses a challenge to Irish identity in that we tend to think of ourselves as a homogenous group. But with the arrival and settlement of half a million immigrants in Ireland in the last decade we must redefine our identity as one which is a product of more heterogeneous influences. By incorporating the 'new Irish' into the political system and accepting, and possibly celebrating, the cultural practices of others, we can benefit from a more diverse Irish society. This will robustly reinforce our cherished image of Ireland as an attractive, welcoming place to visit and live, a country that does not succumb to the vice of xenophobia even when times are tough.

5

A Return to Managing the Irish Economy

Stephen Kinsella and Ronan Lyons

Introduction

What will the Irish economy look like in a generation? What kinds of opportunities to work and invest will be available to our children once they enter the workforce? What might be the economic priorities by the mid-2030s? How can we know? To gain some perspective on these seemingly intractable questions, consider the following scene from 1985. Two economists deliver their thoughts on what the Irish economy might be like in 2010. The first economist rises, clears his throat and begins:

> We have come to realise, since independence, that the Irish economy cannot sustain a population much greater than 3 million people. Living standards have risen at an average of 3 per cent a year over the past generation, and they will probably continue to do so between now and 2010, as long as our population stays in check. We have traditionally exported our young, but in the future we will just have fewer children, because of increased wealth, education, and demographic change. In the last few years, the birth rate has dropped sharply from 22 per 1,000 to 17 per 1,000 this year. In all likelihood, it will continue to drop and may be as low as 8 per 1,000 by 2010.

The second cleans his glasses, take a sip of water, and responds:

> To discuss how living standards in Ireland have risen since the 1960s is to ignore the challenges it currently faces. Unemployment has risen in the last five years from 7 per cent to 17 per cent. Net borrowing by the

government next year is projected to be 12 per cent of GDP. Ireland is unlikely to have unemployment of less than 10 per cent before the turn of the millennium. Large deficits will act on a drag on growth and the high levels of GDP growth between 1960 and 1985 are unlikely to be repeated over the coming 25 years. Instead, we should plan on average growth in per capita output of about 1.5 per cent, which is close to our historical average.

Judged on the economists' awareness of past trends, and the economic situation as they understood it in 1985, both positions taken seem reasonable. One focuses on the birth rate and population, while the other focuses on employment, unemployment and government finances. Neither predicts hoverboards for all, personal jetpacks and holidays on the moon. But neither predicts that, of all developed countries, Ireland would enjoy the greatest growth in income per head over the period 1985–2010. And both are wrong in their key predictions. While Ireland's birth rate fell slightly in the 1980s, it then rose again and in 2010 stood at 17 per 1,000 inhabitants, the same level as a generation ago. Ireland's unemployment and government deficit problems had disappeared by 2000 before re-emerging during the recession starting in 2008.[1]

How Ireland developed from 1985 to 2010 highlights four key lessons for anyone looking to contribute to the debate on Ireland's economic policy over the coming generation:

- The first is the importance of **global trends**. Ireland grew faster than any other developed world economy over that period because of its exploitation of favourable global trends, including European integration, US-led globalisation and technologically enabled trade in services. Both of the analyses above viewed Ireland in isolation, rather than as reacting to global trends.
- The second is the importance of a **long-term vision**. Let us define a vision as a dream with direction, a clearly articulated, results-oriented picture of a future we as a society intend to create. Ireland's capacity to exploit global trends depended on actions towards a vision taken over the course of a generation, including opening up the economy, a business-friendly tax policy, free secondary and tertiary education, and seeking a future in Europe via the European Union.
- The third is the importance of **adaptation and ongoing decisions**. Over the course of the last 25 years, Ireland has made decisions that have kept it to the forefront in attracting and retaining both capital and labour. This includes the decision to join the Eurozone,

opening the labour market to new EU member states and adopting an economy-wide corporation tax rate of 12.5 per cent.

- The fourth lesson is that **unknown factors matter**. No one writing in Ireland could know about the importance for Ireland of interest rate decisions taken in the US in the early 2000s that shaped the global financial environment for the rest of the decade. Put another way, if this chapter had been written in 2005, before the financial and economic crisis, it would undoubtedly have had a very different tone. The combination of the end of Ireland's property boom, from late 2006, and a global financial crisis which triggered a global recession in 2008 and 2009, have altered the Irish economy most dramatically.

Together with other chapters in this book, this chapter aims to build in these four lessons from Ireland's experience of growth over more than a generation into a more coherent, future-oriented picture for the Irish economy over the coming generation. Many aspects of Ireland's economy need to be changed to ensure that Ireland enjoys prosperity over the coming generation. Two important aspects discussed in detail in other chapters are Ireland's competitiveness (see Chapter 6) and the transformation of Ireland's public service (see Chapter 3). This chapter focuses on how the government raises money and spends it, on the growing importance of data and statistics for the economy, and on what role the government should play in managing supply and demand in the Irish economy.

The next section reviews Ireland's recent economic policy and assesses where things went right and where they went wrong over the last generation. Key mistakes were made in not planning for life within the Eurozone, not controlling public expenditure and not managing some of the most important markets in the economy. To ensure future prosperity, these mistakes need to be addressed and the following section outlines five key principles that should underpin Ireland's economic policy: adapting to life in the Eurozone, particularly in fiscal policy; turning taxes into prices; the importance of data; understanding that Ireland is a small number of regions in a larger economy – the EU; and managing systemic markets in the economy.

Assessing Ireland's Recent Economic Policy

By most measures, Ireland has had one of the most successful economies of the past generation. Measured by growth in population, employment, income or output, Ireland has had an enviable recent economic history.

And yet Ireland is used as a poster child for the so-called Great Recession of 2008–2009. The fall in output, measured by real gross domestic product (GDP), between 2007 and 2010 was twice as large in Ireland as in any other Organisation for Economic Co-Operation and Development (OECD) member state apart from Iceland.[2]

Conditions in the domestic economy are worse than even these figures suggest. The fall in gross national product (GNP), reflecting the economic activity of Irish citizens, was even larger (almost 25 per cent by mid-2010). Based on GNP, the domestic economy was smaller in 2010 than it had been six years previously, in 2004. Even excluding bank recapitalisation expenditure, Ireland's budget deficit is the largest in the OECD for each of the years 2009, 2010 and 2011, while the unemployment rate in 2010 is projected to have been the highest of any developed country apart from Spain. Figure 5.1 shows the fall in GDP and GNP, with the growth in unemployment on the right-hand axis. The huge change in Ireland's economic circumstances beginning in early 2008 – before the onset of the global financial crisis – is clear.

Figure 5.1: Overall Change in Size of Economy, 2007–2010, and Unemployment, Selected OECD Countries

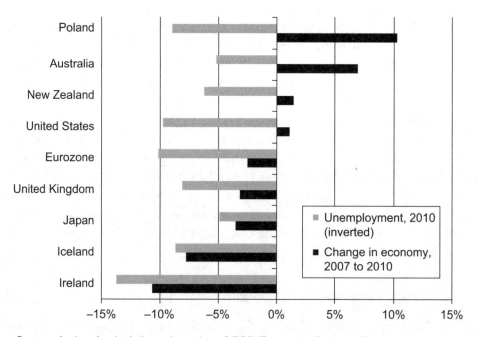

Source: Authors' calculations, based on *OECD Economic Outlook*, September 2010.

It is important, both to understand how this unprecedented economic collapse happened and with a view to shaping future economic policy so that it can't happen again, to know where things went right and where things went wrong.

Where Did We Get It Right?

No economy can grow faster than its peers consistently for more than a generation by accident. While it is easy for commentators to write off the achievements of the so-called Celtic Tiger period, its achievements form a long and impressive list. Even accounting for jobs lost since the collapse of the property bubble, the Celtic Tiger created 400,000 new jobs and brought 50 per cent more women into the labour force. Ireland has been ahead of its peers in growing its services exports, which were almost half of all exports in 2009, and in using technology to enable sales, with one-third of turnover coming from e-commerce. The period also saw huge investment in infrastructure across health, education and transport, and Ireland now has more motorway per capita than most other European countries.[3]

Ireland enjoyed a demographic dividend over the Celtic Tiger years, as younger, more educated workers came into the workforce in record numbers. The 'Pope's children', born in the mid- to late 1970s, began working and consuming at the right time. A confluence of investable capital, a growing supply of skilled labour, and propitious policy decisions with regard to tax and regulation, coupled with EU-driven infrastructural investment, created the Celtic Tiger. This period of growth allowed Ireland to catch up with the OECD average standard of living.[4]

These achievements are the results of two generations of decisions. Ireland made the decision in the late 1950s to abandon self-sufficiency and seek a future as a small open economy in the world market. Shortly afterwards, the government decided to introduce free secondary education for all. Membership of the EU (and its predecessors) reduced Ireland's traditional economic dependence on the UK and prepared Ireland for a more open world economy, which came about via the General Agreement on Tariffs and Trade (GATT) and the World Trade Organization (WTO). All the while, Ireland's investment promotion agency, the Industrial Development Agency (IDA Ireland), performed very well. In 2008, a year that finished with global economic turmoil, Ireland attracted more jobs per capita through foreign investment than any other country.[5] Ireland's investment attraction policies have definitely been one area where Ireland has got it right.

One landmark decision that has had very significant implications, for better and for worse, has been Ireland's decision, made in the early 1990s, to enter into European Economic and Monetary Union (EMU) and adopt the euro. Membership of a currency union brings large benefits to a small open economy, including greater economic integration with currency partners, which is good for exporters. However, it is important to remember that EMU removed perhaps the two most significant tools of immediate response at the disposal of most governments: the interest rate and the exchange rate. The current generation of macroeconomists views the interest rate as the single most important economic tool for policy-makers in their attempts to avoid cycles of boom and bust. Raising the interest rate can cool an economy down, by increasing the cost of borrowing and thus tempering the willingness of firms and households to borrow, for a new business project or a new home. Conversely, lowering the interest rate can provide a boost to a stagnant economy.

As a tool of economic policy, the exchange rate can be used by open economies primarily to give a boost to a country's exporting sector via devaluation. Ireland devalued three times in the ten years to 1993, but often these devaluations were more the result of external pressure and currency speculation.[6] One of the key motivations behind joining EMU was to place Ireland beyond the reach of currency speculators. It is worth pointing out that, at the height of global uncertainty in late 2008, countries such as Iceland, Denmark and Sweden viewed membership of the Eurozone as a key advantage in surviving the economic crisis.[7] In Ireland's case, in the 1990s, loss of exchange rate policy was regarded almost unambiguously as a good thing. Loss of interest rate policy was, at least implicitly if not explicitly, regarded as a price worth paying, particularly if Ireland would be in a position to enjoy a low and stable interest rate environment. Either way, entry into EMU was an action with consequences, many benign, but not all of which have been factored in.

Where Did It Go Wrong?

Ireland experienced an unprecedented economic collapse between 2007 and 2010. Irish economic policy was deficient in key areas before and during this collapse. This section highlights five key areas where Ireland's economic policy went wrong over the past generation. They reflect both the consequences of Eurozone membership, in particular the lack of a plan for life in the Eurozone, and recent control of fiscal policy, as well as failings with respect to specific markets, in particular the housing and banking markets and the public sector labour market.

Life in the Eurozone

Naturally, as part of the Maastricht criteria, Ireland had to prepare itself for entry into the Eurozone. This took the form of commitments about interest rates, deficits and debt. But for all the preparations for entry into the Eurozone, there were no preparations made for life once entry had been secured.

Economies without their own monetary policy face different challenges. For an economic theorist, one of the most significant is that monetary unions can exacerbate different patterns of business cycles across the different regions in the union. For economic practitioners, this was a real concern for Ireland during the 2000s, as Ireland boomed while the Eurozone core was experiencing sluggish economic conditions. Inappropriately low, and often negative real interest rates[8] for Ireland acted as a further asymmetric shock, fuelling unsustainable growth in investment and consumption.

Figure 5.2 shows real interest rates and economic growth in Ireland and in selected other economies for the period 2000–2010. As higher interest rates can cool down an economy, the two series should be moving together, as is the case with the UK. Between 2000 and 2007, the average growth rate in the UK was 2.7 per cent while the average real interest rate was 3.4 per cent. In Ireland, however, economic growth averaged 6 per cent, while the real interest rate was negative for the entire period until 2009. And then, precisely when the economy needed negative interest rates, during the severe recession, they moved positive, thanks to deflation. Whereas the two statistics moved together in the UK – as a macroeconomist would advise – in Ireland, they moved in opposite directions.

In an environment without monetary policy, fiscal policy becomes the primary economic tool. Wages, consumer prices and house prices are key indicators of relative cost competitiveness. With an unprecedented boom, the government's key policy targets should have been restraint of fiscal policy specifically and more generally restraint of house prices, wage levels and consumer prices. However, government policy priorities were backwards. Greater fiscal expansion was the target, as discussed below, while rising house prices were regarded as a sign of greater wealth rather than poorer competitiveness.

Fiscal Policy

The single biggest failing of Irish economic policy was not, however, its sin of omission in neglecting to put in place a new policy system for life in the Eurozone. Rather, its biggest failing was throwing out the painful

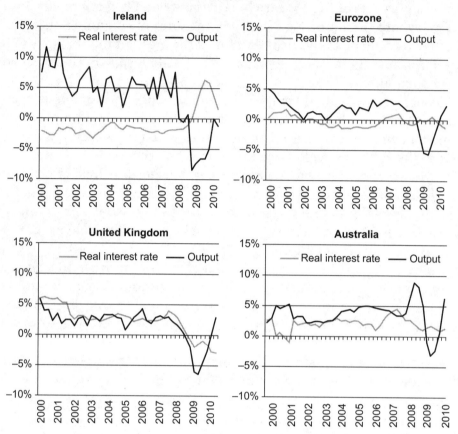

Figure 5.2: Economic Growth and the Real Interest Rate in Selected Economies, 2000–2010

Source: Authors' calculations based on data from CSO, Eurostat, fxstreet.com, Reserve Bank of Australia and Australia Bureau of Statistics.

lessons of the late 1980s and 1990s – that Ireland as a small open economy needs prudential fiscal policy. The lack of prudence is best captured by the philosophy of one Minister for Finance, Charlie McCreevy: 'When I have money, I'll spend it. When I don't, I won't.'

Spending

On the one hand, public sector expenditure ballooned. Gross public sector expenditure rose by an average of 10 per cent a year in the decade to 2008, from €27.1 billion to €76.4 billion. Expenditure on health rose by 250 per cent in the decade to 2008, while expenditure on education rose by 171 per cent. Public sector pay rose by over 70 per cent during that period, more than equivalent increases seen in what had, even before the increases, been lower paid sectors such as business services (58 per cent) and manufacturing (63 per cent). The increases in expenditure sanctioned by government far exceeded those seen in other developed economies. The increase in total government spending in those ten years, 182 per cent, dwarfs the increases seen in countries such as Austria (34 per cent) and the Netherlands (62 per cent) and is about twice as large as increases seen in two other economies now regarded as having unsustainable increases in government expenditure during that decade – the US (which saw an increase of 84 per cent in the same period) and the UK (98 per cent).[9]

Taxation

At the same time, Ireland's taxation policy actively strayed from best practice. The goal should have been to ensure a broadly based taxation system that preserves the incentive to work and provides a solid base of revenues, with ample room for counter-cyclical fiscal actions. Instead, during the 2000s, the Irish taxation system was converted to one where the majority of workers paid little or no income tax and the overall taxation system became dependent on an unsustainable level of transactions in the property market.

The OECD *Taxing Wages* publication outlines just how lopsided Ireland's direct taxation system became. In 2000, Ireland already had one of the most attractive income tax regimes in the OECD. A couple with one earner and two children would pay, after all transfers such as child benefit have been counted, just 5.4 per cent of their income in tax. Only a handful of economies had lower rates. Despite a comparative advantage already, this 'all-in' tax rate was reduced steadily over successive years so that by 2007, the tax rate was significantly negative: a family with one earner on the average industrial wage and two children was being paid by the state a further 8.4 per cent of income, by far the most generous income taxation system among developed countries (see Figure 5.3).[10]

Ireland is also unusual in that it is one of the few developed economies where property owners do not pay an annual property tax, despite the vast majority of wealth in the country being held in property.[11] Instead, property transactions are levied. During the 2000s, the number of property transactions increased significantly, with the total number of loans issued for property rising from below 75,000 in 2000 to over 110,000 in 2006. The total tax revenue from stamp duties, capital taxes (Capital Acquisitions Tax (CAT) and Capital Gains Tax (CGT)) and VAT on new buildings rose from about €3 billion in 2001/2002 to about €9 billion in 2006/2007.

Figure 5.3: Average 'All-In' Tax Rates in Selected Economies, 2000–2007

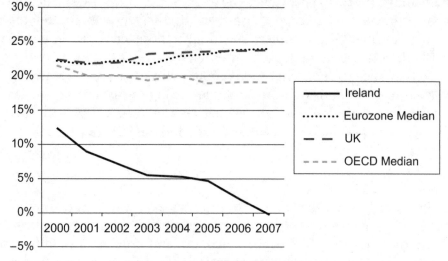

Source: Authors' calculations based on OECD, *Taxing Wages*.

This increase in taxation revenues from the property market was almost as large as the combined increase in income and corporation tax revenues, which had traditionally constituted a much greater part of tax revenues. What is most frightening is that Ireland's government finances did not become precarious by accident – they became precarious by design, albeit a design oblivious of the consequences.

Managing Markets

How was the government able to expand its expenditure by such large amounts while simultaneously reducing the income tax on the average worker? The answer lies in the growth in tax receipts in other areas, specifically from the early 2000s on, due to Ireland's domestic housing boom. The boom in construction is just one example of how the Irish economic policy apparatus failed to manage well markets that are key to Ireland's economic well-being.

Housing

Ireland's housing boom was the result of both rapidly rising house prices and increasing numbers of new properties being built each year. While the true number is almost impossible to know, the total number of new homes needed by the state was in the region of 10,000 every three months. However, every single quarter from the start of 2002 until the end of 2008,

Ireland's construction sector overbuilt. During 2005 and 2006, there were more than twice as many units built as needed, with over 20,000 units built per quarter. If 10,000 units every three months was indeed the correct number, the total number of excess homes built between 2002 and 2008 was close to 200,000. A July 2010 report by the National Institute for Regional and Spatial Analysis at NUI Maynooth estimated that there was a property overhang at that time of over 120,000 units or, on average, 3.5 years supply across the country.[12] The overshooting of construction output, well beyond any reasonable measure of demand, was only able to happen because there existed a widely held belief that Ireland needed these units and because tax breaks existed that enabled developers, both individual and large-scale, to write off the costs of construction against their tax bill. These tax breaks meant that those building properties were not worried about having to sell them immediately. To answer the broader question about why Ireland believed it needed all these homes, it is necessary to look at the banking sector.

Banking

In Ireland's housing boom, property oversupply was only one part of the equation. Indeed, on its own, the oversupply of property would more than likely have depressed house prices, as opposed to further fuelling the housing boom. The other part of the equation was rapidly rising house prices, which were only possible due to increasingly generous and ultimately unsustainable mortgages, which meant that people were lent greater multiples of their annual income. The ratio of residential mortgage debt to the size of the economy (GDP) trebled to 75 per cent in the decade to 2007.[13]

The change in mortgage environment reflected a combination of factors. A signficant part was deregulation and financial innovation, which were not only beneficial but necessary for Ireland's economic development. However, many innovations, such as the introduction of 100 per cent mortgages and unsustainable tracker interest rates, were not 'future-proof', in that they could not be sustained in anything other than extremely favourable market conditions. As the Regling–Watson report on the collapse of the Irish financial system showed, the system was so out of control by 2007 that 'serious stress in the financial system was almost unavoidable'.[14] While what happened in Ireland also happened to varying degrees in other countries, deregulation and innovation cannot excuse a lack of overall control of the financial sector, which, as Ireland has learnt throughout its economic history, plays a pivotal role in the economy.

Public Sector Labour Market

A further failing is the political system's over-dependence on social partnership. Clearly, ongoing strategic engagement between the government and various stakeholders affected by its policies is a necessary and welcome part of a well-run society. However, the heart of social partnership in Ireland was employer–employee negotiations, predicated on an insider–outsider model that diminished Ireland's flexibility in response to changing circumstances. (See Chapter 3 for a discussion of the type of employer the state will need to become over the coming decades.)

The biggest cost to the Irish economy of this over-dependence on social partnership has been the benchmarking exercise. Introduced in 2001, at a time of booming private sector activity, the annual cost of benchmarking has risen with increments and public sector wage agreements to over €1.5 billion a year. In a stunning deviation from the principles of evidence-based policy-making, these permanent increases were introduced despite a lack of evidence of retention problems in the public sector and in the face of existing statistics that showed that public sector pay was above equivalent private sector pay.[15]

The above analysis shows that, while Ireland got many decisions right over the past generation, a significant number of aspects of Ireland's economic system were subject to flawed economic decision making. These decisions have cost Ireland dearly in the economic collapse that started in 2007.

Principles for Ireland's Economic Policy

In addition to policies addressing Ireland's international competitiveness and public sector transformation, which are discussed elsewhere in this volume, the experience of Ireland over the past generation – plus international best practice – would suggest that the following five principles need to be at the core of economic policy-making here, over the coming generation:

- Fiscal policy is the main economic tool for a small Eurozone country.
- Taxes should be viewed as the prices of social market services.
- Modern economies require a much greater level of data.
- Ireland is ultimately a small number of regions in the EU.
- Important markets need to be managed well.

Adapting to Life in the Eurozone: The Importance of Fiscal Policy

Modern economies grow over time at an average rate but in any given year are generally either above or below that trend rate. Much economic policy can be thought of as either contributing to the long-run average rate or else as smoothing the fluctuations around that rate. An economy without its own monetary policy or exchange rate policy is reliant solely on fiscal policy and prudential regulation to smooth its economic growth over time. How Ireland designs its fiscal policy needs to reflect this fact.

A Target Level of Government Expenditure

The starting point for fiscal policy has to be the setting out of a vision for Ireland's public finances. Ultimately, fiscal policy is about expenditure and income, i.e. ensuring a country's government lives within its means. A government's income is based on private economic activity and is subject to some uncertainty. But a government's expenditure can be much more easily controlled and therefore should form the cornerstone of fiscal policy. Targeting a level of government expenditure is a natural starting point.

Certainly a single value target is simplistic and thus not without its limitations. Nonetheless, setting a target level of government expenditure as a percentage of national income would provide clarity to all citizens and other stakeholders, including international bond markets, about how much the government will be spending over the cycle and where the economy is in that cycle. It would also have prevented the excesses seen in government expenditure over the past fifteen years: Ireland's government expenditure was in 2010 one of the largest in the EU relative to national income.

Such a target would need to be relatively binding. Otherwise, it would be ignored, with politicians, suffering from 'present bias', convincing themselves that this time is, indeed, different. Given the limitations of a single target, though, it should be very different to, for example, the June 2010 German constitutional amendment, which requires a federal government deficit of no more than 0.35 per cent of GDP from 2016 onwards.[16] This requirement would give a small open region like Ireland no room to adjust to asymmetric shocks.[17] Ireland's target should be a rolling average and concern overall expenditure, rather than the balance between expenditure and receipts. The target should be set independent of government influence, and be binding, unless exceptional circumstances, such as war, pertain.

Establishing an Independent Fiscal Policy Committee

One suggestion in relation to achieving a relatively binding commitment in relation to target levels of expenditure is to delegate to an independent fiscal policy committee. The logic follows from recent developments in monetary policy, whereby to credibly set monetary policy optimally and thus reduce economic fluctuations, governments delegated interest rate decisions to an independent central bank or monetary policy committee of experts. The analogue for an economic region without its own monetary policy is to establish an independent Central Fiscal Policy Committee, with a high-profile leading board and sufficient support staff for research.

The Central Fiscal Policy Committee would set a target level of spending for the government for the coming calendar year. The committee would be tasked with considering current growth conditions and future projections, and estimating the economy's approximate location in the business cycle. For continuity, the committee would also provide current estimates of Year 2, Year 3 and Year 4 expenditure. As with monetary policy committees, it is likely that the Committee's formal announcements, and ultimately the minutes of its meetings, would be of interest to international markets.

It would not be appropriate for the Committee to specify targets for subheadings of expenditure or indeed target revenue. While it would certainly be possible for a Central Fiscal Policy Committee to set targets for particular headings of government expenditure, such as health or education, this may not only be overly political, it would also interfere with best management practice in organisations responsible for expenditure in those areas (this theme is explored in more detail in Chapter 3). Also, while estimation of taxation revenues is a natural complement to setting expenditure targets, the margin for error is far greater. Expenditure is within the direct control of government, while taxation revenues depend on private sector conditions. For revenues, estimates rather than targets should be published.

There are certainly issues surrounding implementation of any fiscal committee. The statutory basis of such a committee would need to be closer to a central bank than an advisory committee, for example. The committee's funding and powers would have to be ring-fenced, with its work being apolitical. As discussed below, European Commission plans for fiscal policy 'peer review' would also potentially affect its work.[18] There are also concerns, as there are with independent central banks, about the accountability of unelected officials, which would need to be overcome via transparent processes and regular reporting to the government or Oireachtas, as well as to the media.

Fiscal Policy in the Eurozone

As a member of the Eurozone, Ireland will also have to get used to greater coordination of taxation and spending between member states. This is all the more pertinent as Ireland's macroeconomic position, relative to its Eurozone neighbours, is precarious. For example, unemployment was already nearly one-quarter higher in Ireland than in the Eurozone average in 2010 and it is estimated it will be over one-third higher by 2014.[19] The scale of macroeconomic adjustment already entered into on a European level, and planned for the future, is onerous on the public, the government and the civil servants who must implement government policy. Figure 5.4 shows the proportion of government spending in 2009 not covered by government revenues, across a range of Eurozone countries.

Figure 5.4: Percentage of Government Spending Not Covered by Government Revenues, 2009

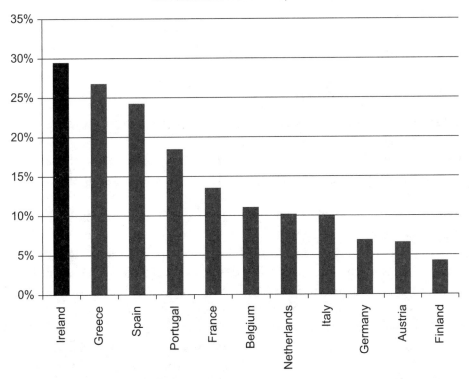

Source: Authors' calculations, based on *OECD Economic Outlook*, September 2010.

All of this fiscal adjustment takes place, of course, in the context of monetary union, and direct oversight from the relevant authorities in the European Commission. Coordination of member states' fiscal policies has been mooted and is sure to become realised in some form if the currency union is to survive as the US dollar currency union has for so long across fifty economically heterogeneous states. The Commission is investigating the likelihood of national fiscal frameworks to better reflect the priorities of EU budgetary surveillance. To quote the European Commission directly:

> To prevent the occurrence of severe imbalances within the euro area, it is therefore important to deepen the analysis and expand economic surveillance beyond the budgetary dimension to address other macroeconomic imbalances, including competitiveness developments and underlying structural challenges. It is proposed to upgrade the peer review of macroeconomic imbalances now carried out by the Eurogroup into a structured surveillance framework for euro-area Member States .... This framework will imply deeper surveillance, more demanding policy co-ordination and stronger follow-up than envisaged under Europe 2020 for all EU Member States.[20]

The intent of the Commission implies that the work of a Central Fiscal Policy Committee, the principal recommendation of this section, must take the European context into account.

Turning Taxes into Prices

Expenditure is one element of Ireland's main policy tool; revenue is the other. Taxation originally started out as a way for the ruling classes to support their lifestyles. In some sense, little has changed and there is very little connection between where most taxes are raised and the services they fund. However, that is unsustainable and many government revenues are now effectively prices for public services. Over the coming generation, the principle of the social market, with taxes acting as the price signal, needs to become embedded in all the services the government provides.

This idea is already deeply embedded in other developed economies. In the Eurozone area, about one euro in six is given to the state in the form of social insurance, a service run by the government. In the US, county-level property taxes, as well as state and municipal borrowing, directly fund services that local residents avail of, such as schools, and waste and emergency services. In Ireland, however, the disconnect between taxation and the associated service remains. Property tax revenues from stamp duties, for example, are pooled centrally and are not used to fund amenities and services enjoyed by residents. Indeed, as discussed in Chapter 3, local government in Ireland spends more than most of its counterparts elsewhere in the OECD, while raising less in revenue.

Certainly, some key tax revenues are required to pay for public goods and the need for a direct income tax on workers' and companies' earnings, and capital gains and acquisitions, will remain, as will the need for an indirect tax on consumption (VAT). However, the dominant principle for government raising revenue should be to price as close to social cost as possible on average, and to price progressively where possible, so that wealthier households pay more. This proposal turns on its head how successive Irish governments have thought about raising revenue. Currently, income and consumption taxes provide the bulk of government revenues. Instead, the government should have as its aim that, by the 2030s, income and consumption taxes are only high enough to cover the shortfall between total costs of non-market activities (externalities) and those that can be priced accurately and fairly.[21]

The accurate pricing of publicly provided amenities requires complicated economic and statistical methods. However, advances in economics, statistics and computational power mean that this is no longer something beyond the bounds of possibility. For many public services, valuation methods exist to reveal how much people value being close to, for example, green space or public transportation. These methods can help the public service understand better the value it creates in wider society. An example is research by the Economic and Social Research Institute (ESRI) on the value of parklands and green spaces in Dublin, which helped the city's park services understand the economic value of what they do.

In 2010, a significant example of the transition from taxing to pricing took place. Ireland introduced a carbon price of €15 per tonne. It is likely that this price will change over time, as science produces a better understanding of the social costs, from direct pollution to climate change, incurred when we use carbon. (See also Chapter 7 for an in-depth discussion of carbon pricing and Ireland's environmental and climate change policy.) Carbon emission is a primary example of an activity that falls outside the marketplace but which imposes costs on society. A local carbon tax complements the approach at an EU level, where there is a carbon trading scheme for the EU's largest emitters of carbon.

There remains, however, a long list of activities that fall outside the market system currently financed by general taxation, rather than dedicated pricing. Four examples are discussed below: water usage, road charges, property taxes and financial systemic risk. They are feasible, as the experience of other countries shows, and they are designed to gradually replace income taxes and VAT, which are ultimately indiscriminate means of raising revenue.

Water

Water is a scarce resource and thus requires an allocation mechanism, like any other scarce resource. In 2007, for example, German and Danish consumers paid US$2.25 per cubic metre of water.[22] For historical and infrastructural reasons, water is publicly supplied to all buildings in Ireland. While commercial entities pay water rates to their local authority, there are currently no charges for residential water, meaning there is no system for allocation of resources when it comes to residential water usage in Ireland. A flat fee might actually be worse for the allocation of water, as it does not incentivise the consumer to use the next litre of water in such a way that might reflect its scarcity, but does give people the feeling that they have paid and thus are entitled to use the next litre. With Dublin running out of drinking water, Ireland needs to put in place a pricing system that encourages sustainable use of what is a scarce resource.

Road Space

Road space is a scarce resource and road usage by one vehicle imposes costs on the rest of society. The clearest example of this is rush-hour congestion, where each car takes up finite road space, to the detriment of all other road users. Different types of costs are currently imposed on road users, such as fuel duties and registration tax, but none achieves the desired result of bringing the private cost of an action in line with the social cost imposed. Toll roads, for example, are essentially an arbitrary revenue collection mechanism that may do little other than encourage people to use other roads for the same journey. A one-off vehicle registration tax or an annual motor tax may achieve some environmental benefits, by taxing based on capacity to pollute, but this does not affect the decisions made by drivers once the car is bought and tax paid. Taxation of motor fuel, lastly, may go some way to discouraging road usage. However, it does not discriminate between someone using a litre of motor fuel to drive a full car on empty streets with no public transport alternative available to them and that person using the same litre instead to drive an otherwise empty car on congested roads, when they had a public transport alternative available for the same journey. To align private and social costs in relation to road usage, these costs should be replaced with a system of electronic road pricing, as Singapore is now doing, discussed below, based on congestion levels on the roads used, the availability of public transport alternatives and – where not covered by carbon pricing – other environmental costs incurred.

Property Tax

In relation to property tax, as was outlined earlier, the current system – based on transactions – has proven to be not just unsustainable but also systemically dangerous, as it tricked the government into altering the taxation system so that median earners contributed very little of their income in tax. Figures from the OECD suggest that something close to 10 per cent of core tax revenues (excluding social insurance) comes from property taxes in most developed countries. As Ireland looks to rebalance its government finances, it should emulate OECD best practice where appropriate and thus look to bring in initially about 10 per cent of its core tax revenues from an annual property tax. This can then be adjusted over time, and across regions of the country, to reflect the contribution that local amenities and publicly provided services add. Property tax should raise money without distorting the incentives people have to improve their homes.[23] The most favoured form of property tax in this regard is a land value tax, levied on the value of the land, ignoring any man-made improvements to the land, including buildings. Generally, taxes distort outcomes, for high taxes on labour can affect how much people are willing to work, while high taxes on capital can affect investment. The supply of land is fixed, however, so it cannot be affected by the land value tax. Land value tax is paid regardless of how the land is used and thus promotes efficient use of land, while the fixed supply of land means the tax is not passed on to tenants.

Financial Systemic Risk

Finally, financial systemic risk and uncertainty is a necessary by-product of a financial system based on fractional reserve banking, where the possibility of default exists. As the world has learned since 2007, the potential for low-probability, high-impact events is real and incurs costly risks, yet these risks are not accounted for within the current set of international financial institutions we have. Estimating the risk of financial systemic failure, and pricing the costs imposed on society of that risk, is a complicated actuarial exercise. Its complexity does not diminish its necessity, however, and the experience of Irish and international financial systems during the 2008 crisis provides a timely reminder of the importance of pricing in financial systemic risk, as well as a useful starting point for the estimation of costs.

The Importance of Data Generation and Collection

Much of the requirements for accurate and progressive pricing of publicly provided services may sound onerous. However, a properly digitised system can generate the information required. This underlines a key principle for economic policy-making over the coming generation: the importance of data generation and data collection. Globally, the pace of information and data generation is accelerating. According to International Data Corporation (IDC) *Digital Universe* research, the amount of information in the world will increase from 800 exabytes in 2009 (one exabyte being one billion gigabytes) to 35,000 exabytes in 2020.[24] The creation of huge amounts of data and information has transformed the way the private sector operates and has created entirely new activities that are highly valuable to organisations, particularly in data analysis. The same will be true of economic management over the coming generation.

An example of how new data is being created to the benefit of the wider economy is Singapore's efforts in road pricing. Singapore's current pricing scheme, dating from the 1990s, consists of electronic road-pricing gantries on all roads leading to the city's central business district and other heavily congested roads. When a vehicle passes under a gantry, a road usage charge is deducted from a mandatory CashCard located in the car. The charge for passing a gantry depends on the location and time, the peak hour being the most expensive. This system has, according to the state's Land Transport Authority, decreased traffic by nearly 25,000 vehicles during peak hours and increased average road speeds by about 20 per cent. In 2007, a new road pricing mechanism was tested, using a global positioning system (GPS)-based system as opposed to gantries. The new system would allow greater real-time variability of pricing, based on prevailing and emerging traffic conditions. This means that Singapore will soon be able to align the price the road user pays with the cost they impose on society, based on factors such as public transport alternatives, emissions and congestion.

Such a system brings large benefits to road users, as well as revenues to the state, but requires large amounts of information in real time to work. This in turn highlights the importance of information technology and the digitisation of core systems upon which economies are based. (See Chapter 6 for strategic priorities in relation to information and communications technology in Ireland.) The digitisation of information and communication systems since the 1980s has revolutionised the way we communicate and share information. The same is starting to happen with other core systems, as can be seen in the road pricing example above, in emerging intelligent utility networks or 'smart grids', as Malta is putting in place, or in live registers of property transactions, as exists in the UK and other countries.

The generation and collection of data, more often than not in real time, is a necessary step if Ireland is to reshape its economy to meet twenty-first-century demands. Firstly, as explained above, it will be almost impossible to turn 'public services' into 'social market services' without this infor-mation. Secondly, Ireland's statistics – like so many other countries – are often still structured as they were for an analogue twentieth-century manufacturing economy, despite the fact Ireland is a digital twenty-first-century services-based economy.

The increased complexity of society and the rapid changes Ireland is experiencing mean that there is an ever-increasing demand for reliable statistical information across a greater number of subjects. This requires combining data from various sources thematically and in real time, as is currently done in the Netherlands.[25] Data on Irish social dynamics like demographics, emigration and employment should be mixed with a range of micro-level data, from the quality and quantity of infrastruc-ture to firm-based productivity measures, from spatial statistics to the price and quantity of housing sales. The goal should be to create a system where, when problems arise, they are flagged early, and openly, to policy-makers. (This ties in with points made in Chapters 2 and 3 about targets for the political system and the public service.)

Ireland as a Small Number of Regions in the EU

In addition to management of Ireland's public finances, both expenditure and receipts, and the generation and collection of statistics, economic policy must respond to – and shape – where we live and work in Ireland. Over the past fifty years, Ireland has benefited hugely from its openness to trade, investment, and new technologies and ideas. In the past ten years, Ireland has also benefited hugely from its openness to people with skills. Ireland was one of the only countries to open its labour markets to the new EU member states from Eastern Europe and the Mediterranean when they joined in 2004. This gave Ireland an advantage in attracting foreign investment that required multilingual or translation skills, such as internet localisation. Keeping Ireland open to new talent is an impor-tant foundation for future economic success.

But Ireland needs to do more than just attract people. To be an attractive place to live and work, Ireland needs to develop sustainable communities in different parts of the country. There have been policy statements over the past fifteen years designed to shape where people live and work in Ireland. But these need to be based in economic reality. The aspirations of, for example, the National Spatial Strategy are noble. However, research shows that the goals outlined in the National Spatial Strategy require economies of scale that only occur with communities of a certain minimum size. It is entirely unrealistic, in other words, to try to create nine viable economic hubs in a country of just over four million people. The best way to preserve small towns is not to designate them as hubs or gateways but rather to have them as part of economically viable regions.

In Chapter 2, Eoin O'Malley discusses the need for political reform in Ireland. Parochial politics will have to give way to the reality that only regions with cities of a certain scale can thrive as economic entities. Ireland needs its politicians to realise and communicate to the electorate that there are, at most, five regional economies on the island of Ireland: Dublin, Belfast, Cork–Waterford, Galway–Limerick and, perhaps with the right supports, Sligo–Derry (see Chapter 8 for a fuller discussion of Irish–Northern Irish relations). Currently, on the entire island of Ireland, there is probably only one functioning regional economy, Dublin, and a couple of sector-specific exporting hotspots, such as Galway and Cork. This is not to say that people will not or cannot live outside those cities. Rather, it is to recognise that to be a sustainable hub of economic activity, a region must have its core and a certain scale and density.

In addition to rewriting existing policies such as the National Spatial Strategy, waking up to this economic reality has major implications for local authorities. Whatever the exact number and nature of 'hubs' of economic regions, for them to be viable, they need coherent decision-making structures. This would require major reform of local authority institutions and potentially the redistribution of powers away from county councils and national government to a new level of regional administration. (Chapter 3 discusses the desired powers these new local authorities would have.) The experience of Dublin's directly elected mayor may prove decisive in this regard. A reorganisation of the country into a small number of regions has implications for data collection and organisation as well. Currently, most types of data are collected according to the EU-designated nomenclature of territorial units for statistics (NUTS) regions. For effective policy management of viable economic regions, policy-makers in those regions need relevant statistics.

Managing Markets

A policy mix that affects where people live and work can be said to be the 'demand side' of economic policy. The 'supply side' refers to conditions which, if improved, would lower costs in the economy. Lowering costs is a key element of strengthening Ireland's competitiveness, a topic explored in greater detail by Michael King in Chapter 6. The lessons of the past generation teach us that a key part of economic policy must be the management of the country's systemic markets.

Central to ensuring that markets work as society wants them to are a well-enforced competition policy and a clear regulatory framework. Competition policy has developed beyond recognition over the past generation and Ireland's competition policy framework is part of the broader EU framework, one of the strongest in the world. Competition policy needs to remain a priority for Ireland's economic policy. Likewise, a further priority must be to ensure that Ireland has a consistent regulatory framework, with a focus on minimising the associated administrative burden. Aside from these general principles, though, there are systemic markets whose lack of active management by the government over the past generation has cost the country dear.

Public Sector Labour Market

From an economic perspective, the government is the largest employer in the country and the wages earned in the public service have knock-on direct and indirect effects on wages and prices throughout the economy. Ireland simply cannot afford to have another episode like the 2002 benchmarking exercise. The topic of the state as a twenty-first-century employer is discussed in greater detail in Chapter 3, but it is worth noting here that the public sector labour market needs to be integrated into the broader labour market, so that public service managers can access the skills they need for as long as they need, while public service workers get a fair wage.

Banking

The financial system is at the heart of modern economies and is arguably the single most important market in the economy. Fractional reserve banking systems are inherently fragile, though, as the spectacular collapse of Ireland's banking system shows. This cost imposed on the rest of society needs to be priced in, as discussed above. Pricing the financial risk should form one pillar of an overall strategy for the management of this key sector. A full strategy for Ireland's financial system must stabilise the conditions under which lending occurs but must not prevent competition and sustainable innovation among financial institutions.

Ireland's financial system effectively collapsed between 2008 and 2010, held up only by money from a government that was already heavily in debt. The ultimate problem for the banks following the financial crisis is that their liabilities (i.e. money they owe to those who hold deposits, bonds or shares in the bank) exceeded the best estimate of the value of their assets (the likely repayments on their loan book).

The first step of reform of banking involves not only implementing the write-down of the banks' assets and large-scale recapitalisations, but also new capital requirements. In 2010, for example, the Central Bank set new 'core tier 1' capital requirements. This first round of measures will almost certainly mean the creation of new, cleansed lending entities, with elements of the older institutions either sold to international buyers, or hived off into 'bad banks' to be paid out of the public purse.

However, cleaning up one mess is a different job to preventing another. And preventing future banking collapses will mean tackling root causes. The root cause of the collapse of Ireland's banks in the late 2000s was similar to the root cause of Ireland's fiscal collapse: a lack of preparedness for life in the Eurozone, which in the case of the banks meant abundant and cheap credit. Rebuilding Ireland's financial system requires financial institutions that are able to lend sustainably.

The second part of banking reform will involve putting in place a stable regulatory environment for when the Irish banking system has been cleansed of the traces of the current collapse. This will invovle, for example, essentially fixed rules about the quantity to be lent for mortgages (e.g. a maximum fraction of after-tax income to be spent on mortgage repayments each month). It will not be possible to prevent bubbles and financial crises outright. However, policy can make them far less likely.

Housing

The legacy of a violent boom-and-bust cycle in construction is an over-supply of commercial and residential property. It seems likely that between 2002 and 2008, Ireland built twelve years' worth of supply. It should be remembered that our 'built environment' is of a much higher quality following the boom, however overvalued some of that may be. Looking to the next generation, it may be worthwhile to view this stock as a 'gift', a one-off increase in construction given to the next generation. The question policy-makers must ask and answer is: what do we do with all this? Three answers come to mind. We can use the stock of residential capital to re-house some of the population. We can demolish it, and thus restrict supply and maintain artificially high prices. Or we could be inventive about the uses of this stock, which for much of the 2010s will be impossible to sell as a commercial product. Simple solutions are to use the over-supply of residential investment for social housing. Other popular solutions include the use of under-used hotels for nursing homes. Clearly, a national dialogue has to be had on just what to do with all this extra construction, now that it is there. Either we let it rot, or we use it. Just what that use should be is a matter for public debate.

As we look ahead, beyond the fall-out of the construction boom of the 2000s, systems need to be put in place that ensure Ireland's housing stock grows at a rate sufficient to meet new demand and that the new houses are built in places where there is demand. This requires an overhaul of planning and local government which is underway but would – if suggestions from earlier about the need for regional economic powers were implemented – require significant strengthening.

All in all, markets are excellent mechanisms for allocating scarce resources. But they are not perfect. Markets that are systemic to Ireland's economy and society need management by the government, and this management must form a cornerstone of economic policy over the coming generation, if we are to avoid regressing to repeat our economic history littered with lost generations.

Conclusion

Centuries ago, George Herbert wrote: 'Cities seldom change religion only.' As with religion, so too with economic policy, which does not and cannot exist in isolation from the rest of the country. Recognition of the type of economy that Ireland is now and the transformation of our economic policy to reflect that, as outlined above, would surely have a far greater impact on the country than just the sum of the individual measures themselves.

The last twenty years have been an economic rollercoaster for Ireland, with recent years seeing a dramatic property boom followed by the largest economic recession of any modern developed economy. Not all economic management decisions made since the 1980s have been bad, as attested by Ireland's ongoing foreign direct investment performance. However, Ireland's economic policy-making suffered from numerous significant mistakes, in particular a failure to adapt to life in a currency union and a seemingly reckless approach to fiscal policy, with permanent spending commitments paid for in boom times from temporary revenue sources.

To rebuild economic policy over the coming generation, it is most important that fiscal policy be overhauled to reflect the fact that it now represents the most important tool of economic policy. A Central Fiscal Policy Committee, a small region's analogue to a monetary policy committee, would provide the necessary stability and economic logic to the country's public spending plans. A second key principle of transformation concerns taxation. Taxes should be based not on the current principle of raising enough money to pay for whatever permanent spending commitments exist. Instead, taxes should be viewed as price signals that help social markets – in, for example, water, road usage and carbon – use a scarce resource well.

Regardless of the exact form of a Fiscal Policy Committee or particular taxes, the next two decades will witness an explosion in data and information across the whole economy. The government needs to ensure it is at the vanguard of data generation and collection and that its statistics reflect the twenty-first-century economy and society it manages, rather than get trapped with legacy structures reflecting how the economy used to work.

Economic policy also needs to reflect where we live and work, and reflect the economic realities of an island economy of six million people. True balanced regional development can only occur when the political system accepts economic realities about the scale and density of people needed for a viable economic region. Lastly, a major lesson for all governments from the past five years is that markets need to be managed well, particularly systemic markets. Generally, EU standard competition policy, well enforced, and an efficient and consistent regulatory regime will suffice for most markets. However, for systemic markets – such as the public service labour market, and the housing and banking markets – more fundamental transformations will be needed.

Only by making these changes and laying the right economic foundations can Ireland hope to address the significant economic challenges it faces and, who knows, once again become the envy of its economic peers.

6

Ireland's Treasure by National Competitiveness

Michael King

Introduction

As one of the directors of the British East India Company, Thomas Mun (1571–1641) rewrote the basics of seventeenth-century economic thinking by arguing that foreign trade was the key driver of economic development. His thesis stood contrary to the economic thinking of many of his contemporaries, in particular Bullionist writers such as Thomas Milles and Gerard de Malynes, who argued that countries should seek to accumulate precious metals rather than allow 'leakage' abroad in exchange for foreign goods. Mun justified the pursuit of foreign trade on the grounds that an even greater amount of money will be generated for the home economy. His thesis was published posthumously in 1664 under the title *England's Treasure by Forraign Trade*. The following quote captures Thomas Mun's advocacy of the benefits of foreign trade:

> Behold then the true form and worth of foreign trade, which is, the great revenue of the King, the honour of the kingdom, the noble profession of the merchant, the school of our arts, the supply of our wants, the employment of our poor, the improvement of our lands, the nursery of our mariners, the walls of the kingdoms, the means of our treasure, the sinews of our wars, the terror of our enemies.[1]

While many contemporaries considered Mun an apologist for the activities of the East India Company and a self-interested stakeholder, his belief in the centrality of foreign trade to economic growth and improving living standards has been vindicated by both subsequent economic progress and recent economic theory.

Following independence in 1922, Ireland was slow to understand international trade as an opportunity. In the late 1950s, the young Irish state finally adopted an export-oriented strategy with some initial successes. Following the turbulent 1970s and 1980s, it was not until the 1990s that Ireland fulfilled its potential, building significant market share in world export markets and catching up with the standard of living of our European peers for the first time since the gains of the nineteenth century industrial revolution bypassed the majority of the island of Ireland. By 2000, the Irish economy was considered super-competitive, consistently ranked in the top five most competitive economies in the world.[2] Seventy-five years after independence, with living standards reaching levels above many of our European peers, the honour of our republic was finally realised.

However, with the dawn of the new century, to quote Yeats, 'all changed, changed utterly'. Ireland's economic growth post-2001 was founded on a credit-fuelled construction and consumer boom that led Ireland into significant property and stock market crashes, a fiscally expensive banking crisis and a recurring budget deficit problem. As a result, unemployment reached 13 per cent in 2010, up from 5 per cent two years previously.

Nonetheless, there remain many reasons to be positive. Ireland's export sector performed remarkably well during the global economic crisis in 2008 and 2009, softening the extent of the contraction in the Irish economy. In addition, there is broad agreement on what should be the focus of a next-generation competitiveness policy. Broad consensus prevails in public discourse around the need to build the knowledge economy through education, investments in research and development (R&D) capabilities, information and communications technology (ICT) and support for the internationalisation of Irish business.

Seldom has Ireland lacked the necessary high-level vision or aggregate targets in recent decades. The challenge for Ireland, though, lies in developing the sophisticated and holistic policy solutions and the inner political and institutional strength to push through difficult reforms. The great imponderable is whether Ireland can display the necessary ambition, courage and solidarity to navigate these challenges and deliver a platform for reducing unemployment and continuing the pursuit of higher living standards. Obstacles block our path, many of which are discussed elsewhere in this book, such as an outdated political system (Chapter 2) and the reluctance of the public sector to reform (Chapter 3).

We do start with one advantage, however. The economic crisis will undoubtedly lead to the emergence of a new generation of decision makers in business and politics, who – having learned lessons from Ireland's economic collapse – can avoid the mistakes of the past and perhaps more importantly be the catalyst for the essential reforms Ireland must implement. Our success will be determined not by the colour of our economics nor the party of our leaders but by the politics of change and the ability of our leaders to push through challenging reforms. Nothing less is at stake than the dignity and reputation of all our people.

This chapter aims to outline how Ireland can develop the policies required to deliver on our competitiveness goals. The next section outlines what exactly national competitiveness is and reviews Ireland's competiveness performance from the early 1990s on. It concludes by outlining the key competitiveness challenges facing the Irish economy. The following section reformulates the competitiveness pyramid used by the Irish government to understand Ireland's competitiveness performance. It then outlines three areas – education reform, ICT promotion and the cost of doing business – each of which represents one area of competitiveness policy essential for recovery. In each case, practical suggestions are recommended for how Ireland can reach its vision of re-establishing and maintaining a position as one of the most competitive and successful economies in the world.

Understanding Ireland's Competitiveness

What Is Competitiveness?

While the concept of competitiveness is universally referenced in public debate, it is often misunderstood and frequently subject to subtle nuances in definition. This is not helped by the absence of an underlying economic theory behind competitiveness or a widely agreed understanding of why some countries grow at certain times and why others do not. This lack of clarity is reinforced by the approach taken by international competitiveness rankings, published each year by the World Economic Forum (WEF) and the Institute for Management Development (IMD), which measure competitiveness using hundreds of indicators.

Competitiveness refers to the ability of firms to compete and succeed in international markets. Competitiveness policy, therefore, encompasses all the factors that influence the performance of businesses, from tax rates and levels of infrastructure to levels of trust and cooperation in society. In addition to the WEF and the IMD, Ireland's National Competitiveness Council (NCC) produces annual reports documenting Ireland's performance through scores of indicators reflecting the broad reach of the components of competitiveness.

To understand competitiveness, it is useful, as is often the case with macroeconomic issues, to compare a country to a household. Imagine a standard household in Ireland earning money from wages and spending it on consumption. Ignoring for the moment income from investments, the household's income determines how much it can spend each year. And to earn money, the household needs to possess skills that are in demand. If the household wants to increase its living standards year-on-year, it has to each year increase its productivity, i.e. it has to produce more value for every hour worked. Other strategies to increase income exist, but they are largely unsustainable. For example, the household could simply work more hours or borrow to fund consumption today, but these are short-term strategies at best.

The competitiveness challenge for a small open economy like Ireland can be similarly understood. To enjoy a higher standard of living – which involves importing more goods and services from abroad, as we can't make everything at home – Ireland needs to offer world markets products and services that meet international consumers' ever-evolving needs. This can be achieved by becoming more productive at what we currently export or by moving into higher value-added exports.[3] In each case, there is an increase in the overall productivity of the Irish economy, as measured by the value of output (goods and services) produced per unit of input (human, capital and natural resources).

There are of course short-term options to improving competitiveness. Echoing the example of the household, we could raise our standard of living in the short term through unsustainable borrowing – something Ireland did between 2001 and 2007. Another option is devaluation, an option Ireland has lost, at least in the sense of currency devaluation, with the adoption of the euro. Devaluation and deflation, the options open to a region in a monetary union, can be useful in the short term to correct prices when they become out of line with key competitors, but they are not the basis of a long-term sustainable competitiveness strategy. In fact, low wages often indicate a lack of competitiveness in the quality and productivity dimensions that underpin high standards of living.

As can be elicited from the example of the household, while many elements contribute to competitiveness, it is **export performance** and **productivity** that are the critical indicators that ultimately define the competitiveness of an economy. In this spirit, Ireland's NCC argues that 'Growing exports and raising productivity across the economy is the only sustainable path to reducing unemployment and securing long-term economic growth and prosperity.'[4] Michael Porter places the emphasis on productivity more specifically, describing competitiveness as the productivity with which a nation uses its human, capital and natural resources. In the discussion on refocusing our competitiveness policy below, a reconfigured competitiveness pyramid highlights the central importance of export performance and productivity for a new competitiveness policy.

Ireland's Competitiveness Performance

Deterioration in Ireland's competitiveness since 2001 has pre-empted the deterioration in the wider economy. By dissecting Ireland's performance and analysing it over three time periods, the real Celtic Tiger (1993–2001), the spurious Celtic Tiger (2001–2007) and the recession (2007–2010), the key strategic challenges facing the economy can be unearthed.

The Celtic Tiger: 1993–2001

Ireland's trade performance between 1993 and 2001 was remarkable. Over the period, Ireland's average annual growth rate for exports was 16.7 per cent, compared with 7.4 per cent for Organisation for Economic Co-Operation and Development (OECD) countries and 7.6 per cent for the world. Despite our small size, Ireland enjoyed 1.25 per cent of the global trade in goods and services in 2000. Significantly, between 1995 and 2002, net exports contributed on an annual basis around 2 percentage points to economic growth. Underlying this trade performance was significant productivity growth recorded between 1994 and 2001, primarily in the multinational sector of the economy. Between 1990 and 2000, Ireland enjoyed productivity gains of over 4 per cent annually, more than twice the US, the UK and the EU-14 (the EU-15 less Ireland).[5]

The Spurious Celtic Tiger: 2001–2007

While the credit-fuelled boom in construction and consumer spending maintained growth rates at an annual average of 5 per cent during the period 2001–2007, the underlying competitiveness of the Irish economy was subtly but steadily eroding. Some of the headline export figures disguised the decline in competitiveness. Exports continued to grow but no longer ahead of our international peers. Between 2001 and 2007, Ireland recorded export growth rates of 5.2 per cent compared with 4.6 per cent for OECD countries and 6.4 per cent for the world. The transition to a service economy was reflected in the fact that over this period Ireland lost market share in merchandise trade but gained significant market share in services trade.

Importantly, in contrast with the 1990s, between 2003 and 2007 net exports did not contribute to economic growth. Similarly, Ireland's productivity performance weakened after 2000. Between 2000 and 2005, productivity growth slowed to its lowest levels since 1980, at a time when productivity growth accelerated in the US and remained strong in the ten new EU entrants of 2004.[6] Despite convergence on average with EU and US productivity levels, Ireland's productivity levels lagged EU and US levels in several sectors of the economy, such as miscellaneous manufacturing, transport, wood/paper products, utilities and agriculture.[7]

Since 2000, Ireland's international competitiveness rankings have steadily fallen (see Figure 6.1). By 2006, while Ireland enjoyed annual gross national product (GNP) growth rates of 5 or 6 per cent, our competitiveness rankings fell over the decade to twenty-second (WEF) and eleventh (IMD) from top five positions in both rankings in 2000. While Ireland's performance in the international competitiveness rankings could not have predicted the nature and severity of the recession to come, our poor performance indicated the likelihood of future economic reversals. In particular, what appeared to be a stable period of economic growth between 2001 and 2006, with annual growth rates of circa 5 per cent, was in fact characterised by real declines in competitiveness as defined by the WEF and the IMD.

Figure 6.1: Ireland's Competitiveness Rankings and GNP Growth Rates (2000–2010)

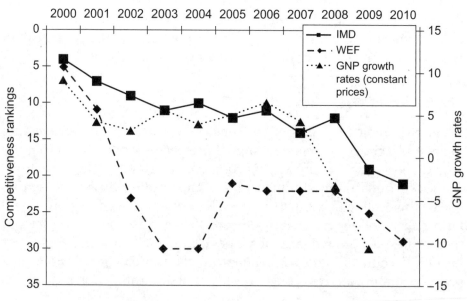

The Recession: 2007–2010

When the domestic economy entered severe recession in 2007, Ireland's export sector did not experience a similarly severe contraction, and in international terms our export sector was relatively unscathed by the downturn. Ireland's decline in exports in 2009 (-2.2 per cent) was very mild compared to the average decline in the Eurozone (-14.1 per cent) and the OECD (-13.6 per cent).[8] In fact, with exports steady but imports falling because of the recession, net exports contributed over 2 percentage points annually to economic growth over this period.

Services

The emergence of internationally traded services as the key driver of the economy will be a lasting legacy of the first decade of the twenty-first century. While services had long since become the major sector for employment, by the end of the decade services exports were about to outstrip merchandise exports. In 2009, services exports accounted for 45.4 per cent of total Irish exports, compared to 21 per cent in 2000.[9] Ireland now enjoys a significant share of the world market in business services, computer services, and financial services and insurance. The importance of services to the Irish economy was acknowledged in the 2008 Forfás publication *Catching the Wave: A Services Strategy for Ireland*.

Key Strategic Challenges

Within this context a number of strategic competitiveness challenges emerge. These challenges include:

- How can we improve the export performance of indigenous firms?
- How can we continue to attract foreign direct investment into key exporting sectors?
- How can we drive productivity gains in non-exporting sectors and the public sector in particular?
- How can we increase the proportion and number of workers employed by exporting companies?
- How can we make Ireland a world centre for services exports (energy and education are two examples)?
- How can we maintain and develop high-skilled manufacturing in Ireland?

- How can Ireland overcome key weaknesses in access to finance, indebtedness and macroeconomic certainty to allow the private and public sectors to invest in the future?

While specific policy directions addressing each of these challenges should be pursued, many of the key interventions for each challenge actually form part of cross-cutting themes, relevant across all the challenges. In the following section, I identify three key cross-cutting areas of policy action that can address Ireland's competitiveness challenges: reform of the education system, ICT capabilities and cost competitiveness. First, though, I outline a refocusing of Ireland's competitiveness policy for the modern world economy.

Refocused Competitiveness Policy: Building New Strengths

A Reconfigured Competitiveness Pyramid

To build a vision of a new competitiveness policy for Ireland, it is worth considering where the focus of competitiveness policy should be for a country at Ireland's stage of development. Distinguishing between nations at different levels of income, the WEF's *Global Competitiveness Report 2009–2010* argues, 'strengths in competing at earlier stages of development become weaknesses at more advanced levels of development.'[10] The report recommends that policy in high-income countries should prioritise the sophistication of enterprise and innovation systems and move away from focusing on policy areas more relevant to countries at an earlier stage of development, such as school enrolment rates and physical infrastructure.

This change in focus for policy makes sense when we consider Ireland's performance across policy inputs such as regulation or infrastructure. Putting aside for a moment the lack of availability of finance in the Irish economy, apart from enterprise sophistication and innovation systems, none of the other WEF components represent long-term critical determinants of the competitiveness of the Irish economy.[11] For example, prices and costs are moderating and our physical infrastructure has all but caught up with the OECD average, with planning underway to complete the few remaining critical infrastructure projects.

Figure 6.2 outlines a new competitiveness pyramid for Ireland, one that builds on the existing pyramid developed by the NCC (see Figure 6.3), which is used for current competitiveness policy.[12] The new pyramid takes into account our stage of development and current strengths and weaknesses. It reflects the required emphasis on business R&D and on knowledge infrastructure, and the primacy of export and productivity performance for a small country like Ireland. The pyramid is not meant as a linear system. For example, business support services such as the Industrial Development Agency (IDA Ireland), Enterprise Ireland and the country enterprise boards), regulation and taxation are all important in fostering business research and development.

There are three main innovations from the existing NCC competitiveness pyramid:

- Firstly, a distinction is made between what the government does (policy inputs) and what business does (business inputs). Policy inputs clearly have an influence on business inputs, such as the impact of banking regulation on the cost and availability of finance or the impact of government investment in infrastructure on logistics costs.
- Secondly, as discussed above, the critical competitiveness indicators – export performance and productivity – are elevated above other indicators of business performance, such as output, investment, foreign direct investment (FDI) and R&D activity.
- Lastly, the knowledge/innovation wing of the pyramid is highlighted to depict that it is now the policy priority for Ireland as a high-income country. As discussed below, Ireland's education and ICT systems are the bedrock of our knowledge and innovation systems.

In short, Ireland's new competitiveness policy should focus on driving innovation, and ultimately exports and productivity, by making the oft-mentioned 'knowledge economy' a reality, through building a world-leading skilled labour force and inspiring research and development in domestic and foreign-owned companies.

Building a Second-to-None Education System

Developing a world-class knowledge infrastructure to drive innovation, and ultimately exports and productivity, is currently a key focus of government policy. It is a cornerstone, for example, of the Department of Education and Science's *Statement of Strategy 2008–2010*, the Department of Enterprise's *Strategy for Science, Technology and Innovation 2006–2013* and the government's *Towards 2016* social partnership agreement. But to move beyond statements of intent and to actually deliver that system, we must imagine what it will look like and plan the journey from the current system to the system required.

Figure 6.2: A Reconfigured Competitiveness Pyramid

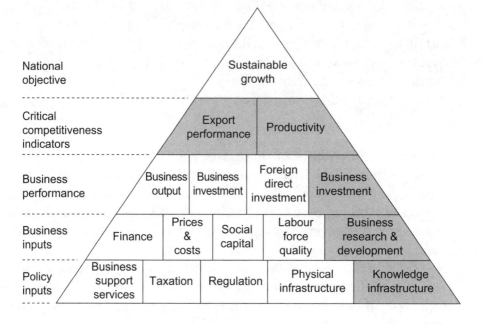

Figure 6.3: The Original NCC Competitiveness Pyramid

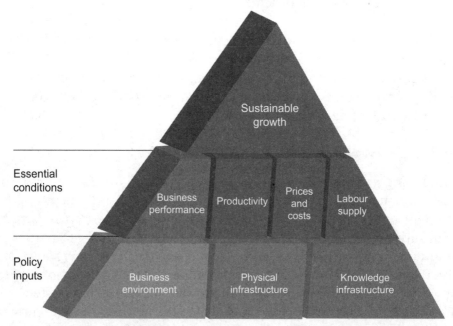

Source: NCC, *Annual Competitiveness Report 2010 – Volume 1: Benchmarking Ireland's Performance*, p. 20.

Imagine Ireland as a home to universities on a par with the best in the world in terms of research and student development. Imagine Ireland as a country where pre-school and primary education provides students with the highest scientific, numeracy and ICT skills in the world. Imagine a secondary school system that facilitates the emergence of a multilingual globalised society in Ireland, through sophisticated learning techniques and overseas exchanges. Imagine an end-to-end education system that inspires creativity, multicultural teamwork skills and international management and entrepreneurial skills. However, in each of these areas Ireland's performance is currently less than world class.

There is cause for optimism. Ireland does have a track record of giant leaps in educational outcomes. Investments undertaken in the 1960s across the education system played a key role in laying the foundation for the educated workforce and greater labour force participation rates that underpinned the rapid economic growth of the 1990s. In 1967, the then Minister for Education, Donagh O'Malley, unilaterally introduced free secondary education and free school buses for rural areas. This was complemented by the founding of the first regional technical colleges in 1970, which opened up higher education to significantly more school-leavers. Even with emigration in the 1970s and 1980s, significant labour demand in the 1990s meant that Ireland belatedly benefited from previous investments in education when emigrants returned to Ireland in the 1990s.

The current performance of the Irish education system, however, is very mixed at all levels. At pre-primary level, where the returns to education are greatest, Ireland lags international peers in pre-school performance by an alarming rate. The percentage of three-year-olds in state-funded education in 2005 was 1.7 per cent, compared to an EU-14 average of 82.2 per cent.[13] Fortunately, a 2009 announcement to give one year free pre-school education to all children is an important first step in ensuring quality pre-school for all, transforming pre-primary from childcare into early education. The next step is the development of sophisticated teaching methods that broaden cognitive development and prepare students for primary level.

With universal participation in primary education, the policy focus must be on raising standards. Ireland has a poor record in internationally comparable studies of student ability, evidence that the system is not at a world-class standard. The amount of time spent on the key skills of mathematics, science and technology at primary level is among the lowest in the OECD. Unsurprisingly, then, evidence from the Programme for International Student Assessment (PISA) 2006 assessment suggests that Irish fifteen-year-olds lag peers in other OECD countries in scientific and mathematical literacy.[14] At secondary level, while more students study mathematics than any other subject (95.7 per cent in 2009), just 16.2 per cent took the higher level exam in that year, about half as many as took higher level Irish (32.4 per cent), although both subjects are offered at three levels (higher, ordinary and foundation).[15] In Irish schools, the availability of computers is very low relative to leading comparator countries and ICT is not effectively integrated into teaching practices.[16]

Ireland's performance at higher education is again mixed. On the plus side, compared with an OECD average of 35 per cent, 41 per cent of 25–34-year-olds in Ireland have a third-level qualification. Also, both the number of Ph.D. graduates per 1,000 people and the number of mathematics, science and computing graduates as a percentage of all graduates are high in Ireland in comparison to other EU countries.[17] However, despite a large increase in actual expenditure on R&D, reaching 1.5 per cent of GNP in 2006, Ireland is well below the OECD average (2.34 per cent) and has a considerable distance to achieve the 2013 target of 2.5 per cent of GNP, outlined in the *Strategy for Science, Technology and Innovation*.

This mixed performance outlines the necessity for the big push towards superior educational outcomes. Developing a plan designed to achieve the vision outlined above will require not just broad stakeholder involvement, but also open-mindedness towards the best research and an appetite for reform not evident prior to the crisis.

A Capabilities Approach to Education

Two economists, Ricardo Hausmann and Cesar Hidalgo, have put forward a 'capabilities' approach to understanding economic growth, hinted at by Adam Smith but left largely undeveloped since. They suggest that changes in an economy's structure can be understood as capabilities already present in the economy being combined to form new goods and services.[18] For example, Singapore has combined capabilities from its infrastructure provision and its international trading activities and is developing exports in smart road systems.

As countries develop, certain capabilities become increasingly important, such as innovation, business sophistication and higher education, while others – such as basic transport and market size – become no longer sufficient for continued economic progress. As the Irish economy develops and becomes increasingly services based, labour force skills become the predominant determinant of local capabilities. NCC figures show that labour makes up three-quarters of inputs in services industries, compared to one-quarter in manufacturing industries.[19] Therefore, skills – and the education system – are more important for Ireland's competitiveness now than ever before.

There has been a tendency to consider maths, science and ICT skills as sufficient for Ireland to be a competitive knowledge economy. While they are undoubtedly important, a more holistic perspective on core competencies should form the basis of the Irish education system. Table 6.1 identifies eleven core competencies that should take centre stage in any reform agenda. The competencies have been chosen as the key educational outcomes necessary to develop a scientific, globalised and innovative workforce central to underpinning future competitiveness. Apart from the usual focus on mathematics, science and ICT skills, the framework emphasises the role of languages and includes soft skills such as teamwork and creative thinking. It is unlikely that current teaching methods can deliver real improvements in some of these areas so curriculum reform will be required, including the integration of ICT and 'service learning', where students participate in outreach activities designed to meet the needs of the community. In this latter model of education, service to the community occurs within the context of specific educational goals around critical thinking and the development of civic responsibility.

Table 6.1: Competencies for Competitiveness

Scientific	Globalised	Innovative
Mathematics	Languages	Multi-skilled
Science	Understanding of history/civics	Creative thinking
Literacy	Cross-cultural teamwork skills	Management skills
ICT skills		Entrepreneurial skills

At present, Ireland is importing many of these competencies from abroad rather than developing these skills in young Irish people. In short, Ireland needs an education system that delivers a world-class and ever-improving set of local competencies as identified in Table 6.1 to allow our business community to succeed in international markets.

With this in mind, Ireland requires consecutive six-year **Education System Development Plans** (ESDPs) to set ambitious targets and to plot a set of integrated reforms designed to achieve ambitious targets and provide the necessary funding to design and monitor accurate measures of outcomes. Targets should be set for cohort performance over the lifetime of their education, teacher performance and appropriate intermediate targets and should be set for future ESDPs as well as for the initial six-year period. Innovations in teaching practices should be built into the plan, evaluated and then adopted and modified as appropriate.

The adoption of the first ESDP should form part of the new wave of public sector transformation, a theme explored in greater detail throughout Chapter 3. Below are outlined three sets of policy recommendations, concerning school reform, maths, science and ICT skills, and teamwork and creative skills, which should be part of the first ESDP.

School Reform

A comprehensive reform of school management practices and teacher contracts needs to happen so that the incentives of educators are aligned with student attainment and development. Such reform would include empowering and rewarding successful school management, incentives for teacher performance based on effective evaluation, renewable contracts rather than permanency (see also Chapter 3) and flexible working practices. Such reform should be complemented by an initiative measuring the effectiveness of teachers.[20]

Empowerment of school management and flexible working practices can lead to better outcomes. When the incentives of school principals are aligned with student performance, a range of features can improve and adapt to students' needs, such as locally adapted school hours, after-school services, and allocation of teacher time to areas of specific needs, in a way that produces better student outcomes. Similarly, flexibility in labour contracts can ensure that teacher prerogatives do not take precedence over student needs when it comes to local educational priorities.

Effective teacher evaluation can play a central role in the drive for better educational outcomes. If the evaluation process is robust and widely accepted, it can help reward the better teachers and when combined with renewable contracts rather than permanency, can weed out underperforming teachers. The most effective teachers should be rewarded with longer contracts and promotions with associated pay increases, as opposed to promotions simply given to teachers on the basis of years of experience or indeed educational qualifications.[21]

Mathematics and ICT Skills

Poor results in mathematics in the state examinations lead to annual calls for the re-introduction of bonus points for honours maths, cumulating in the 2011 decision of Ireland's seven universities to award 25 additional points to all students who achieve a D grade or higher in honours mathematics. The problem with this approach is that, while mathematics is very important, it is not the sole key competency of the knowledge economy. Plausible arguments for bonus points for all science and ICT subjects can be made even before a debate starts on which subjects inspire other skills needed for the modern labour force. Ireland requires a step change in student outcomes not only in mathematics but in science and ICT, languages and key soft skills such as creative skills, teamwork, management and entrepreneurial skills. When the wider competencies for competitiveness are considered, a system of bonus points for maths is rendered a less effective policy.

In September 2008, the National Council for Curriculum and Assessment (NCCA) began a pilot project called Project Maths, designed to ensure an appropriate balance between understanding mathematical theory and concepts and developing practical application skills. In June 2010, the *Report of the Project Maths Implementation Support Group* was published and recommended that Project Maths be rolled out to all schools in Ireland.[22] The report makes a number of recommendations to ensure greater participation in higher level mathematics in all schools through the provision of specialist teachers, to raise awareness about the importance of maths and to ensure that all post-primary students at all levels are taught mathematics solely by teachers who hold a qualification in mathematics by 2018. This later recommendation is based on the premise that in the absence of any robust form of teacher evaluation, teacher qualification is the best proxy for assessing likely teacher effectiveness. As argued previously, the best maths teachers, as illustrated through effective teacher evaluation, should be retained, not simply those with certain qualifications. The report provides a good starting point for recommendations. The next part is the more challenging part: the integration of the recommendations into a comprehensive and integrated reform package that is measured against specific targets in the years ahead.

In the area of ICT, the reliance on computer science labs that are remote from the normal classroom and used infrequently, or at best within a strict timetable, is a tangible example of how existing practices impose constraints that neutralise much of the power of ICT in learning.[23] Efforts to reform curricula and increase ICT investment at primary and secondary level have taken place in the first decade of the twenty-first century. Such efforts have been slowly evolutionary rather than revolutionary. According to an EU-wide report, Ireland has a lower proportion of computers and internet connections than the EU average.[24] Ireland also has a poor record of integrating ICT into the curriculum; according to the OECD, a lower proportion of Irish students use spreadsheets, word documents and ICT applications than the OECD average.[25] Looking forward, a recent report by the Institute of International and European Affairs (IIEA) provided a series of recommendations on improving ICT skills among students in schools. The most worthy of these include the swift rollout of a digital curriculum at primary and secondary level and a system of complementary teacher training. The introduction of weighted marks at Leaving Certificate level for ICT-related subjects was also recommended, emphasising the importance of a number of subjects to the competitiveness of the Irish labour force.[26]

Teamwork and Creative Skills

The teacher-led and individualistic approach to classroom interaction in the Irish education system is not suited to the development of teamwork, creativity and entrepreneurial skills, key skills necessary for the knowledge economy. In addition, the importance of cross-cultural skills cannot be overstated, as Ireland's most important exporters draw skilled staff from all around the world. Such skills are essential to the innovation process and will ultimately determine the success of efforts to pursue productivity-enhancing R&D activities on the island.

Building on the current strengths of our education system, Ireland should seek to integrate styles of teaching that promote collaboration, student-to-student learning, empowerment and the creative use of technology. Project-based group work facilitated through technology is particularly suited to the pursuit of these objectives. An example of innovation that should be integrated into the primary and secondary level education systems, in parallel with the formal integration of ICT into curricula, is the award-winning Bridge2College programme based at Trinity College Dublin. Bridge2College aims to improve attitudes towards personal learning and education, to improve third-level access for young people from socially disadvantaged areas, and to champion an advanced education model for all schools. In 2010, the programme was extended from an after-schools programme in 30 schools to become part of the formal curriculum in a small number of pilot schools.[27]

In this section, I have simply focused on three components of what should ultimately form part of a new comprehensive ESDP. If pursued, each set of recommendations can lay the foundation for future success in productivity growth and export performance. Furthermore, if a series of ambitious, integrated and reform-driven plans are implemented an opportunity exists for our generation to leave a world-class education system as a legacy to future generations.

Our Digital Being: Where Is the 'Seoul'?

In the later decades of the twentieth century, a small number of the 150 or so countries originally left behind by the Industrial Revolution transformed themselves into modern high income economies. South Korea is one such country. A combination of foresighted policy interventions and favourable market geography, institutions and demographic changes has turned South Korea from a poverty-stricken nation in the 1960s into an economy ranked twenty-second in the world in terms of income per capita.[28]

South Korea is widely considered a global leader in information and communications technology (ICT), standing side-by-side with a small number of the world's wealthiest countries. But it is an example of a middle-income country that has, through a series of development plans since 1987, become a leader in ICT. The lesson from the South Korean case is clear: cutting-edge ICT systems are not simply the luxury of the world's wealthiest nations but a feasible goal for aspiring nations.

South Korea's ICT advances can be attributed to a consistent three-pillared policy intervention: significant **investment in ICT** in education and universal broadband, complementary aggressive **legislation** and a commitment to **continuous policy evaluation**, research and development. Each pillar has formed part of the series of national development plans, from the initial *National Basic Information System* (1987) to the more recent *Cyber Korea 21* (1999) and *Global Leader, e-Korea* (2002).[29] While the role of investment is important, Korea has passed over 150 laws related to ICT since the introduction of the Framework Act on Informatization Promotion in 1995. An example of such transformative legislation is the 2002 Act on Closing the Digital Divide.

The relative performance of South Korea in ICT illustrates, firstly, how, despite a generation of budget surpluses, Ireland was unable to position itself at the forefront of ICT and, secondly, how a country with fewer resources was able to make the giant leap to become a global ICT leader in a generation. Figure 6.4 traces the historical broadband penetration rates for four countries of interest: Ireland, South Korea, Sweden and Switzerland. The success of the South Korean policy is evident from the turn of the century, achieving broadband penetration rates of over 25 per cent by 2002, whereas Ireland, by 2010, had yet to reach this milestone.[30] The second most striking point is the advances by Sweden and Switzerland, which have caught up with South Korea since 2006.

There is, of course, more to ICT than broadband, for example the integration of ICT skills into the existing labour force, the way businesses work and access to additional technologies via broadband. To help gain a

Figure 6.4: Broadband Penetration, Historical Time Series

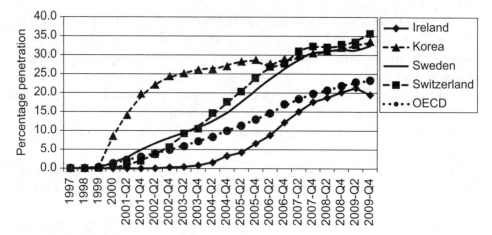

sense of Ireland's performance in these areas, Table 6.2 records Ireland's ranking in the international competitiveness rankings for availability of latest technologies (WEF), for firm-level technology absorption (WEF) and for information technology skills (IMD). For each indicator, Ireland is ranked behind its leading European peers, as well as behind South Korea, with the sole exception of ICT skills.

The South Korean story presents a success story Ireland can emulate. With a commitment to rigorous policy evaluation, key legislative supports and modest investment, Ireland has the potential to make giant strides in the area of ICT. In the era of burgeoning budget surpluses, Ireland tended to use financial resources as the primary policy tool and, as Figure 6.4 and Table 6.2 show, we still fell behind key competitors. As Korea's experience shows, money is only one element in an overall strategy and Ireland should seek to develop an integrated ICT development plan.

Improving Ireland's ICT performance can play two roles in the economy, both through ICT as a sector itself and through its impact on productivity in other sectors. In Ireland's case, the ICT sector is a critical contributor to exports already, but new and significant business opportunities exist in digital media, cloud computing and ICT-related green technology.[31] Secondly, ICT is making significant advances into traditional sectors of the economy and dominates social interaction like never before. Ireland should seek to be an ICT leader and ensure that policy is primed to place us at the centre of future ICT innovations. Specifically, Ireland should seek to develop niche ICT clusters, provide a world-class ICT network and foster digital instincts through the education system. The following three paragraphs outline steps Ireland can take in these three areas.

Table 6.2: International Competitiveness Indicators in ICT, Country Rank in 2009–2010

	ICT in Business				Broadband			
	Gross National Income per capita, purchasing power parity	Availability of Latest Technologies, WEF Ranking	Firm-Level Technology Absorption, WEF Ranking	Information Technology Skills, IMD Ranking	Percentage of Fibre Connections (OECD Rank)	Median Broadband Speeds (OECD Rank)	Broadband Subscribers per 100 Inhabitants (OECD Rank)	Average Ranking
Sweden	$37,780	1	2	4	23% (4)	10,240 (18)	32.4 (7)	6.0
Switzerland	$39,210	5	4	20	1% (16)	10,240 (18)	35.6 (3)	11.0
South Korea	$27,840	23	9	34	49% (2)	51,200 (2)	33.5 (5)	12.5
Ireland	$35,710	34	32	24	1% (17)	3,072 (30)	19.5 (22)	26.5
Indicator/ Source	Current international dollars, world development indicators, 2008	Are the latest technologies available in your country? 2009–1010 weighted average (WEF, 2010)	Do businesses in your country absorb new technology? 2009–2010 weighted average (WEF, 2010)	Information technology skills are readily available, 2009 (IMD, 2010)	Percentage of fibre connections in total broadband, December 2009	Median advertised broadband download speed, kbit/s, October 2009	OECD fixed broadband subscribers per 100 inhabitants, December 2009	

Developing Niche ICT Clusters

Fostering clusters of companies has been at the centre of IDA Ireland's policy in recent decades and has been highly successful in life sciences in Cork, medical devices in Galway and financial services in Dublin. Clusters of similar firms can increase productivity and the capacity for innovation and can stimulate and support new business formation through improving access to specialised suppliers, skills, training, and research and development.[32] Through IDA Ireland and Enterprise Ireland, efforts should be stepped up to build global market share in digital media, cloud computing and ICT-related green technology. As part of a wider cluster policy, the transformative role of relevant legislation should not be underestimated. For example, in their 2008 report on digital media, the IIEA recommended the establishment of a legal hub and global rights clearance centre that would facilitate the development of locally based intellectual property rights.[33]

World-Class ICT Network

The median broadband speed in Ireland lags considerably behind key competitor countries. Historically, this is in part due to Ireland largely missing out on the fibre-optic revolution pioneered by South Korea and Japan. But technology develops fast. Emerging wireless technologies may replace fibre optic cables as the infrastructure of the future and Ireland will need to be, for the first time, an early adopter in whatever next-generation technology emerges. In order to achieve this, Ireland will need to participate in the development of these new technologies, be highly strategic in any investments and ensure that the regulatory regime is sufficiently nimble to not only avoid hindering new technologies but to encourage private investment in new infrastructure.

Fostering Digital Instincts

ICT is revolutionising our relationship with knowledge, with our work colleagues and clients and even with our family members. It is fundamentally changing the essence of business and rewriting traditional concepts of innovation and productivity gains. To underpin Ireland's culture of innovation and higher productivity in the years to come, the education system should be transformed to foster 'digital instincts' at primary and secondary level. Originally coined in the IIEA's report, the term is used here to represent the instinctive mindset of future generations to process knowledge, analyse challenges and drive innovation through the medium of ICT, as is discussed in more detail in the section on education above.

These recommendations represent a starting point in efforts to turn Ireland from laggard to leader in ICT. As technologies change, Ireland's ability to adapt and innovate in ICT policy will ultimately determine if Ireland will remain a slow adopter in the generations to come. If Ireland can learn from the successes of South Korea, it is possible in a fiscally constrained environment to make giant leaps in ICT capabilities.

Cost Competitiveness

Cost competitiveness may seem against the spirit of competitiveness presented in this chapter. High costs need not be a problem for an advanced economy if productivity is high and the goods and services exported are sufficiently differentiated by quality on international markets. Nonetheless, a strategy on cost competitiveness is included for two reasons. Firstly, while the majority of the price and wage increases since 1993 are a benign outcome of the process of economic development, there have been a number of examples of price increases caused at least in part by domestic policy constraints, such as a lack of competition, insufficient capacity and the oversupply of credit. Secondly, while an island at the edge of Europe is likely to face higher prices for certain internationally traded goods due to additional transport and distribution costs, this should be no more than absolutely necessary and Irish citizens and companies should not have to automatically face paying 10–20 per cent more than their counterparts in other EU member states.

Ireland experienced a significant loss in cost competitiveness between 2000 and 2008, reflecting higher price inflation in Ireland and the appreciation of the euro. According to Eurostat, prices in Ireland were the highest in the Eurozone in 2008.[34] While deflation during 2009 moderated some costs, particularly property costs, a number of issues remain. The cost of waste and of public services such as health and education continues to rise.[35] Legal costs have failed to moderate after the boom years, while transport costs, such as public transport and taxis, are relatively expensive in Ireland compared with our main trading partners.[36]

As discussed in Chapter 5, a consequence of the adoption of the euro is no longer being able to devalue our currency to realign cost competitiveness and boost exports in the short run. As a result, an increased emphasis on the supervision of prices is necessary. Some efforts have been made in this regard. In the last few decades, various anti-inflation groups have reported to the government. For example, as part of *Towards 2016*, the 'anti-inflation group' previously established under the *Sustaining Progress* agreement was reconstituted with the same membership and mandate.[37] But this group has lacked sufficient independence, adequate resources for research and policy analysis, and the involvement of leading experts.

Costs Council

A measure to guard effectively against excessive costs is the establishment of an independent National Council for Business and Public Sector Costs (NCBPSC), comprising senior academics and business leaders. This independent advisory group would monitor costs facing business both directly and indirectly, through public sector costs, and make policy advice on ensuring costs are no higher than necessary. This suggestion is based on three core arguments. Firstly, the advent of the euro means that the management of costs has been elevated to an essential component of economic policy. Secondly, there has been significant evidence of domestic policy constraints playing a key role in inflating prices and costs, for example a lack of competition, insufficient capacity and the oversupply of credit. Thirdly, the importance of independent checks on policy has been illustrated to devastating effect during the financial crisis of 2008–2010.

While the *raison d'être* of every so-called quango should be carefully examined, we should take a cautionary note from the excessive culture of consensus during the 2000s. Even at the risk of creating new quangos, Ireland actually needs new advisory groups specifically designed to independently and publicly provide long-term advice and analysis on key areas of policy. One example is an independent Central Fiscal Policy Committee, discussed in Chapter 5. The proposed new NCBPSC, or 'Costs Council', should sit alongside the Central Fiscal Policy Committee as a key institutional innovation designed to improve long-term economic policy-making in Ireland. Another formulation would be for both the costs and the fiscal remits to fit under the guise of a broad-based Council of Economic Advisors.

The Costs Council would also fit in with existing mechanisms. The merged Competition Authority and National Consumer Agency will continue to enforce Irish and EU competition law and defend the interests of the consumer, and Forfás should continue its comparative study of the cost of doing business in Ireland. The proposed NCBPSC could receive research and secretarial support from both Forfás and the combined Competition Authority and National Consumer Agency. It would also be mandated to contribute to discussions on public service pay rates. Such an innovation could have prevented the costly and unjustified bench-marking exercise of 2002.

With wages making up a significant majority of input costs for many sectors, particularly service activities, a subtle understanding of wages and productivity is required. Indeed, high wages can help attract the best international talent to our shores. The Council's remit in relation to wages would be to ensure wage increases do not exceed productivity gains, while ensuring a competitive general cost of living.

Conclusion: Delivering Change

Restoring Ireland's competitiveness, defined in this chapter as reignit-ing productivity growth and delivering further increases in exports, is the only long-term strategy to reduce unemployment and continue the pursuit of higher living standards. Restoring competitiveness will require significant reform in many areas of policy. Three strategic directions have been outlined that, if pursued, will provide the basis for ensuring Ireland's competitiveness. Firstly, Ireland needs a series of Education System Development Plans to deliver ongoing reform to establish its education system as a global leader. Secondly, a comprehensive strategy to place Ireland at the forefront of ICT capabilities is recommended, one that goes beyond just public investment. Lastly, to reinforce the competitive effect of these reforms, this chapter proposes a new approach to business costs, to ensure that costs in the Irish economy are not unnecessarily inflated. Taken together, the three policy directions highlighted will help improve Ireland's competitiveness.

The ideas and recommendations set out in this chapter are more often than not widely suggested and often debated. In the era of centrist poli-tics, a policy direction itself is seldom original as commentators and politicians compete in the realm of priorities, timing, nuance and techni-cal detail. The future prosperity of future generations will be determined by neither the colour of our economics nor the party of our leaders but by the politics of change and the ability of our leaders to push through challenging reforms.

Over history, the defining characteristic of successful civilizations has been their capacity to change. Reinvention is the lifeblood of longevity. Societies unwilling to change in the face of new realities can stagnate and decline. For change to occur, Ireland needs to rediscover its ambition, courage and solidarity for wide-ranging reforms. Indeed, economic his-tory shows that crisis is often the best opportunity for reform and our opportunity is now. Evidence of ambition for change was weak in the immediate aftermath of the onset of recession in 2007 and 2008. The initial reaction of interest groups to the Budgets of 2008–2010 has shown that solidarity was in short supply. And with arguably the economic fate of the country in the balance, the first year following the Croke Park Agreement in early 2010 saw very little progress on agreed reforms.

The hope remains that from the crisis, a new generation of decision makers, businesspeople and political leaders will emerge who – having learned the lessons of the crisis – can in the years to come provide the ambition, courage and solidarity to make the difficult decisions that will help Ireland thrive again. Nothing less than the honour of our republic is at stake.

7

A 'Green' Ireland?
Energy Security and Climate Policy

Joseph Curtin

Introduction: A Danish Comparison

The members of the Organization of Petroleum Exporting Countries (OPEC) initiated their first oil embargo in October 1973, a response to the decision taken by the US government to resupply the Israeli military during the Yom Kippur War. The price of oil quadrupled over the following year. A second oil crisis soon followed. The Iranian revolution of 1979 and the disruption to oil supply which followed led to oil reaching its highest real price ever recorded until March 2008.[1] The combined effect of these shocks sent the global economy into a tailspin of stagflation – deflation combined with widespread unemployment – from which it did not emerge until the mid-1980s.

But the lessons from this crisis were soon forgotten. The triumph of short-term thinking around the cabinet tables and boardrooms of the world, encouraged perhaps by demanding electorates and shareholders, meant that business as usual soon resumed. In Ireland, for example, 68 per cent of our total energy needs came from imported fossil fuels in 1990. This had risen to 89 per cent by 2006, when imported oil alone accounted for 60 per cent of the country's total energy requirement.[2] In 2008, energy use in transport was over 99 per cent dependent on oil products, all of which were imported. The warnings of the 1970s and 1980s seem to have receded from the collective Irish consciousness as the economy boomed.

This critical exposure to imported energy is yet another unwelcome gift bequeathed by the Celtic Tiger to the next generation, another surprise hidden beneath the froth of the boom years.

Denmark serves as a useful counterpoint. When the first oil crisis struck, more than 90 per cent of all Danish energy supplies were imported – among the highest dependency ratios of any country. In the midst of the crisis, the Danish government launched a strategic response with the publication of its first energy strategy, *Danish Energy Policy 1976*, with the objective of securing Denmark against future crises in supply. This was followed by *Energy 81*, *Energy 2000*, and most recently, *Energy 21*, which sets out an ambitious energy policy agenda for the coming years.

The overriding objective was to secure Danish energy security against the backdrop of uncertainty in international energy markets. A number of highly successful energy policy initiatives were launched to deliver this objective. Among the areas targeted were combined electricity and heat production, improving the energy efficiency of existing and new buildings, supports for wind and other renewable energies, strategic investment in energy research and development (R&D), district heating based on gas, and the ambitious use of green taxes.

The results have been dramatic. Since 1997, Denmark has become a net exporter of energy. Energy efficiency improvements have meant that gross energy consumption has been stable for a long period despite solid economic growth, and Denmark now gets more gross domestic product (GDP) per unit of energy used than any other European country. Renewable sources of energy (renewables) account for 18 per cent of Denmark's total energy needs and 28 per cent of its power generation, chiefly due to the incorporation of wind into the power mix. And exports of Danish energy technology more than tripled from 1998 to 2008, and now make up around 11 per cent of total Danish goods exports.

This is an excellent example of the impact of a government's vision on its country's competitiveness, a theme taken up in Chapter 6. The Danish wind turbine industry consists of more than 200 companies and manufactures 35 per cent of all wind turbines. The world's two largest producers of enzymes to bio-ethanol (covering a combined 70 per cent of the world market) are Danish. Denmark's Riso National Laboratory for Sustainable Energy is leading the world in hydrogen fuel cell research. And Europe's largest producer of thermal solar energy (SolarCAP) is located in Denmark.

Danish policy has given rise to a new industrial cluster. This is clearly not a result of a natural competitive advantage (Ireland's wind power resources are superior to Denmark's), but rather as a result of strategic and targeted long-term policy. It happened because Denmark, led by an imaginative and entrepreneurial political elite and with widespread support from society, had the desire to be a leader. This could be described as a comparative societal advantage.

More than 30 years since Denmark's first energy strategy in the aftermath of the oil shock of 1973, it is now commonly accepted in energy circles that a period of increased oil price volatility may be on the horizon and that higher prices will become the norm. In the words of Chris Huhne, UK Secretary for Energy and Climate Change, 'The world we're going into ... will be a world where we will have very substantial oil price spikes ... exactly as they did in the 1970s and 80s.'[3]

The picture for natural gas, Ireland's second most important source of energy, is somewhat different. There have been huge investments in liquefied natural gas (LNG) from 2005 and technological breakthroughs in the US have made the extraction of 'non-conventional' or 'shale gas' possible in large quantities. According to the International Energy Agency (IEA), the resultant gas glut will see depressed prices until 2015 at least, perhaps beyond.

The mainstream view is, therefore, that the era of cheap oil has almost certainly come to an end, and high prices and increased price volatility will become the norm in the coming years. The story may be somewhat different for gas, and we may be entering a period where gas and oil prices become increasingly divergent.

There is another impetus for diversification of our energy supply: self-preservation. The *Fourth Assessment Report* of the Intergovernmental Panel on Climate Change (IPCC), published in 2008, warned that warming to the planet is 'unequivocal' and that it is 'very likely due to the observed increase in anthropogenic greenhouse gas (GHG) concentrations'.[4]

According to the US National Ocean and Atmospheric Administration, the first eleven months of 2010 were the warmest since records began in 1880, 2000–2009 was the warmest decade on record, and in total seventeen countries experienced record temperatures in 2010, including the highest temperature ever recorded in Asia, 53 degrees Celsius in Pakistan.[5] The observed impacts of climate change are in fact occurring faster than had been predicted by the *Fourth Assessment Report* of the IPCC.[6]

This chapter seeks to explore the likely ramifications of climate change and energy security for Ireland in the period to 2020, and beyond to 2050. In the 2010s, climate change and energy security will pose comparable policy challenges to the oil shocks of the 1970s. How Ireland responds to these challenges will go a considerable way to determining the economic success of this country in the new millennium. It will be argued that radical, long-term strategic thinking, combined with profound institutional reform, will be required if these challenges are to be effectively met.

The next section of this chapter explores Ireland's early responses to the energy and climate challenges in the pre- and post-Kyoto period and catalogues the missed opportunities of this period; and the following section outlines the EU's energy and climate change package and assesses the successes and failures of the Fianna Fáil–Green coalition government. The final section outlines four 'big ticket' challenges for the country which can be turned into opportunity: greening agriculture, reducing and decarbonising building energy use, transitioning to zero-carbon transport and upgrading the electricity grid. The political and legislative reforms required to achieve success are also outlined in this section. Some brief concluding remarks follow.

Environmental Laggard: An Overview of Ireland's Response

Ireland's initial response to these challenges can be divided into three distinct phases: the pre-Kyoto period, the decade following the agreement of the Kyoto Protocol and the period from 2007 to the present time.

Pre-Kyoto

Prior to the negotiation of the Kyoto Protocol in 1997, there was no consideration of environmental issues in energy policy formulation, though energy security considerations appeared on the radar intermittently. The first temporary blip of awareness of the energy security challenge can be detected on the radar in the late 1970s. In a discussion document published by the Department of Industry, Commerce and Energy in 1978, the country's then 75 per cent dependence on imported oil was acknowledged to leave Ireland 'dangerously exposed' and it was argued that it 'should be reduced as quickly as possible'.[7]

Wind power received fairly short shrift. Wind turbines are very briefly discussed and the conclusion is reached that they may pose a 'danger to life and damage to property from their use'.[8] Meanwhile in Denmark, the installed generation capacity for wind increased over 300 times from 1 megawatt (MW) at the beginning of 1980 to 326 MW by the end of 1990.[9]

Conservation of energy was not dismissed quite so comprehensively: the document concluded that energy conservation could yield substantial savings and that 'effective energy conservation measures are required to achieve these savings'.[10] However, none of the specific measures identified

– like combined heat and power, district heating or heat pumps – were pursued.

The document concludes that 'Coal-fired and nuclear-powered generating plants ... appear the only realistic alternatives.'[11] Energy was dropped from the departmental title in 1980, an indication of the profound neglect by successive governments in planning for Ireland's energy future. Moreover, climate change was effectively a non-issue in Ireland in the pre-Kyoto period.[12]

Post-Kyoto

The agreement of the Kyoto Protocol in 1997 was a watershed in the development of Irish energy and climate policy. Under the protocol, the EU15 agreed to cut GHG emissions by 8 per cent on 1990 levels for the period 2008–2012, and Ireland agreed to limit emissions to a 13 per cent increase on 1990 levels as its share of the target. In the following decade, environmental concerns were officially considered and acknowledged in policy documentation, though they continued to be largely overlooked in favour of other considerations in decision making. The primary concern during the immediate post-Kyoto period was the introduction of competition into energy and gas markets, leading to the 1999 establishment of the Commission for Energy Regulation.

The first official attempt to address the environmental component of energy policy was attempted by the Department of Public Enterprise (then responsible for energy policy) with the publication of the *Green Paper on Sustainable Energy* in 1999. This paper argued that on business-as-usual trends, Ireland's chances of meeting its Kyoto target were slim. It therefore proposed a budget of IR£126 million for GHG mitigation and the establishment of the Irish Energy Centre on a statutory basis (now the Sustainable Energy Authority of Ireland (SEAI)).

A specific climate change strategy (as distinct from an energy policy with a climate component) soon followed. The then Minister for the Environment, Noel Dempsey, commissioned a report from Environmental Resources Management (ERM), a consultancy firm, that demonstrated it would be possible to reach Ireland's target at little or no cost to society given an appropriate policy response.[13]

The report found that the least costly and most equitable options were economic instruments that affect the price of carbon-based products across the whole economy. It therefore advocated the introduction of a carbon tax, and acknowledged that additional government action would be required to offset market failures in certain areas. This expert report served as a basis for the public and political debate which followed and (notwithstanding the dropping of some political hot potatoes such as the proposal to phase out burning peat) the report formed the basis of Ireland's first National Climate Change Strategy, published in 2000.

This well-thought out strategy paper did not, unfortunately, form the basis of the policy which followed. Many of the policies outlined in this strategy now read like a list of missed opportunities: the promised progressive introduction of carbon taxes from 2002; the rebalancing of vehicle registration tax (VRT) for cars; a modal shift to public transport; comprehensive strategies to deal with energy-inefficient housing; achieving higher residential densities; or negotiated agreements with industry to increase efficiency and reduce emissions.

The failure to introduce a carbon tax can largely be attributed to a vociferous campaign of opposition from special interest groups, the Irish Business and Employers' Confederation (IBEC) and the Irish Farmers' Association (IFA) in particular, supported by the Department of Enterprise, Trade and Employment and the Department of Agriculture respectively. The main argument used against the tax – as with most environmental regulation – was that it would undermine the competitiveness of Irish industry.[14] The balance of evidence both then and now suggests that these concerns were largely misplaced. According to a meta-analysis that reviewed evidence from the World Bank, the Organisation for Economic Co-Operation and Development, national governments and academics, good environmental regulation stimulates cost reduction for industry and business, creates markets for environmental goods and services, drives innovation, reduces business risk, assists competitive advantage and creates competitive markets.[15]

Further evidence is provided by the European Commission-funded Competiveness Effects of Environmental Tax Reform (COMETR) project, which assessed the competiveness implications of introducing a carbon tax in the seven EU countries which had done so (Germany, the UK, Denmark, Sweden, the Netherlands, Finland and Slovenia). This study found that 'carbon leakage' – where emissions are not reduced, rather displaced to another location – had been very small and in some cases negative and that the GDP effects were positive in five of six countries, especially when revenues from the tax are recycled.[16]

The early introduction of a carbon tax was not the only missed opportunity: the commitment to higher residential densities was never realised. Examples of urban sprawl, one-off housing and new communities without adequate public transport, social infrastructure or amenities came to blight the entire country in the years after the publication of the strategy.

The abject systems failure of planning policy over this period has been well documented.[17]

So bad had Dublin's urban sprawl become that by 2005 the European Environmental Agency had begun using Dublin as an example of a 'worst-case scenario' of the impacts of poor planning so that the new EU member states in Eastern Europe would avoid making the same mistakes.[18] The resulting car-dependent lifestyles of the majority of Irish citizens make addressing emissions from the transport sector all the more difficult.

In addition, the 900,000 or so new houses built since 1982 have been built to low standards of energy efficiency, a consequence of lax building regulations. Indeed, statistics show that Ireland suffers from having among the worst housing standards in Europe in terms of energy efficiency.[19] Given the lax inspection regime, it is perhaps unlikely that many houses were built in compliance with what building regulations there were.

The priority in this policy area, as with so much of public policy, was to ensure that no costly regulations were imposed on the building sector, to 'keep the show on the road'. Imposing societally beneficial costs on the vociferous, organised, well-connected and well-resourced property development sector would have been politically unpalatable. The big-ticket item – the closure of Moneypoint power station from 2008 – was also shelved as the implications for energy security would probably have made this proposal untenable.

By 2007, according to the Environmental Protection Agency (EPA), emissions were 25 per cent above 1990 levels, twice the Kyoto target increase of 13 per cent by 2012. A new National Climate Change Strategy (NCCS) for 2007–2012 followed, which recycled some of the commitments from the first strategy, such as the rebalancing of VRT. Additional measures, including a levy on incandescent bulbs, revised building regulations and the installation of smart meters in the homes of electricity users, were also mooted.

The net result of these failures is that economic activity was as dependent on imported carbon as ever towards the end of the 1990s. It appeared as if the failure to implement the first National Climate Change Strategy would also cost the state hundreds of millions of euro, and the government designated €270 million under the National Development Plan 2007–2013 for the purchase of carbon credits.

From Laggard to Leader?

In 2007, two events led to a marked shift in Irish energy and climate change policy. At an EU level, the European Commission published the first of its Energy and Climate Packages. Domestically, energy and climate change had been moving up the political agenda in any case, but the formation of a new coalition government that included the Green Party hastened this process.

Galvanised by the EU

Ireland's room for manoeuvre on energy and climate was increasingly tightening. A package of measures to address these challenges, which has far-reaching consequences for Ireland and the EU, was agreed by the European Council in December 2009, and later ratified by the European Parliament.

This combined legislative package is considered the most significant emanating from Brussels since economic and monetary union. It will require nothing short of a fundamental reorganisation of how economic activity is organised and sustained by member states. Its main components relate to emissions reductions, the promotion of renewables and energy efficiency. In order to encourage an international agreement on climate change, the EU made a commitment to reduce emissions by 30 per cent of 1990 levels by 2020, or 20 per cent if an international agreement was not reached.

The Emissions Trading Scheme (ETS), which covers nearly 40 per cent of EU emissions, was also reformed. This scheme requires companies to surrender permits equal to their emissions over a given period. If a company's emissions are greater than their allocation of permits they must invest in emissions reduction technology or purchase more permits. After 2012, companies will progressively stop receiving free allocations of permits, and the European Commission will control the allocation of an ever-decreasing number of permits. The sectors covered – including the Irish energy, cement, metal processing and paper sectors – will therefore come under increasing pressure to reduce emissions.

Each member state received an emissions reduction target for emissions not covered by the ETS. Ireland is required to reduce 'domestic sector' emissions by a minimum of 20 per cent on 2005 levels – the most challenging emissions reduction target of any member state. An agreement that 20 per cent of all energy consumed in the EU would come from renewables by 2020 was also reached. Ireland's share of this target is to achieve 16 per cent all energy consumed from renewables by 2020, from a base of 3 per cent in 2005. As a component of the overall renewables target, 10 per cent of fuel used for transport must also come from renewable fuels by 2020. Finally, a target to achieve 20 per cent energy efficiency savings by 2020 was agreed. Unlike the renewables and emissions reduction targets, however, this target is not legally binding. The climate and energy package of measures have become known as the 20/20/20 goals for 2020.

Ahead of the Curve

As the climate change and energy package was being negotiated in the EU, the first comprehensive Energy White Paper was published by the Irish government in 2007, entitled *Delivering a Sustainable Energy Future for Ireland*. Many of the goals in this strategy pre-empted what was being negotiated in Brussels. In a sense, the White Paper sets out a blueprint for how Ireland's energy efficiency and renewables commitments under the climate and energy package would be achieved.

The White Paper, along with the *National Energy Efficiency Action Plan* published in 2009 and the draft *National Renewables Action Plan* published in 2010, are the key documents of Irish energy policy. All contain the Brussels imprimatur. Credit is due to a small yet efficient energy section in the Department of Communications, Energy and Natural Resources for pre-empting the EU's new direction.

This White Paper establishes a framework for achieving the three strategic goals of security of supply, sustainability and competitiveness of energy supply in the period 2007 to 2020. This document is considered by one senior government official as 'the first time that we looked energy policy objectives on a much broader basis ... and the first time that a real strategic understanding of the energy policy issues was bedded down in a government strategy document'.

Modern energy policy is, in effect, about finding the right balance between these objectives. While the goals of energy security and sustainability are generally mutually reinforcing, achieving competitive and affordable energy supplies can sometimes come into conflict with achieving these goals, particularly in the short term.

Among the more significant objectives for 2020 set out in the strategy are ambitious targets for renewables: 33 per cent for electricity generation (subsequently increased to 40 per cent in 2008 by Minister Eamon Ryan), 10 per cent in transport and 12 per cent in heating. Together, these targets should ensure Ireland achieves the overall 16 per cent renewables target demanded by the EU. A 20 per cent efficiency savings target by 2020 was also included in the document. Accelerating energy research, establishing the all-island energy market and continuing to strengthen the regulatory framework were also identified in the strategy as priorities.

Unlike energy, no climate change strategy has been published which deals with the post-2012 period. Transport and agriculture account for 70 per cent of 'domestic sector' emissions. These two sectors – often considered the most intractable from an emissions mitigation perspective – must be the focus of policy in the period to 2020. The 2007 Programme for Government, however, contains a political commitment that Ireland will reduce its GHG emissions on average by 3 per cent per annum over the period of the government. It was also agreed that a 'carbon budget report' would be presented in conjunction with the annual Budget statement. Ireland's first Carbon Budget was presented on 6 December 2007.

These innovations have not succeeded in integrating climate change considerations into the government's budgetary policy to any great extent, though they have helped to provide some measure of the progress made towards meeting national targets, and perhaps also increase public understanding of climate policy.

Although there has been considerable progress on energy policy, Ireland's chances of meeting its 2020 climate commitments remain negligible.

Implementation

The early signs are that the energy strategy will be implemented effectively. According to the Irish Wind Energy Association, Ireland's total installed capacity in 2010 was 1,679 MW, generated from 143 wind farms in 25 counties, almost a trebling of installed capacity since 2005. Total renewables are anticipated to provide in the region of 15 per cent of total electricity generation in 2010 and the target of 40 per cent of all energy generated from renewables by 2020 is likely to be met. This will require an enormous effort: approximately 300 MW of wind power will have to be added to the grid annually, which poses a range of technical, economic and political challenges. Ireland – already among the world's leading countries for wind power generation – would be at the very frontier by 2020.

Lower fossil fuel prices in 2010 will mean that wind power will marginally increase electricity prices for the first time in 2010/2011. This cost is passed through to consumers through a public service obligation. It should be noted, however, that nearly twice as much will be spent subsidising peat. Both wind and peat are domestic fuels and therefore enhance security of supply. Peat, however, is the most carbon-intensive fuel used in electricity generation and there is an increasingly strong case for phasing out peat-fired electricity generation, as was recommended in the ERM report in 1999. These savings might be used to subsidise wind power. Wind power continues to make sense as a hedge against future fossil fuel price increases, and it is required in order to meet Ireland's legally binding EU targets for renewables in any case.

Work to improve the energy performance of new housing stock is also well under way. Revised building regulations were introduced in 2008, which required a minimum 40 per cent increase in the energy performance of new housing. According to the Carbon Budget statement of 2010, work on proposals to go beyond this level to achieve a 60 per cent improvement relative to 2005 standards is now at an advanced stage as of late 2010. The ultimate goal is to achieve a carbon-neutral building standard for dwellings by 2013.[20]

Progress has also been made on the far bigger challenge of upgrading the existing building stock. The SEAI Home Energy Saving Scheme was launched in 2008 to provide grants to homeowners to upgrade the energy efficiency of their housing and received substantial funding in 2008 and 2009. Additional residential insulation schemes overseen by the Department of the Environment and the SEAI have also received substantial increases in funding, and a number of exemplar retrofit programmes in large industrial, commercial and public sector buildings have also been part-funded through the SEAI's Energy Efficiency Retrofit Fund.

In the transport sector, a commitment has been reached that electric vehicles will make up 10 per cent of all private motor vehicles by 2020. The Electricity Supply Board (ESB) will provide a nationwide electric car charging infrastructure of 3,500 charging points by 2011, Renault-Nissan will supply the vehicles, and government incentives – including a €5,000 grant and VRT exemption – will ensure demand.

Subsequent to the Energy Act 2010, all motor fuel sold in Ireland as of 1 July 2010 must include at least a 4 per cent biofuel blend. The draft Renewable Energy Action Plan foresees an increase in the biofuel blend to 6 per cent in 2012. Rebalancing of VRT to take account of carbon dioxide (CO_2) emissions was finally introduced in Budget 2008 and has been hugely successful in reducing emissions. Since July 2008, the average emission performance of new vehicles sold has decreased by 13 per cent to 145 kilogrammes of CO_2 per kilometre.

The claim by special interest groups and high-profile businesspeople that this measure somehow destroyed the car industry after its introduction in the summer of 2008 does not hold up to even basic scrutiny. Statistics from the European Automobile Manufacturers' Association show that, for example, passenger car sales fell faster in Spain than they did in Ireland in 2008, despite a far more severe economic contraction in

Ireland.[21] Spain made no changes to its motor taxation or vehicle registration taxes in 2008. It did, however, win its first major soccer championship that year but this success is no more correlated to the collapse in new car sales than the introduction of the new taxation system in Ireland.

What the new system achieved is a rebalancing of sales in favour of cleaner cars. After the introduction of the change, in July to December 2008, the share of lower emissions vehicles rose from 43 per cent to 73 per cent.[22] Because of the availability of a near-perfect substitute for a high emissions car (a lower emissions car) the cost to society is positive. Emissions are reduced, dependence on imported energy is minimised and car owners can run their car at a lower cost over its lifetime.

Another positive move was the long-awaited introduction of a carbon tax in Budget 2010. As is discussed earlier in this section and in Chapter 5 on economic policy, a carbon tax brings about a better allocation of a scarce resource, the atmosphere, by rebalancing private incentives to pollute in order to match social incentives.

Significant progress has, therefore, been made in achieving Ireland's energy and climate policy objectives. Enormous challenges, however, remain. Ireland remains at record levels of exposure to imported energy and up to 12 million tonnes of carbon dioxide equivalent (CO_2-eq)[23] must be found if 2020 targets are to be met. To put this in context, this 'worst-case scenario' distance to target figure would be comparable to emissions from the entire transport sector in 2008 (14 million tonnes).[24]

Transformation

The imaginative policies and measures brought forward so far can be considered no more than a launching pad and not sufficient to secure Ireland's future. The challenge ahead is to fully unwind the high levels of exposure to imported energy and to effect a transition to a low-carbon economy. It is likely that developed countries will be required to reduce emissions by at least 80 per cent of 1990 levels by 2050 if the global temperature increase is to be kept within 2 degrees. This target is enshrined in the draft climate legislation.

In order for a transformation of this magnitude to be achieved, the power generation, transport and residential sectors will have to be operated at close to carbon neutrality and emissions from the agriculture sector will have to be reduced dramatically. There are four 'big-picture' issues which must be addressed within this context. They are:

- A comprehensive climate strategy for the agriculture sector
- A national retrofit strategy to deliver carbon-neutral buildings by 2050

- A strategy for zero-carbon transport by 2030 built around electrification
- Overcoming the obstacles to upgrading the electricity supply grid, which is the biggest stumbling block to decarbonising electricity supply

Finally, political and legislative changes necessary to facilitate the transformation to a near zero-carbon economy are identified.

Greening Agriculture

Ireland is unique in the EU in that 40 per cent of domestic emissions come from agriculture, compared to an EU average of 11 per cent. Agricultural emissions are divided between methane, nitrous oxide and carbon dioxide. Methane emissions arise from enteric fermentation (an animal's digestive process) and manure management, while nitrous oxide arises from synthetic fertiliser use and animal manures. The relatively small quantity of carbon dioxide emissions arise from on-farm machinery use.

On the positive side of the equation, sequestered emissions from forestry planted since 1990 (which absorbs CO_2) can be counted in meeting Ireland's commitments under Kyoto. This will yield 2.7 million tonnes of sequestered CO_2 emissions per annum between 2007 and 2012. However, the rules have yet to be determined for the post-2012 period. Of greater concern is that the reduction in agricultural emissions since 1990 has been driven by external factors, rather than domestic policy, in particular reform of the Common Agriculture Policy, which has reduced cattle numbers and synthetic fertiliser use.

Although EPA projections forecast a marginal decrease in agricultural emissions by 2020, the abolition of milk quotas combined with higher global demand for agricultural produce may limit any reductions. The Department of Agriculture has, however, suggested that the increased output envisaged in the national dairy herd could increase emissions by 12 per cent.[25] The uncomfortable reality is that an increase in emissions from Ireland's largest polluting sector would scupper Ireland's climate change policy and render achieving Ireland's target impossible.

What will be required of the agriculture sector is its transformation through a comprehensive mitigation strategy. Because of the relatively high proportion of emissions from agriculture in Ireland, immediate and significant emissions reductions are required. This should not, however, be looked upon as a threat. Much as Denmark looked on the energy crisis as an opportunity, so too can the agriculture sector proactively engage with the emissions reduction and sequestration agenda. It can be used as an opportunity to develop the skills, expertise and knowledge required for sustainable food production on a mass level.

Thought leaders in the sector, including industry leaders, Bord Bia, Teagasc and the Department of Agriculture, have begun to drive the required transformation. In 2010, Bord Bia published an excellent analysis of the shifting trends in the sector, *Pathways for Growth*. The subsequent Department of Agriculture's *Food Harvest 2020: A Vision for Irish Agri-Food and Fisheries* recognises climate change as 'the biggest environmental challenge that we collectively face'[26] and sets out to apply the smart economy to the agri-food sector in Ireland.

Food Harvest 2020 proposes linking particular farming practices to the national emissions inventory, and using life-cycle analysis to demonstrate the carbon intensity associated with Irish food and drink products. As the paper acknowledges, agriculture stakeholders would need to be given the appropriate advice, information and incentives to enable altered production methods and the reduction of carbon intensity per unit of product. This could also result in increased profitability. The report acknowledges that research into emissions from agricultural systems presents a business opportunity for Ireland. This paper is a promising start which must be built upon. As part of a comprehensive climate strategy, the agriculture sector must take on realistic yet challenging emissions targets.

In relation to methane emissions, an animal's digestive process clearly cannot be manipulated effectively. Therefore, the focus must be on reducing methane emissions from manure management, and particularly nitrous oxide emissions associated with the use of oil-based synthetic fertilisers. This will have benefits for food security and energy security, as synthetic fertilisers are entirely dependent on imported oil. Reducing and eliminating fertiliser will require a number of tactics, including use of clover and joining up waste management with agricultural policy. One million tonnes of waste must be diverted from landfill in the coming years in order to comply with EU directives, and the linking of waste policy and fertilisation must be enhanced in Ireland, as it has been with great success in countries such as Israel.

Integrated whole-farm strategies will be required, embracing numerous mitigation techniques such as extending the grazing season, reducing animal finishing times, changes in slurry management, etc.[27] To reward farmers who move to more sustainable production systems, a domestic trading scheme should be established for the sector. Such a scheme would reward farmers who, for example, progressively eliminate synthetic fertiliser use, set aside land for forestry (permits can be used to create an annual income stream from afforestation) or use bio-diesel for farm equipment, by awarding them credits for such behaviour, which they might sell on to farmers who might wish to increase their herd (and therefore emissions). Such a scheme has been established in New Zealand, the only developed country in the world with an emissions profile comparable to Ireland.

The application of such a comprehensive strategy is necessary if Ireland is to credibly brand itself as a true leader in sustainable food production and would enhance the natural advantage of a grass-based herd, enabling product diversification in an increasingly competitive marketplace.

House of Tomorrow

Approximately seven million tonnes of emissions come from the Irish residential sector (not including electricity use in buildings). While new buildings are built to ever-higher standards of energy efficiency, the great challenge is upgrading the existing building stock. But there is also an enormous opportunity in the period to 2020 as the investment required can be recouped from energy savings.[28]

An Institute of International and European Affairs (IIEA) report found that up to 1 million buildings could be retrofitted by 2020 under a national programme and that such a programme would have several benefits.[29] A new multi-annual National Retrofit Programme was subsequently announced in the December 2009 Budget. The new programme brings together all existing domestic micro-generation and retrofit programmes into a single framework. Homeowners will receive an upfront discount for works such as improving insulation or changing their heating system, funded from a dedicated energy efficiency fund, administered by the SEAI, 'closely associated' with the carbon tax. Furthermore, energy supply companies will be given energy saving targets, based on delivering a certain number of retrofits.

The real challenge, particularly within a 40-year time frame, will be moving the entire building stock towards carbon neutrality. Can householders and businesses be encouraged to invest much more in retrofit than the current average of €3,000, which is mainly for attic and/or wall insulation? To bring a pre-1990 house up to a relatively high standard of energy efficiency, an investment of €15,000–€25,000 will be required. To incentivise this level of investment, the government must ensure that there is a higher up-front discount available to customers who wish to undertake 'deeper' retrofits.

One way of incentivising a deeper retrofit is to connect the level of a property tax with the property's building energy rating (BER), much as annual car tax and VRT are related to a vehicle's emissions. In the UK, for example, all new homes meeting the zero-carbon standard costing up to £500,000 pay no stamp duty.

On-bill financing options as well as a range of green financing options must also be made available to customers as part of the 'package' that they are offered. The ESB and Bord Gáis Éireann (BGE) have already begun to transform their offerings to customers and will continue to do so in the coming years. BGE, for example, will deliver a range of energy-saving measures, including an on-bill financing measure where they will lend up to €2,500 to customers to make the necessary investments. To facilitate deeper retrofits, BGE has also promised to work with financial institutions to make further loan offerings available to clients.

Property-assessed clean energy (PACE) financing is another instrument with great potential that must be investigated further. Under this model, bonds are issued by a local authority or 'municipal financing district' and the proceeds are lent to commercial and residential property owners to finance retrofits. The building owner repays the loans over twenty or so years to the local authority in question. (In the US, this is added to the property tax bill.)[30] The PACE bond market is backed with a federal loan guarantee in the US and has the potential to accelerate the energy retrofitting of the US's building stock. For homeowners, the attraction is that the upfront costs are zero, and the loan is attached to the property, not the homeowner.

The potential of PACE financing to facilitate 'deep' retrofitting under a national programme is significant. Under current legislation, however, local authorities in Ireland cannot issue bonds and many legal issues would need to be overcome (for example, PACE could affect a bank's beneficial interest in a property where a prior charge exists). Legislation would therefore be necessary and further research required.

Other policy priorities for retrofitting include ensuring the highest building standards; addressing issues related to moisture and ventilation; ensuring that appropriate incentives are available for all types of dwellings, whether owner-occupied, social or rented (rented accommodation presents particular challenges); and building supply chains for products and services. The development of one-stop-shop retrofit companies that can provide a whole range of services to consumers and of a market of energy services companies, for larger buildings, are also important.

While the National Retrofit Programme correctly focuses primarily on 2011–2013, and to 2020 thereafter, it is imperative to integrate a long-term perspective into the programme. One trajectory for a zero-emissions building sector by 2050 is that 60 per cent of emissions reductions would come from efficiency, 20 per cent from on-site renewable energy sources and another 20 per cent from zero-carbon electricity. Other pathways are possible. Policies and incentives must be designed and be compatible with this long-term objective.

One implication of taking a medium- to long-term objective is that investing in all oil-fired heating systems would be discouraged, perhaps by regulation, in favour of biomass boilers, heat pumps and the electrification of heating in highly insulated buildings. Currently, homeowners are actually incentivised to invest in high-efficiency oil boilers under the Home Energy Savings scheme. Ireland has a uniquely high proportion of oil use for domestic heating within the EU due to past policy failings. These investments may bring short-term dividends but will be an increasing burden in the medium- to long-term future.

Going Electric

Approximately 14 million tonnes of emissions come from Ireland's transport sector and the sector is almost entirely dependent on imported oil. These emissions must be reduced to zero by 2050. Several measures discussed earlier will reduce the level of emissions from the sector in the period to 2020, yet the overall trajectory for emissions is still to increase during this period. Some of the measures introduced will therefore have to be built on, and the measures outlined in the sustainable transport action plan require an effective implementation strategy. Some areas will be highlighted for attention here, rather than a complete analysis.

Firstly, there is little doubt that the electric vehicle (EV) is set to displace the standard motor vehicle in the coming decades and the magnitude of the opportunity is potentially enormous. According to one senior government official, the EV is considered the big solution to the problems of energy security and emission in the transport sector. The official in question saw the transition to EVs as inevitable, stating:

> The rules of the game have now changed. As soon as you get critical mass, government will tax the buggery out of all non-electric vehicles. Range anxiety is only an issue for the next five or ten years. It's going to come; we know it's going to come. It's not going to be an issue by 2030.

The attractions from the Ireland Inc. perspective are particularly striking. EVs are effective at reducing transport emissions in that the electricity used to charge the batteries comes from the power generation sector and is therefore counted within the EU ETS. This alleviates the pressure to reduce emissions in the constrained 'domestic sector'. By acting as an 'early' or even 'first mover', Ireland can position itself as a test bed for new 'smart grid' applications for electric vehicles. The package for consumers is also attractive: for an average family car, EVs operate at somewhere between 10 and 15 per cent of the cost of a standard motorcar, though the upfront costs currently compare unfavourably with the standard motor vehicle.

It is very realistic that with a replacement ratio of approximately 8 per cent, all vehicles should be electric by 2030. While it is true that Ireland is a technology taker in this sphere and that enunciating a target for 2030 would have little or no impact on the pace of technological change, announcing Ireland's intention to have a fully electrified transport fleet by 2030 would complement current policy initiatives and cement Ireland's emerging reputation as a green leader.

Reform of the motor tax and VRT system has been a highly effective instrument in modifying consumer choice. The current reforms, however, do not go far enough. Given the urgent requirement to reduce emissions from transport and the increasing choice available to consumers in the lower emissions vehicle segment of the market, further reform of the VRT and motor tax system will be required.

The EU has set a long-term target for new car emissions of 95g/km for the year 2020. Within this context, the government could identify a target average vehicle efficiency level to be achieved by 2020, and identify a VRT and motor tax reform pathway compatible with achieving this objective.

Public transport projects, measures to encourage modal shifts (particularly the delivery of high-quality cycling infrastructure) and planning reforms to ensure higher density communities better serviced by public transport must also be delivered if the transport sector is to play its part in reducing emissions and the dependence on imported fossil fuels is to be alleviated.

Getting Connected

Transformation of the transport and building sectors rely at least in part on de-carbonising the electricity supply. If targets for 2020 are met, in some weather conditions, wind will provide 75 per cent of supply, while at other times wind will supply close to zero. This presents all sorts of daunting and exciting technical challenges for Ireland's engineers.

Apart from the the key issue of baseload supply[31] which much be addressed (namely whether Moneypoint is replaced with a nuclear power station or a coal-powered station with carbon capture and storage capacity around 2025 or so), grid connection is the biggest single obstacle to delivering Ireland's and Europe's energy policy targets in this area. According to one senior policy-maker involved in the space, 'This is a common view held within industry and energy policy-making circles in Ireland and throughout Europe.'

There is both a national and an international dimension to this challenge. A priority for creating a functioning internal European market for energy is connecting the often atomised European grid systems. This is particularly the case in Ireland, which as an island state is more disconnected from the European grid than other EU member states.

International grid interconnection allows surplus energy to be exported. This helps balance supply and demand, which is particularly important when high proportions of intermittent wind energy are being added to the grid. In this sense interconnection and renewables are intricately linked: no interconnection, less renewables.

The two main interconnection projects currently on the table are the East–West Interconnector to Wales, which is due to be finished by 2013, and the North–South Interconnector to Northern Ireland, which has been beset with planning difficulties and local objections. According to Eirgrid, the semi-state body that maintains and develops the island of Ireland's electricity network, at least one further interconnection project will be required to the UK or France by 2025.

The national dimension involves upgrading the all-island electricity network to facilitate increased proportions of on-shore, off-shore and wave energy to facilitate the transmission of dispersed renewable power generation to consumer centres.

According to Eirgrid's *Grid25* study, an investment of at least €4 billion will be required to upgrade the grid between now and 2025 and, if this investment is not forthcoming, Ireland's climate goal objectives will be seriously undermined.[32] In addition, high-tech industry that requires secure, high-quality energy supplies would be limited to locations with strong grid infrastructure, the power system will not be able to guarantee security of supply, and access to the market will not be possible for all low-cost generators, limiting competitiveness in the electricity market.

The main stumbling blocks to upgrading the national grid and improving international interconnection are political coordination, local objections to planning laws and financing. According to the senior expert working with grid issues: 'There is a clear recognition that something needs to be done' and that, 'Notwithstanding the progress in coordination in recent times, there remains a gap in coordination in this area. Little thought seems to have gone into devising a step-by-step approach to implementation.'

Attempts have also been made to address the planning issue. The introduction of the Strategic Infrastructure Act 2006 removes county councils from the planning process and gives overall responsibility to An Bord Pleanála (the Planning Board). According to this expert, it is too early to tell if this process is working. Much of what is required comes down to political leadership. A concerted effort to counter the misinformation and scaremongering which characterises the debate on interconnection is necessary. A positive approach would involve drawing a clearer parallel between renewables and interconnection – everyone loves renewables but no one is too keen on pylons. Engaging with local government more effectively is important to get political buy-in across all levels of government, and a more streamlined process of negotiation on compensation might also be beneficial.

Climate for Reform

Considerable institutional reform across both energy policy and climate policy is required if goals in both areas are to be achieved.

In relation to energy policy, there is a sense that the various components of the Irish energy policy landscape – the Department of Energy, Communications and Natural Resources, the SEAI, the Commission for Energy Regulation (CER), Eirgrid and the ESB – are pulling together to achieve strategic objectives. According to one senior government official,

> I don't think any policy-maker would ever say that there isn't room for improvement. I think certainly all the bodies are now talking more than they have ever talked ... every time we come up with a new policy initiative the dialogue gets better, stronger and closer.

This view was echoed by another senior policy-maker involved in the area, who recognised the transformation in policy-making which has occurred. He also gave credit to the Department of Energy, Communications and Natural Resources for its 2007 Energy White Paper, which recognised the direction being taken by the EU.[33] Proactively engaging with this process had 'bought Ireland a couple of extra years to respond' in his view. He was critical, however, of the overall direction sometimes offered by the Department, particularly in the area of grid connection.

Both officials highlighted a number of institutional obstacles to effective policy-making. Resourcing is a key issue. The energy section of the Department has approximately 40 full-time equivalents. They are collectively responsible for, among other issues, the corporate governance of the ESB, BGE and CER, energy efficiency, renewables, affordable energy, the National Oil Reserves Agency, peat and implementing Europe legislation.

One solution would be to create a cadre of highly talented and mobile individuals who can be moved around the system and address new issues as they arise. Another stumbling block to implementation is the interaction between government departments. Often budget allocation is made to an area which has been identified as a political priority, but officials must apply for sanction to spend that money, a process that can delay projects for many months. Making ministers and departments directly responsible for their budgets, and having the Department of Finance supervise rather than micro-manage is one solution discussed in more detail in Chapter 3, along with ideas on enabling public service organisations attract the talent they need in a flexible manner.

Multi-annual spending commitments are also vital for the successful implementation of long-term policy objectives, as has been consistently pointed out by the IEA, for example in its Energy Policy Review of Norway in 2005. It is not hard to imagine why companies making investments in new areas require regulatory certainty. Yet multi-annual spending commitments are almost impossible to secure under the current system. Clearly, within the context of budgetary constraints there are good reasons for annual controls on spending, but this rule must be implemented with some imagination and flexibility.

The current system is far too focused in achieving short-term objectives. A transformation of thinking in our body politic – a cultural transformation of sorts – is required, as is discussed in Chapter 2. An element of risk-taking must be encouraged. If Ireland's current approach to achieving policy objectives was so successful, we would hardly be experiencing the dire straits that we now find ourselves in. In how Ireland makes energy policy, the *status quo* is not an option.

In relation to climate policy, there are serious questions about the institutional capacity to deliver, where, for example, the resourcing issues are more prominent than in energy. The climate unit in the Department of the Environment is a small, committed unit, badly affected by the catastrophic policy of decentralisation.[34] Two key experts who amassed considerable expertise in their specific areas requested transfers to avoid relocation to Wexford. One of these – Ireland's key negotiator at international negotiations – moved on just in advance of the Copenhagen climate change conference.

On climate change, the Department of the Environment must coordinate work across several government departments, including Finance, Agriculture, Enterprise, Trade and Employment, Transport, and Energy.

Coordination is currently attempted through a senior officials group, and a cabinet sub-committee on climate change oversees this group's work. There are question marks over the extent to which this institutional arrangement is capable of delivering the transformational policy change required. It is the experience of many experts working both within and outside of the public service that this group is sometimes nothing more than a forum for zero-sum negotiations between participating depart-ments. For example, a private sector expert with experience working with several government departments and stakeholders on climate policy development highlighted a number of issues:

> In Ireland, as a small country, there is a very limited amount of data available. In the agriculture sector, for example, the system is to some extent reliant on the interpretation of data from organisations seen as aligned to specific interests.

In his view, there is no sense of a unified approach to dealing with a national strategic challenge: 'Often there is a sense that certain sectors engage with the process only to get the answers that they want.'

Some of these issues may be addressed in the Climate Bill, which would ideally establish an independent Climate Change Advisory Group seated in the EPA. This group would be responsible for making an annual report to the Minister for the Environment identifying progress on achieving emissions targets and for recommending appropriate measures in cases where a 'distance to target' is seen to emerge. The group would also be primarily responsible for devising a medium-term strategy for achieving targets, and possibly for establishing sectoral targets within this context.

The aim of this Bill would be to ensure that climate policy is, to some extent, removed from the cut and thrust of everyday politics, that it is based on the best available independent research, identifying which measures should be implemented and in what order. The final decisions on which measures should be implemented must, of course, remain in the hands of elected representatives. If a measure recommended by the expert body were not introduced, however, the minister responsible would need to provide a clear and cogent reason, and she or he would also be required to bring forward an alternative measure to bridge the 'distance to target'.

A flaw in climate legislation is that it often sets out far too many targets. In addition to the EU target for 2020, a 2050 target might be enacted in legislation, as well as medium-term 'strategies', which would effectively set five- or seven-year targets, and often an annual reduction commit-ment (of 2.5 or 3 per cent). Apart from the obvious question of whether these targets actually coincide, the annual reduction target undermines the core value-added objective of the Bill – establishing seven-year strategies, or carbon Budgets. It is vital to retain flexibility within this five- or seven-year period. The emissions reduction may be front-loaded or back-loaded, and a 2.5 or 3 per cent target creates an unnecessary annual constraint and would increase the cost of achieving targets.

One final reform which would greatly aid the development of a coherent energy and climate change policy would be the establishment of a new government department. The UK government created a separate new Department of Energy and Climate Change in 2008. In the words of a senior Irish official:

> [There is] a lot of work to be done on aligning policy. The two should be one. The UK has a department which is looking at energy and climate change. I absolutely think that we should move in this direction.

Conclusions

Significant progress has been made in addressing two of the biggest challenges on the policy horizon: energy security and climate change. Yet Ireland remains at record levels of exposure to imported fossil fuels and faces increasingly demanding emissions reduction targets.

To deal with the challenges presented, four 'big ticket' measures were outlined above. They will build on policy initiatives rolled out in recent years, for example, in the building and transport sectors where promising initiatives have been undertaken. In other cases, such as devising a comprehensive climate strategy for the agriculture sector, a fundamental rethink is required. In the case of building interconnections, the body politic knows what needs to be achieved, but important issues remain, including developing public understanding and trust.

What is necessary above all else, in order to achieve success, is the incorporation of a strategic long-term perspective into policy decisions. Societies that are able to understand the necessity for a strategic and coordinated approach to global challenges would appear to have a comparative societal advantage. Cost-benefit analysis is a vital tool for policy-making but is imperfect and may never capture the full dimensions of a decision in a medium- to long-term time horizon. Multi-goal cost-benefit analysis at least attempts to overcome some of these shortcomings.

The same caveats apply to another useful tool for informing policy decisions: marginal abatement cost curves, which are used to evaluate the cost of reducing emissions from various sectors though the use of various technologies. There is often an assumption in policy circles that once this analysis has been undertaken, one simply starts with the cheapest measure to reduce emissions and moves towards more expensive measures over time. This simplistic approach ignores co-costs and co-benefits of policy decisions. A shift to cycling, for example, not only reduces emissions but also congestion and ill-health. The co-benefits to retrofitting buildings include lower fuel poverty, job creation, better health and increased security of supply.

It is likely that whatever polices are identified for the next climate change strategy, the way in which policy is formulated and the agencies involved in its formulation will require considerable reform. Radical institutional reform is vital to rationalise decision making and to ensure that difficult decisions are not sacrificed at the altar of political expediency. There is a gaping implementation deficit within Irish energy and climate policy that needs to be addressed.

Again, a comparison with Denmark is illuminating. In September 2010, the Danish Commission on Climate Change Policy provided a detailed blueprint for how it will become a fossil-fuel-free economy by 2050.[35] The strategy is built around electrification, integration of off-shore wind, micro-renewables and district heating systems powering zero-emissions homes, a battery-powered transport system, and the development of an intelligent and interconnected energy grid.

As Denmark shows, solutions are there. This chapter has suggested new directions in four main areas. In agriculture, ideas include linking waste and agriculture policy and a domestic emissions trading scheme for the sector. For Ireland's building stock, a model of property-assessed clean energy could incentivise deeper retrofits, while in transport, a major energy consumer, the switch to electric vehicles will be central in the drive to carbon neutrality. This is dependent on de-carbonising electricity, which in turns requires deep integration of Ireland's energy supply with Europe's. To achieve these transformations, the policy-making institutions will have to be reformed: a dedicated Department of Energy and Climate Change is suggested.

The question for Irish policy-makers and wider society to consider is how long we can afford to lag behind and what price we will pay. It can often be difficult to imagine the end of a reality in which we are completely immersed, the late Celtic Tiger standing as a salient example. There is no excuse, however, for sleepwalking into the next catastrophe when the alternatives are so self-evidently available.

8

The Republic, Northern Ireland and the UK: A Little Less Conversation, a Little More Action Please

Aoibhín de Búrca

Introduction

Over the past thirteen years, there have been a number of historic days in both the peace process and in the relationship between the Republic, Northern Ireland and the UK. These days happened because of previous years of well-planned policy, careful diplomacy and political engagement. They led to events such as Prime Minister Tony Blair and Taoiseach Bertie Ahern standing together on the steps of Castle Buildings at Stormont to announce the 1998 Belfast or Good Friday Agreement (the negotiated peace deal and new political settlement in Northern Ireland), which Blair saw as an opportunity: 'the burden of history can at long last start to be lifted from our shoulders'.[1] The establishment of the North/South Ministerial Council (NSMC) satisfied long-standing nationalist demands for Irish government involvement in the North and cross-border bodies. The first meeting of the NSMC, which was held in 1999, was infamously referred to as a 'mafia wedding' by the journalists involved, due to the simultaneous arrival of a snaking procession of 22 Dublin-registered Mercedes into Armagh and the government helicopter, carrying the Taoiseach, Tánaiste and Minister for Foreign Affairs.[2]

Some incredible developments took place in Northern Ireland: the first day of the Northern Ireland Assembly, Irish Republican Army (IRA) decommissioning and the inclusion of Sinn Féin in government. There was also the sight of the 'Chuckle Brothers', the title given to Ian Paisley of the Democratic Unionist Party (DUP) and Martin McGuinness of Sinn Féin, former enemies, who became First and Deputy First Ministers respectively in 2007. But there were also darker days when the peace process nearly derailed, when there was violence on the streets and when it seemed like frustrating political negotiations would remain deadlocked.

Overall, the peace process is arguably one of the most successful of all Irish government policies. It was a process of deliberate, strategic and planned policy by consecutive Irish governments and international assistance. The 1998 Agreement itself was a testament to the years of painstaking negotiations and political engagement at the highest levels. But, in recent years, a combination of factors has led to the policies and the focus being less coordinated, less urgent and less proactive.

There are a number of reasons for this. One is that peace on the island is seen to have been achieved, and politicians and the Irish public have moved onto other areas of immediate concern. Another is that, during the thirteen years, the stop–start nature of the Northern Ireland Assembly, and the effects on the NSMC and its implementation bodies became perceived as being almost the norm rather than as something to worry about. There has also been a dramatic improvement in British–Irish relations, whereby good relations are now taken for granted. However, a general sense of satisfaction with regard to past achievements masks an alarming complacency over the coordination of all-island and border region policies, and the lack of proactive political engagement at all levels. This is a serious cause for concern and is leading to missed opportunities. The 1998 Agreement has not delivered on its potential. The issues that remain at a North/South and Northern Irish level threaten to cause serious problems into the future, and there remain those in the shadows who will exploit any opportunity to breathe new life into the ashes of conflict.

Getting to Good Friday: The Three Strands and Issues of Concern

'When did the conflict begin in Northern Ireland?' This question typically demands a long and diplomatic answer. It relates to the motivations and the grievances of the disparate groups involved, so is potentially a loaded one. The complexity of the issues in question meant the 1998 Agreement had to find solutions for everyone involved, despite the fact that each phase of the conflict had moved everyone further apart. In this regard, the conflict has been described as moving from a 'multiphased conflict to multilevel settlement'.[3] There were three different phases to the conflict, each creating a political context which led to the next. The first phase was the sixteenth-century reassertion of English control over Ireland and the seventeenth-century plantations in Ulster. The second phase consisted of nationalist uprisings, partition and the formation of two separate centres of government (eventually known as the Republic of Ireland and Northern Ireland), and the third began with the 1968 civil rights movement in Northern Ireland.[4] Given the context, you have to admire the ambition of those who instigated the peace process, who persevered and who foresaw an agreement which could be inclusive.

For the new Irish state in the 1920s, partition led to remarkably quick state building on both sides of the border and to an ever-growing gulf between the two jurisdictions on the island. The Government of Ireland Act 1920 had already effectively partitioned the island into two entities: Northern Ireland and Southern Ireland. Under the terms of the Anglo-Irish Treaty in 1921, Southern Ireland became the Irish Free State and obtained dominion status within the UK. The Boundary Commission, set up under the terms of the 1921 Treaty, implemented partition. What was striking about the post-partition administrations was how quickly and systematically they happened, with Dublin and Belfast creating entirely different administration and governance systems, with little reference to or contact with one another.[5] There were secret discussions between certain individuals and parties, but they didn't affect the overall direction of government policy and state administration, north or south. The new Irish Free State was intent on differentiating itself from its former colonial power. The minority nationalist community in Northern Ireland was left to deal with the consequences behind the border. It was not until 1965 that Taoiseach Seán Lemass broke with the anti-partitionist rhetoric and went to Northern Ireland to meet his counterpart, Terence O'Neill, the Northern Irish Prime Minister. Lemass knew the political risk he was taking and didn't tell anyone of his decision, not even his wife. The first his driver knew of the trip was when Lemass got into the car and ordered him to drive to Belfast. Both Lemass and O'Neill knew they were taking a big risk.[6] Neither leader could have foreseen that the visit, as well as being a major diplomatic breakthrough in North/South relations, would also set in train a series of events which led to the outbreak of 'the Troubles' in 1969.

The British and Irish governments' initial attempts at negotiating a settlement for the Troubles didn't end in success, but did provide the building blocks. The Sunningdale Agreement in 1973 lasted only five months and was defeated by loyalist strikes and unionist opposition. Sunningdale was followed by the Anglo-Irish Agreement of 1985, particularly reviled by Unionists for establishing the precedent of Dublin playing a formal, albeit very limited, advisory role in Northern Irish affairs. The principles outlined in the 1993 Joint Declaration/Downing Street Declaration by the British and Irish governments formed the basis of the eventual 1998 Agreement.

The 1998 Agreement has been described as a mixture of all the old initiatives, ideas and principles from the peace process being cobbled together and packaged up in the hope that it might be made to work. It is comprised of three strands: Strand One, which deals with the democratic institutions in Northern Ireland; Strand Two, which deals with North/South cooperation; and Strand Three, which deals with the British–Irish relationship. Referenda in May 1998, in both jurisdictions, passed the Agreement, by 94 per cent in the Republic of Ireland and by 71 per cent in Northern Ireland, giving it a clear and overwhelming democratic mandate.

Strand One: Institutions in Northern Ireland

Strand One has been the most visibly contentious of all the strands, and has been the most precarious and fragile. It set up the democratic institutions in Northern Ireland. It is regarded as a form of consociationalism, which is an arrangement whereby parties representing rival ethnic blocs can share executive power or enter a grand coalition together, and have mutual vetoes, proportionality and community autonomy.[7] In Stormont this means that there is a First Minster and a Deputy First Minister, each representing either the unionist or the nationalist section of the community, and the executive members are cross community. There is both parallel consent and a weighted majority voting system in the Northern Ireland Assembly, which ensures mutual vetoes. The d'Hondt system, whereby the parties nominate ministers according to the number of seats each party holds respectively, is used for executive appointments and the election system is Proportional Representation by Single Transferable Vote (PR-STV), which allows for proportional and minority representation. However, the issue of community autonomy in Stormont frequently becomes a source of antagonism, because it relates to issues of culture and identity. One of the most common criticisms of both consociationalism and the manner in which it is practised in the Northern Irish Assembly is that it institutionalises sectarianism, rather than creating a transformational context.

The Assembly has been brought to the brink on many occasions; it has been suspended repeatedly and has required vast amounts of attention from the Dublin and London governments. It started shakily with the unionist leader David Trimble from the Ulster Unionist Party (UUP) and

Seamus Mallon of the nationalist Social, Democratic and Labour Party (SDLP) as First Minster and Deputy First Minster respectively. But the issue of IRA decommissioning, or, rather, the lack of IRA decommissioning, was a major stumbling block and the discussions grew increasingly antagonistic and confrontational. The issue festered and eventually Peter Mandelson, then Secretary of State for Northern Ireland, suspended the Assembly in 2000, much to the dismay of nationalists and the Irish government. The DUP leader Ian Paisley, in particular, was insistent on photographic proof of decommissioning. He called for the IRA to be 'humiliated' and forced to wear 'sackcloth and ashes, not in a backroom, but openly'. The IRA did eventually declare the war was over in 2005, and it injected some momentum into the peace process, leading to the St Andrew's Agreement in 2006.

St Andrew's Agreement, 2006

In October 2006, three-day multiparty talks took place in Fife, Scotland between the Northern Irish parties (notably both the DUP and Sinn Féin) and the Irish and British governments. The talks focused primarily on devolution and restoration of the democratic institutions, including the Assembly, which hadn't been in operation for four years at this point. It laid out deadlines for restoration (which came and went), and all parties eventually signed up to the issues of policing, power sharing, changes in the Assembly, future legislation and a financial package. The British and Irish governments had alluded to the threat of 'Plan B' if deadlines and commitments were not kept, whereby they would go over the heads of the Northern Irish politicians and impose a solution. This did not come to pass, but it did serve to focus minds.

Following the St Andrew's Agreement, the elections in 2007 ushered in the DUP and Sinn Féin as the majority parties. In line with the St Andrew's Agreement, they met and devolution took place on 8 May, with Ian Paisley (DUP) and Martin McGuinness (Sinn Féin) as First Minster and Deputy First Minster respectively. This represented a massive change from the days when unionists refused to shake hands with McGuinness, or even look at the former IRA leader and his Sinn Féin colleagues in TV interviews.

Strand Two: North/South Cooperation

This strand involves the Irish government having a joint role with the Northern Ireland executive through the North/South Ministerial Council

(NSMC) and its implementation bodies, and being involved in cross-border policy. It was one that the Irish government fought hard to get in the multiparty talks, and it is one that nationalists had been demanding for years in some form or other. Unionists were most hostile to this strand and attempted to limit North/South cooperation. During the negotiations, it appeared as if the entire strand might be coming unstuck when the UUP declared it too expansive and the formal cooperation areas had to be reduced from over sixty to six. The UUP didn't want tourism to be a seventh implementation area and the Irish government did. As a compromise, an all-island private company dealing with tourism, Tourism Ireland,[8] was set up. The implementation bodies that now exist are Waterways Ireland, Safefood, InterTrade Ireland, the Special EU Programmes Body (SEUPB), the language bodies (Foras na Gaeilge and Tha Boord o Ulstèr-Scotch), and the Foyle, Carlingford and Irish Lights Commission (FCILC). These bodies are overseen by the joint secretariat of the NSMC, which is staffed by Northern Irish and Irish civil servants, based in Armagh and funded by both jurisdictions. The NSMC is answerable to the Northern Irish Assembly and the Houses of the Oireachtas. The six areas of cooperation that the NSMC work on involve aspects of transport, agriculture, education, health, environment and tourism, and policies are implemented separately in each jurisdiction.

North/South cooperation is jokingly referred to as the 'go low and go slow' approach, and over the last decade this strand has been working away quietly without attracting as much attention as the other strands. But it has faced difficulties, including, most obviously, unionist hostility, the suspension of the Northern Irish Assembly and the resulting lack of political leadership and direction. It has also been used as a bargaining tool by unionists, given its importance to nationalists. David Trimble, as First Minster, tried to prevent Sinn Féin ministers attending the NSMC in 2000 in an effort to pressure the IRA to decommission. But Sinn Féin proceeded with their meetings in education and health on a bilateral basis with the Irish government until the First Minister's action was ruled unlawful.[9] Also, initially, the DUP boycotted the NSMC outright and didn't attend any of its meetings. Now the DUP do attend and the meetings are increasingly constructive, in terms of policy decisions and delivery.

When the Assembly was suspended in 2002, the Irish and British governments decided that the implementation bodies would operate on a 'care and maintenance' basis. In effect, the two governments would take caretaker responsibility for the implementation bodies, rather than suspend them and their staff of several hundred people.[10] While the period

2002–2007 was one deprived of political direction and leadership on North/South cooperation, the time was used for an overhaul of the implementation bodies. The Secretariat brought the implementation bodies and relevant government departments together (North and South) and took a collective look at how the implementation bodies were governed, how they could cooperate better, share services and deal with procurement, recruitment, staff relations, budgeting, and so on. The result was that, when suspension was lifted in 2007, the implementation bodies had developed a collaborative method of decision making and had improved corporate governance.

Strand Three: The British–Irish Relationship

Strand Three is concerned with the British–Irish relationship. It has been the least controversial and least problematic of the three strands for the Irish government. In the 1998 Agreement, it was agreed that the British–Irish Intergovernmental Conference (BIIC) would incorporate and replace the Anglo-Irish Intergovernmental Council and the infrastructure of the 1985 Anglo-Irish Agreement. The unionists disliked the Anglo-Irish Agreement and, in particular, the Maryfield Secretariat,[11] and were insistent that it be shut down. There was a surreal moment during the 1998 Agreement negotiations when Tony Blair thought they wanted to shut down Murrayfield, and winced at the thought of demolishing the Scottish rugby stadium.[12] However, the confusion was eventually cleared up, and the Maryfield Secretariat was shut down and replaced by a joint secretariat of Irish and British civil servants based in Belfast.

The 1998 Agreement also established the British–Irish Council (BIC), which is also referred to as the Council of the Isles, given the number of islands involved: the Channel Islands (Guernsey and Jersey) and the Isle of Man, as well as the UK, Scotland, Wales, the Republic of Ireland and Northern Ireland. It was seen by nationalists as a concession to unionists who were concerned about the NSMC and the North/South element of the Agreement.[13] However, it has no statutory power, operates by consensus and is dependent on political will for it to be utilised to its potential. It is intended to promote the relationships of the governments involved and to increase cooperation and consultation among them. Areas which it has worked on or has had discussions on are spatial planning, demography, digital inclusion, energy, environment, housing, language, drugs, social inclusion and transport.

As well as the BIC and the BIIC, which are part of the 1998 Agreement, there is also the British–Irish Parliamentary Assembly (BIPA), which was initially created in 1990. It was designed to connect the British Houses of Parliament and the Oireachtas, and promote cooperation in the relationship between the British and Irish governments. However, in 2001, it was enlarged and now includes the Scottish Parliament, the Welsh Assembly, the Northern Ireland Assembly, the legislature of the Isle of Man, and the states of Guernsey and Jersey. It has a biannual plenary and it also has four committees that work on sovereign matters: European affairs, economics, and environmental and social issues. It is more systematic and structured in its engagement with the parliaments than the BIC.

The British and Irish governments have been working on the Northern Ireland conflict together for a solution since Sunningdale (1973), and the relationship has greatly improved over time. As well the years of negotiations and intense contact with regard to the Northern Ireland conflict, the two governments are also now close neighbours and trade partners. This is reflected at a popular level, as the British Council Ireland's 2004 report *Through Irish Eyes*[14] showed. It found that 81 per cent of Irish people surveyed thought the relationship between the governments had never been so good. The personal favourable feelings of people were as a result of their closer contact with friends and relatives living in the UK, and a sense of shared culture and interests. This is reflected at the highest diplomatic levels also. In recent years, successive Irish Presidents Mary Robinson and Mary McAleese have both made official state visits to the UK and have met with the UK head of state, Queen Elizabeth II. The 2011 visit of Queen Elizabeth to the Republic is the ultimate step in this high-level diplomacy.

The Main Issues of Concern

The main objective of the 1998 Agreement for the Irish government was to achieve peace and prosperity on the island. These notions of peace and prosperity are intertwined, and each contributes to the likelihood of the other. So it is in everyone's interest to ensure it delivers. Complacency in either area will have consequences for the other. A return to the violence of the past and a failure to realise the financial potential of North/South cooperation because of complacency would be both reckless and foolish. The Agreement was the result of a top-down approach by governments and parties, with the referenda as the constitutional sign of approval from the people. But it still needs to deliver on its promises and in the day-to-day reality of people's lives.

People living in border regions are particularly affected by the lack of delivery in relation to hospital services, broadband provision and so on.

They have to deal with an uncoordinated, complex web of bureaucracy and administration, as well as a debilitating economic disadvantage. Cross-border mobility is also a major issue for people and obstacles still remain with regard to pensions, taxation, banking, public services and other areas. Efforts have been made through initiatives such as www. borderpeople.info, a website that supplies information regarding commuting, working, living and studying in the border areas. There have also been studies and reports commissioned on these subjects, but, like all cross-border and all-island policy areas, there is not one single centralised body to ensure all of the polices work at an administrative level, and work systematically. Also, the lack of coordination regarding legislation between the governments and jurisdictions means that every single new law passed in Westminster, the Oireachtas or Assembly has the potential to be contradictory in the cross-border sense, rather than complementary and effective. It's not just the border counties that are affected by this lack of coordination, the entire island is affected. This is especially true in business. There are immediate impacts on businesses and companies that are being unnecessarily impeded and tied up in red tape as they try to operate in both jurisdictions. The issue of economic coordination is discussed more fully in the section on North/South cooperation.

With regards to peace, Northern Ireland is not immune to the fact that most peace processes have ended in failure,[15] and events in 2010, such as the days of rioting in Ardoyne following Orange marches and the bombings carried out by dissidents, mean there is no room for complacency. Northern Ireland still faces major issues that must be resolved: segregation, sectarianism, parading and security. It was hoped that the divisions would gradually fade away as the peace process took effect, but segregation in Northern Ireland has actually increased since the 1998 Agreement. There has been an increase in peace walls and interface barriers, which separate unionist and nationalist communities from one another. In Belfast, where there were eighteen interface barriers in the early 1990s, there are now eighty-eight.[16] There are also more Northern Irish people opting to live in segregated communities since the 1990s. Overall, nearly 40 per cent of all people in Northern Ireland live in Catholic or Protestant areas; in the context of state-provided housing, this rises to over 90 per cent.[17] Education in Northern Ireland is also very heavily segregated. Over 90 per cent of Protestants attend the state-controlled and voluntary grammar schools, and over 90 per cent of Catholics attend the Catholic Church-controlled and grant-maintained schools.[18] Any attempts to change the education system in Northern Ireland are highly contentious and are strongly resisted. The recently announced Draft Programme for

Cohesion, Sharing and Integration by the Office of the First Minister and Deputy First Minister makes it hard to imagine how segregation and sectarianism will be resolved anytime soon because there is no concrete policy, coherent strategy or real commitments in the document to actually tackle these issues.

The 12 July parades by the Orange Order in 2010 ended in nights of rioting in North Belfast's nationalist Ardoyne area, and these riots spread to other areas. The disturbances cost millions of pounds, businesses were damaged and police officers were injured. The scenes of the riots, with burning cars and flags, were broadcast around the world, creating difficulties for those seeking to attract foreign direct investment. Parading, and the reaction to it, is a yearly issue and needs to be resolved, as it only serves to reignite and escalate divisive identity issues. Not all parades are contentious, but the few that are cause unsustainable economic damage and put Northern Ireland in the news headlines for all the wrong reasons. Rioting and parading are part of the financial cost of the divide in Northern Ireland, which totals £1.5 billion a year according to the 2007 Deloitte report,[19] a figure which includes costs in relation to the provision of public services, transport, housing and education. In the face of an economic recession, such a hole in public money to pay for segregation is not acceptable.

Another cause for concern is the security threat from dissident republicans and the rise in attacks and activity in the last three years. This obviously puts lives at risk, frightens off tourists and potential investors, and diverts attention away from the real governance issues. The dissidents are quite aware of the opportunities provided by sectarianism, segregation and parading and are well placed to capitalise on them. While the security threat is a worry, the main parties have been united in condemning the actions of dissidents and haven't allowed themselves to play into their hands. But in the aftermath of any big attack in the future, politicians will come under pressure to talk tough on security, to act in a repressive manner and to put the Army back on the streets. This, of course, will allow the dissidents to act as defenders of their communities, to escalate attacks and gain more recruits. Reaction and response are very important, and politicians must avoid the short-term gains of inflammatory rhetoric and knee-jerk security measures. The security issue will be discussed further in the final part of the next section, 'Policies for the Future'.

Policies for the Future

As seen above, the two main areas of concern in the Irish, Northern Irish and British relationship are North/South cooperation and the post-conflict situation in Northern Ireland. These issues must be addressed to avoid serious problems in the future, and policies need to proactively engage in finding solutions.

Sharing an Island: North/South Cooperation

The North/South cooperation policy areas were outlined formally in the 1998 Agreement. Decisions regarding how the policy areas are to be approached and implemented are decided at executive level through the NSMC. The policy areas include agriculture, transport, tourism, education, environment and health, as well as the areas where the six implementation bodies have responsibility. The Irish government ministers meet with their Northern Irish counterparts in plenary and sectoral sessions through the NSMC, and agree on common policies and directions, and then implement the policies separately in each jurisdiction. During the suspension of the Northern Irish Assembly (2002–2007), this form of decision making was not possible through the NSMC. The cross-border and all-island policy areas grew without the required sustained political engagement and direction, and they are now desperately in need of coordination and systematisation at both political and civil service level. Furthermore, until recently, hostility and suspicion of cooperation had resulted in delays and obstruction, which again hampered focused policy development.

In the Republic, the leader of each political party is also the spokesperson on Northern Ireland, which, in theory, is symbolic of the importance attached to the relationship with Northern Ireland and the peace process. The same applies to the role of the Taoiseach, who, as well as being prime minister, also acts as spokesperson on Northern Ireland. Within the civil service there are two main policy divisions: the Northern Ireland Division in the Department of An Taoiseach, and the Anglo-Irish Division in the Department of Foreign Affairs. As well as this, each department in the Republic, if it covers one of the NSMC areas of policy, also has a cross-border unit that is supposed to take the lead in terms of cross-border issues within the department. Furthermore, the six NSMC implementation bodies have close relationships with their relevant departments in both Northern Ireland and the Republic.

However, while advances have been made, there is only moderate cooperation, and ideological political opposition remains an issue, including from some DUP politicians.[20] Speaking on the matter of cross-border cooperation at the Joint Committee of the Implementation of the Good Friday Agreement, Andy Pollak, who is the head of the Centre for

Cross-Border Studies, said they received much support from senior level Northern Irish civil servants, but that there was significant slowdown once the DUP were in power. However, '... in the South the problems seem to exist more at the operational level. Civil servants do not really want to do this type of work as they see it as peripheral to their real concerns.'[21]

As well as departmental policy coordination, and NSMC coordination as outlined earlier, there is also the Special European Union Programmes Body (SEUPB), which is one of the North/South implementation bodies. The SEUPB manages cross-border EU structural funds for Northern Ireland and the Republic, as well as Scotland. It requires the Irish and Northern Irish governments to have a 'common chapter', whereby the two governments must synchronise parts of their separate national develop-ment plan programmes when applying for structural funds, to ensure cross-border coordination. The latest programme runs for the period 2007–2013, a time when one-third of the entire EU budget will be spent on structural funds. The All-Island Cooperation chapter of the Irish National Development Plan 2007–2013 specifies a number of key areas of mutual cooperation (energy, communications, science, etc.), as well as the ben-efits of all-island planning.

There is no lack of research available in the area of cross-border planning and cooperation, and there is equally no shortage of agen-cies, departments and policies dealing with cross-border and all-island cooperation. In 2001, the Irish Labour Party published an in-depth and comprehensive all-island *National Spatial Plan*, dealing with issues of energy, industry and transport, land-use planning, settlement patterns, information technology and waste management. InterTradeIreland, one of the six cross-border implementation bodies, is in charge of developing and promoting trade and business on the island. It frequently publishes research and its March 2010 spatial planning report was jointly prepared with the Irish Academy of Engineering and Engineers Ireland. It identi-fied and recommended what infrastructure will be needed for an island of eight million people in order to achieve world-class competitiveness. In 2010, Fine Gael also published their Border Forum policy initiatives, deal-ing with regional spatial planning issues and the cross-border region. In particular, this document is concerned with the lack of strategy in dealing with the economic disadvantages of the border counties.

There is also the Comprehensive Study on the All-Island Economy from 2006, which was compiled by the BIIC. This was launched by Peter Hain, the then Secretary of State for Northern Ireland and the then Irish Minister for Foreign Affairs, Dermot Ahern. It demonstrated the strategic basis and economic rationale for all-island economic collaboration, and identified a number of areas where collaboration and cooperation would be beneficial.

However, there are a number of weaknesses in the Northern Ireland economy, as well as the structural differences between Northern Ireland and the Republic, notably in the area of corporation tax. General taxation differences and VAT differences cause difficulty for cross-border activity, as do differences in currencies and administration systems. Northern Ireland does not raise enough taxes to cover its costs, and receives £7–9 billion of a subvention annually from the UK. The 2008 Central Statistics Office (CSO) report *Ireland, North and South: A Statistical Profile*[22] compared the two jurisdictions and found that Northern Ireland's economy was significantly weaker with regard to employment and private industry. In Northern Ireland, 31 per cent of people are employed in the public sector and the economy is heavily dependent on government expenditure (70 per cent relative to Gross Value Added (GVA)[23]). In the Republic, in 2008, only one-fifth of the workforce were employed in the public sector, and over 13 per cent were employed in financial and business services. During the Celtic Tiger, the Republic had record growth, low unemployment rates and high participation rates, and this also accounts for some of the current differences between Northern Ireland and the Republic.

Both jurisdictions are feeling the impact of the worldwide economic recession in the 2010s, especially in the area of unemployment, which is traditionally high in Northern Ireland and which rose rapidly in the Republic after 2007. The Republic has to find ongoing and substantial savings to reduce its deficit to manageable levels by mid-decade. Northern Ireland is also facing severe curtailments in its budget in the same period, as a result of the UK's Comprehensive Spending Review. The Oxford Economics and Economic Research Institute of Northern Ireland (ERINI) report compiled for the Northern Ireland Council for Voluntary Action (NICVA),[24] points out that, given the state of the finances in the UK, arguing for an exemption due to 'special circumstances' will fall on deaf ears. One area where there is good news is corporation tax. The British Chancellor George Osborne, in his 2010 Emergency Budget, committed to reducing corporation tax from 28 to 24 per cent in Northern Ireland over four years. There will also now be an inquiry and a White Paper on ways to improve the Northern Ireland economy, including the possibility of lowering corporation tax. This did not happen under previous British governments.

In order to coordinate all these economic policies regarding North/South cooperation, there needs to be more systematic administrative coordination and executive government control. This also applies to the myriad of policy areas that have grown up during the last thirteen years, as well as the policy areas specified in the 'common chapter' and in the 1998 Agreement. Whereas traditionally the Anglo-Irish division in the Department of Foreign Affairs took the lead on Northern Ireland diplomatic affairs and have had the larger division, in recent years the initiative on North/South cooperation has shifted towards the Northern Ireland Division in the Department of An Taoiseach. There will always be an overlap between the two departments and they will need to work closely on the interdependent policy areas of Northern Ireland diplomatic affairs, North/South cooperation and the British–Irish relationship. But, in terms of delivering on the North/South cooperation potential of the 1998 Agreement, the obvious choice for a lead department would be the Department of An Taoiseach. It has the structures and, more importantly, the clear authority to deal in a systematic cross-departmental manner, and there is already a policy division team in situ. Therefore, it makes sense that they should take responsibility for the North/South coopera-tion strand from the Department of Foreign Affairs at the coordination and strategic planning level. The Department of Foreign Affairs should maintain the lead on diplomacy (including bilateral relations with the UK government in London) and post-conflict issues in Northern Ireland, such as strategies for reconciliation, dealing with sectarianism and politi-cal security. Responsibility for international diplomacy and getting the message out rests with the Department of Foreign Affairs and its dip-lomats in Irish embassies around the world. Rioting and paramilitary violence, and images of such, can damage the Republic's image abroad and must be dealt with as soon as it happens. The Department of Foreign Affairs also plays a vital role regarding the promotion of the peace pro-cess and conflict resolution at an international level. But North/South cooperation requires a 'whole of government' approach that only the Department of An Taoiseach can deliver on a daily operational basis.

At the executive level, there is no doubting the commitment and dedication of many of the previous Taoisigh when it came to finding a solution in Northern Ireland. A vast amount of their time was spent on the peace process. But the peace process has received less attention in recent years and North/South cooperation urgently requires more. It would be very constructive for the government to have a 'super-junior' Minister for North/South Cooperation within the Department of An Taoiseach. Super junior ministers sit at the Cabinet and have input at an executive level, and this would go a long way towards ensuring the executive bear in mind cross-border and North/South coordination when making decisions. The Taoiseach should continue to be the spokesperson on Northern Ireland, as an indicator of priority and intent. The super-junior Minister for North/South Cooperation in the Department of An Taoiseach would be able to work with the Northern Ireland Division policy team, which is already in place, as well as liaise with the Department of Foreign Affairs. Elsewhere, each government department which has a cross-border unit should be made responsible and report to the Minister for North/South Cooperation, as should the NSMC and the six cross-border implementation bodies. In the Houses of the Oireachtas, the Joint Committee on the Implementation of the Good Friday Agreement should be utilised to full effect by the super-junior minister. The priority areas of cooperation should be closely monitored, with work schedules and measurable objectives for each year in the policy areas. It is also vital that the super-junior minister coordinate actions with the border region bodies and has an efficient report-back mechanism with them.[25]

They Haven't Gone Away, You Know

Out of a population of 1.5 million, over 3,600 people were killed in Northern Ireland in the 30-year period of the Troubles. Many thousands more were injured and maimed, and there was a knock-on effect on future physical and mental health. Segregation, sectarianism and security problems still exist and can only be overcome by tenacious political leadership and diplomacy. The Patten Report[26] showed how sensitive issues such as policing can be dealt with by paying systematic attention to the issues and breaking down the policies into small steps. The same is required for other issues related to segregation and sectarianism. Hoping that they will just disappear is naïve in the extreme, and there needs to be a proactive approach to dealing with them. Rather than reacting in an ad hoc manner to events when it may be too late, Irish policy-makers need to be cognisant of the dangers of complacency. They also need to bear in mind that, although the current set of policy-makers have dealt with the threat of paramilitary violence against the state and potentially explosive diplomatic situations, the next generation will not have that residual knowledge. Therefore, diplomatic policy towards Northern Ireland needs to be ringfenced, reinforced and clearly defined for the future. Currently, the policy division that deals with Northern Ireland in this regard is the Anglo-Irish division in the Department of Foreign Affairs, and they are best placed to do this.

The Irish Department of Justice deals with justice and security policies for Northern Ireland, and it has greatly increased security cooperation with its counterparts in Northern Ireland in recent years. This focus on cross-border security cooperation is because of the current need to constrain dissident republican activity. The May 2010 Independent Monitoring Commission report showed that activity was the highest since the Commission began in 2003, but that this 'was in no way a reappearance of something comparable to the PIRA campaign'.[27] The most active dissident group is the Real IRA (RIRA), which came into being in 1997, following a split with the Provisional IRA (PIRA) leadership over the direction of the peace process. The Real IRA was responsible for the Omagh bomb, which killed 29 people in 1998. The Omagh bomb killed the largest number of people in a single incident during the entire conflict and was carried out after citizens in both jurisdictions voted overwhelmingly for the 1998 Agreement. As a result of the bombing, the RIRA declared a ceasefire in response to the public outcry and revulsion that the bombing sparked, and because of the legal measures adopted by the Irish government and threats from the PIRA. But, in recent years, the RIRA, and the Continuity IRA, have been more active. The Continuity IRA is believed to be responsible for the murder of Constable Stephen Carroll, the first Police Service of Northern Ireland (PSNI) officer to be killed by dissident republicans, in March 2009. The RIRA claimed responsibility for the attack on the British Massereene Army Barracks, also in March 2009, which killed two young British soldiers, who were scheduled to deploy to Afghanistan. They have also been involved in road blocks, pipe bombs and car bombs in the period 2007–2010. One of the car bombs targeted the PSNI GAA team captain Peadar Heffernan, who later had to have both legs amputated.

The dissident activity is not just limited to Northern Ireland; it has been increasing in the Republic in the last three years too. A report published by Europol, the *EU Terrorism and Situation Trend Report (TE-SAT) 2010*,[28] which is based on An Garda Síochána figures, showed the Republic to have the highest level of 'separatist' activity in the EU (including ETA activity in France and Spain).[29] It also showed that An Garda Síochána topped the list with regards to arrests for such activity, indicating the threat is being taken seriously and is being dealt with. Obviously, the benefit of shared intelligence and coordinated security polices by the PSNI and An Garda Síochána is that they protect citizens in both jurisdictions in a more comprehensive way. The border is used by dissidents, and clearly they exploit the disjuncture in jurisdictions and the fact that the border has effectively been 'demilitarised'. It is also important to bear in mind, in relation to the Real IRA Omagh bomb, that 'the car, the explosives, the phones and most of the suspects came from the Republic',[30] and the heavy responsibility of the Irish state to prevent such attacks.

When the new Northern Irish Chief Constable of the PSNI Matt Baggott gave his first interview in 2009, he raised some eyebrows when he said: 'The border is an artificial thing. If I lived down there [border areas] I would probably be less hung-up on the sensitivities providing my family were being looked after. We shouldn't let politics stand in the way of doing what really matters to the families that live in that particular area.'[31] His sentiments on closer security cooperation have been echoed by the Irish Garda Commissioner Fachtna Murphy, and the two police forces have built a working relationship and have shown solidarity in recent years. A sign of this closer relationship was the presence of the Irish President Mary McAleese at a PSNI graduation ceremony in 2010, on the invitation of Matt Baggott. She quoted Fachtna Murphy to the young graduates, saying, 'an attack on one member of one force is an attack on both forces' and told them that they were not alone, and that they had the support of the main political parties and the people of Ireland, North and South.[32]

At a departmental level in the Republic, it is the Department of Justice and Law Reform that deals with cross-border security cooperation. They also work on practical criminal justice cooperation, which is based on the 2005 British–Irish Intergovernmental Agreement (IGA) on cooperation in criminal justice matters. It allows for cooperation in areas such as probation, sex offenders, forensics and so on, and deals exclusively with criminal justice issues. In April 2010, policing and justice were devolved to the Northern Ireland Assembly and David Ford of the Alliance Party was appointed as the new Justice Minister, the first in almost four decades. He and his counterpart in the Republic will now meet once a year to discuss matters. Now that policing and justice has been devolved to the Assembly, the other areas of potential cooperation they could begin to look at include additional joint training exercises, developing cooperation systems for cross-border pursuits and ensuring resource allocation is spread correctly in border areas. They currently have a working group that reports to them twice a year on the progress made in the agreed priority areas and their 2010–2011 work programme for North–South cooperation on criminal justice matters was based on the IGA. The Department of Justice and Law Reform also administers the Remembrance Commission for victims of the Troubles and the Independent Commission for the Location of Victims' Remains (ICLVR), which deals with the 'disappeared'. Other unresolved issues from the past such as collusion, intelligence and border patrols also need to be dealt with. In particular, the British authorities have still not handed over the Dublin–Monaghan bombing files, despite requests by Irish authorities.

Old Fractures Will always Require Attention

There may be a temptation in the future to adopt a purely security–criminal justice approach to the dissident threat and transfer responsibility to the Department of Justice. However, this would overlook the importance of a political–diplomatic response in any strategy to prevent a rise in support for dissident groups. Currently, this responsibility resides with the Department of Foreign Affairs and, in any future restructuring, should remain there. The dissident groups' constituency, the nationalist populace from whom they seek support, has the most likelihood of constraining the actions of the groups. The importance of constituency support did not escape the attention of the Real IRA during the Troubles or following the Omagh bomb. A recent example of this is their attempt to tap into public discontent with the threat to target banks and financial institutions as a strategy, which comes during a time of growing unemployment and anger towards banks.[33] The challenge is to ensure that their constituency doesn't grow, that if there are grievances they are dealt with by the relevant authorities and no opportunity can be given to these groups. At the political security level, the Department of Foreign Affairs must identify and systematically monitor when and where the dissidents are most likely to exploit political grievances, and proactively engage them before it happens.

One of the immediate areas of concern is the younger generation coming through, who were, for example, seen rioting at the 12 July 2010 parades, burning flags and cars and even attempting to set the Dublin–Belfast Enterprise train on fire in Lurgan. The irony of trying to set fire to the only cross-border train service on the island, which is jointly operated by Northern Ireland Railways and Iarnród Éireann, was lost on the rioters. An outreach programme, such the one carried out with loyalists, should be part of this strategy. It must also be borne in mind that everyone who is now under eighteen was not born at the time of the Joint Declaration/Downing Street Declaration in 1993, which outlined the principles underpinning the 1998 Agreement, and they have no memory of the Troubles. Therefore, they could be more likely to have a romantic perspective on the reality of the situation and the consequences of using violence.

While the 1998 Agreement is seen by some as a solution, in reality it is only part of a process which is ongoing. The relationships between the three governments (that of the Republic, Northern Ireland and the UK) will always require patience and careful handling in the future, and political tensions from the past may crop up. An example of this was the Conservative–UUP alliance in the 2010 British general election, where tensions rose over the Fermanagh–South Tyrone unionist pact, which nationalists read as sectarian tribal politics. Ultimately, the alliance was not successful and was rejected by Northern Irish voters. But it did raise worrying questions about the agenda of the British Conservative Party. However, since his election, British Prime Minister David Cameron has impressed with his handling of the Bloody Sunday Inquiry Report on the day of its release, on 15 June 2010, and his speech that day in Parliament.

There is much room for improvement in the Republic–Northern Ireland relationship. An example of this was the 2001 foot and mouth outbreak. It didn't escape the attention of farmers in Northern Ireland how quickly and thoroughly the Irish government moved to seal the border when Irish interests were threatened. Unionists questioned how the Irish had been unsuccessful in the past when it came to sealing the border after republican attacks. For nationalists, it served to emphasise how quickly the Irish could seal off the border when Irish interests were at stake. Partition and its fallout led to a series of events which didn't endear the Republic and Northern Ireland to one another, and evoking that past can lead to a lot of guilt and bad feeling. Much work must be done to build up trust, respect and working relationships between North and South, and it won't always be pleasant or rewarding.

Finally, when dealing with the post-conflict situation in Northern Ireland, reconciliation and victims' rights must be emphasised. Obviously, the lead responsibility for this rests with Northern Ireland's civil society and in the Northern Ireland Assembly. But the Irish government and future policy should be sensitive to the issue of victims. The British government commissioned the Consultative Group on the Past to investigate how best to deal with the aftermath of the conflict. The group consulted across the community in Northern Ireland and the key principle that emerged in the report was that: 'The past should be dealt with in a manner which enables society to become more defined by its desire for true and lasting reconciliation, rather than by division and mistrust, seeking to promote a shared and reconciled future for all.'[34] It also suggested that the Office of the First Minister and Deputy First Minister should work with the British and Irish governments to implement the initiatives in the report, which would take five years to complete, and that the Irish government make a contribution towards costs. However, although many of the recommendations are feasible, there are clearly issues with others, such as the manner of payment for victims (£12,000 each) and the definition of 'victims' in the report, which must be resolved. However, those designing future policy should also be aware of the fact that not all participant responses to the *Report of the Consultative Group on the Past*, which was published by the Secretary of State for Northern Ireland, wished to have Irish government involvement, and this must be respected.

Conclusion

The peace process has been one of the most easily recognisable, albeit immensely time-consuming, successes of Irish state policy in recent times. It is frequently used as an example by other peacemakers who are trying to resolve international conflicts. Consecutive governments spent vast amounts of their time working on possible solutions with their British and Northern Irish counterparts. It has delivered a troubled but enduring peace and led to much better relationships between the different jurisdictions. Given the complexity and extent of the conflict(s), securing and sustaining the 1998 Agreement should be acknowledged as a remarkable achievement.

However, although the 1998 Agreement stands as a powerful symbol of the resolution of the Northern Ireland conflict, the actual implementation of the three strands of the Agreement has been mixed. Strand One, dealing with the democratic institutions in Northern Ireland, has been the most volatile. The Northern Ireland Assembly was suspended on a number of occasions as the peace process teetered along. There are also post-conflict issues that still remain and which need to be addressed. Strand Two, dealing with North/South cooperation, was badly affected by the Assembly suspension (2002–2007) and suspicions about the motivations of North/South cooperation. The third strand, the British–Irish relationship strand, has been the most successful. It has seen a massive improvement in the relationship between the two countries since the days of the Anglo-Irish war and the early days of the peace process.

To address the main issues of concern, which are North/South cooperation and the post-conflict situation in Northern Ireland, there are a number of recommendations that can be used for the future policy framework. Creating the position of super junior Minister for North/South Cooperation in the Department of An Taoiseach would allow for strategic planning and coordination of North/South cooperation in a more focused, cross-departmental manner. Elsewhere, while the Department of Foreign Affairs will always be vital for ensuring good diplomatic relations with Northern Ireland and the UK, it also needs a renewed focus for dealing with security, segregation and reconciliation. It would be advisable for the NSMC and its implementation bodies to proactively inform the Irish public of their work and engage in outreach programmes. This is important for reasons of transparency, and also to ensure support into the future. In the Oireachtas, the Joint Committee on the Implementation of the Good Friday Agreement should ensure North/South and British–Irish cooperation is mainstreamed when it comes to legislation and political initiatives, and should take a more proactive role in this. Finally, the opportunities created by policing and justice being devolved to Stormont should be seized and the close cooperation and solidarity shown by An Garda Síochána and the PSNI should be built on.

The next generation, those who were children during the Troubles in the 1980s and early 1990s, will be responsible for delivering on these policies in the next 25 years. The 1998 Agreement and the peace process have provided huge potential and opportunities. Our generation has enjoyed an environment in which we can develop alliances and relationships outside of traditional divides, and we know they are possible. Ultimately, we have a choice: we can have the agenda set for us, or we can set it. The lessons of our history tell us previous generations thought they had found the solution to the Anglo-Irish conflicts, but they were all proven wrong. This generation should not make that mistake, so let's set the agenda to ensure we deliver.

9

Thinking 70 Million Plus:
A New Relationship with Ireland's Diaspora

Neil Sands and Nicola White

Introduction: Ireland Is Not an Island

The Taglit-Birthright Israel initiative, a public–private partnership, brings thousands of young Jewish people, predominantly from the US, to Israel for ten days, free of charge. Given their age and their background, the trip leaves a lasting impression, reinforcing a strong sense of solidarity felt by Jews throughout the world towards Israel. The successes of the programme have led other countries with large diasporas, such as India, Armenia and Poland, to put in place similar programmes.

A paradox of globalisation is the simultaneous proliferation of nation states. Global trade and migration have never been greater, but people are enduringly clannish. Despite political scientists proclaiming the increasing obsolescence of the nation state, secessionist movements have never been so popular in both the developed and developing world.[1] Economic development and migration have made people keenly aware of their identity. One hundred and eighty million people, 3 per cent of the world's population, currently live in a country other than their own.[2] Denser patterns of migration also mean that the importance of diaspora[3] networks is increasingly being noticed by governments around the world. Diaspora relations are a powerful foreign policy tool, in terms of both political and economic gain. The relationship should, however, be a subtle one, a two-way exchange. Too often, countries view their diaspora as a resource to be tapped – what can we get from our sons and daughters who have prospered in foreign lands – rather than trying to strike a more balanced exchange. Developing ties to the 'old country' should be an experience of mutual benefit and reward.

The Irish diaspora is vast. Although the Republic of Ireland has a population of only 4.5 million, the wider Ireland is in fact a highly globalised entity, with over 70 million members in its transnational community. There are 3.1 million Irish passport-holding citizens living overseas.[4] The Irish can be seen as a global tribe united by history, culture and shared experiences, and increasingly networked through advances in communications technology. However, despite the sizeable numbers, Ireland continues to be ranked behind other countries, such as India and Israel, which have much smaller diaspora groups, in terms of successfully engaging its diaspora.

The potential is obvious; it has lain dormant for far too long. In comparing Israel's success in developing its diaspora relations to that of Ireland, John Harnett of the Irish Technology Leadership Group observed:

> They have about 130 Nasdaq companies, Ireland has about five. We can be the next Israel because we have all the ingredients – education, entrepreneurship and we have a diaspora three times the size of theirs.[5]

Unfortunately, most Irish diaspora projects undertaken to date have been ad hoc, and predominantly limited to the US. The necessity of reform is apparent when one compares the Israeli Taglit-Birthright initiative with the Certificate of Irish Heritage scheme announced by the government in June 2010, under which successful applicants would be issued with a small card which could entitle the bearer to discounts at Irish tourist attractions.

This chapter examines some of the countries that Ireland can learn from, countries that have thought more profoundly about energising their diaspora. India, for example, has a number of different categories of overseas Indians: non-resident Indians (NRIs); people of Indian origin (PIOs) and overseas citizenship of India (OCIs). The OCI scheme was introduced in 2005. While it does not offer anything like 'dual citizenship' – as OCI holders do not receive an Indian passport and have no voting rights – OCI does offer a series of benefits, such as multi-purpose lifelong visas to visit and reside in India. In the first four years of the programme, 400,000 OCI visas were issued. This is an effective way of enlarging the pool of engaged members of the Indian diaspora, recognising their contribution and making them feel part of the global 'Team India'. India's relationship with its diaspora is mutually beneficial, not one-dimensional.

For Ireland to follow suit, we will need to offer a more compelling incentive than tourist discounts. Indeed, one cannot expect the 'global Irish' to play what could be a fundamental role in helping rebuild Ireland over the next generation if they remain disconnected, disengaged and not at least partially in control of that process. The fact that a role for the Irish diaspora was omitted from any part of the government's *National Recovery Plan 2011–2014* is not only a missed opportunity by the government, but is also an insult to our diaspora members. They represent a market, a sales force, a constituency and an ambassadorial corps through which we can bring 'the world to Ireland' and 'Ireland to the world'. The country needs the global Irish to play a central role in constructing its future. Redefining Ireland through a strong diaspora policy as a globally connected nation of over 70 million people, rather than a small country on the periphery of Europe, is not only a powerful way to think, but also tangibly rewarding.

This chapter sets out the role of the Irish diaspora and the government in creating a sustainable and strategic diaspora policy which can harness benefits for all stakeholders. The following section examines the transformation of Ireland's diaspora from the sad farewells of 'live wakes' to an emerging twenty-first-century global network. The third section outlines four key principles that should underpin Irish diaspora policy over the coming generation. The first principle is to recognise the breadth of diversity among the Irish diaspora, from fifth-generation Argentineans to recently returned Poles. The second principle is to ensure that Ireland's diaspora policy is attuned to emerging political and economic trends, i.e. to ensure that the strategy caters for the Irish-born twenty-something in Shanghai as much as more traditional notions of our diaspora. Thirdly, it will remain of vital importance to engage key influencers, Irish versions of Dov Frohman, who is introduced below. Lastly, a relationship must be mutually beneficial and Ireland must develop meaningful initiatives to reward the Irish diaspora for getting involved.

The chapter rests on an exploration of international best practice in the field of diaspora engagement across political, economic, social and cultural spectra. Countries such as India and Israel provide the template on which to build a new and enduring diaspora policy for Ireland and their success is detailed throughout the chapter as reminders that the fundamental ingredient for success is not only policy formulation, but also its execution. Lessons in formulating diaspora policies from other countries such as Armenia and Greece are instructive in reminding us that engaging the diaspora is by no means a silver bullet solution to economic stagnation. There is no one-size-fits-all approach that is likely to be appealing to or effective in interacting with this geographically, socially and economically diverse body of people. Ireland requires a differentiated, but coherent, diaspora strategy, inclusive of civil society and implemented by all relevant government departments and agencies.

From 'Live Wakes' to New Networks

The Origins of Ireland's Diaspora: Emigration and Remittance

All diasporas are held together by a common ethnic and cultural identity. They experience a collective affinity, be it familial, cultural, economic or political, with the original homeland, and this in turn gives rise to transnational citizens and villages.[6] Historically, the Irish diaspora has continually played an important role in the economic development and promotion of Ireland. Several European countries, including Ireland, were heavily dependent on remittances received from their emigrants during the nineteenth and twentieth centuries.

In terms of the dispersal of the global Irish, the numbers are quite staggering in size. In addition to almost 34 million Irish Americans and 5 million Scots-Irish Americans, there are also 3.8 million Irish Canadians, 1.9 million Irish Australians and 500,000 Argentineans of Irish heritage. Within the last three decades, presidents or prime ministers with strong Irish antecedents have held office in Australia (Paul Keating, Kevin Rudd), Canada (Brian Mulroney), Israel (Chaim Herzog), Mexico (Vincente Fox), New Zealand (Helen Clarke), the UK (Tony Blair) and the US (Ronald Reagan). Generally, almost one-quarter of the annual *Forbes* 400 wealthiest individuals in the US have similarly strong claims to Irish descent.[7] Cultural sentiment can play a critical influencing role, in addition to more hard-headed economic rationale, in explaining why US foreign direct investment in Ireland continues to outstrip that in China and Russia combined. Ireland has also long benefited from the philanthropic efforts of its diaspora members. Chuck Feeney, who became a multi-billionaire many times over in the 1960s and 1970s when he founded the Duty Free Shoppers Group, is an instructive example. Feeney has given away most of his vast wealth to universities, research institutions, social programmes, community enterprises and charities around the world, but primarily in Ireland where more than $1.2 billion has been allocated to a wide range of programmes.

There are now over 3.1 million Irish citizens living outside the country and this number is increasing, with 72,000 passports issued to non-residents in 2007 alone. Add to that 800,000 Irish-born people living overseas and an estimated 6 million people in Britain having a close Irish relative and the sheer scale of this diaspora becomes both impressive and daunting. Furthermore, the winds of economic emigration are once again sweeping across the Irish nation, carrying many of the island's brightest and best abroad in search of better opportunities. According to figures released by the Economic and Social Research Institute and Eurostat, for the first time since 1995, 2010 recorded a net outflow from Ireland. Ireland now tops the EU with regard to outward migration. This is both a damning indictment of past policy and a future opportunity for developing global ties. There clearly exists a significant urgency to capture the value of this latest generation of Irish ambassadors within the diaspora.

Current Irish Diaspora Initiatives: Good Intentions, Half-Realised

The Irish government has long invested in diaspora community projects in the US, Britain, Australia and elsewhere to ensure that these groups have the infrastructure (buildings, online facilities, etc.) to develop and grow. The Emigrant Support Programme (run by the Irish Abroad Unit within the Department of Foreign Affairs) supports practical community and heritage projects that foster a greater sense of Irish identity and community abroad. From 2005 to 2010, the Irish government directed over €83 million to the support of these services, including frontline welfare services.

Recognising the need for a more strategic engagement with the diaspora, the Irish government has made recent efforts to redefine the relationship between Ireland and its diaspora by organising the Farmleigh Global Irish Economic Forum, which took place in September 2009. At this inaugural event, a representative group of members of the global Irish gathered with the objective of discussing ways in which Ireland and its diaspora can engage on a range of mutually beneficial dimensions. In advance of the Farmleigh Forum, the non-profit organisation The Ireland Funds produced a comprehensive report for the Forum on diaspora strategies. The government later established an interdepartmental committee to examine and take forward the recommendations that were contained in this report and those made by participants during the course of the Forum.

The most prominent Irish diaspora initiatives include the Global Irish Network, Gateway Ireland and a diaspora bond, as well as cultural and technological programmes. All of these initiatives are welcome, innovative concepts. There is, however, significant room for improvement in terms of the practical implementation of each of these programmes. The Global Irish Network (GIN) was launched in February 2010 and brings together for the first time some 300 individuals from different regions and sectors who all share a strong connection with Ireland, have a record of high achievement in international business or have assisted in the promotion of Ireland abroad through their prominence in the cultural or sporting worlds.

The value of the GIN is obvious: 'This direct access to key private-sector decision makers across the globe has the potential to deliver real, tangible economic benefits for the Irish at home and abroad.'[8] However, the potential success of this network lies in what can be termed 'asks and tasks'. The members of this network need to be engaged in small groups with specific projects over a limited time frame. If not, initial enthusiasm may well prove unsustainable. These GIN members represent a natural resource the government can use as it seeks to bring about Ireland's recovery. However, hosting quarterly meetings across the globe with these members without a specific 'asks and tasks' agenda and follow-up mechanisms will result in nothing more than a networking event for those attending. In order to maximise the potential of the GIN a senior government official should be appointed with responsibility for drafting and implementing an 'asks and tasks' system so that respective GIN members can each make a distinctive and powerful contribution towards Ireland's economic recovery. Moreover, the GIN should be more concretely linked to the Farmleigh Overseas Graduate Programme,[9] which will provide up to 500 graduate placements abroad once fully operational. Members of the GIN can further help with 'talent acceleration' through internships, work placements, exchanges and mentoring, 'internationalising' Ireland's next generation of leadership. The commitment to provide talent acceleration through graduate placements or mentoring should be a pledge met by all members of the GIN as a requirement for membership.

Gateway Ireland, a private sector initiative that enjoys support from the Irish government, is a national online hub that aims to harness the potential of the Irish diaspora and provide a unique central hub for the promotion of Ireland internationally. It channels a range of information on Ireland, including topics such as business, education, tourism and culture. The website will eventually include language-specific 'electronic embassies' which developers say will offer Ireland a unique presence and competitive advantage in its growing relations with the emerging economies of the world, including Brazil, India and China. Again the concept is a good one; however, a significant infusion of resources will be required to market Gateway Ireland successfully. The oft-heard experience of Irish diplomats is that people with 'too much time on their hands' are attracted to diaspora events and networking circles. Gateway Ireland needs to ensure that it is an attractive, operational tool for those with little time and big ideas.

During the course of the debate over the 2010 Budget, the Minister for Finance announced that the National Treasury Management Agency (NTMA) and his Department would develop a National Solidarity Bond. The NTMA, the Department of Finance and relevant departments are examining the feasibility of extending such a scheme to non-residents, including how to successfully market it abroad, possibly through Ireland's network of overseas diplomatic missions. There are several precedents from other countries: The Indian government has consistently pursued diasporic capital. In 1992, the government issued India Development Bonds and in 1998 and 2000 it launched Resurgent India Bonds and India Millennium Development Bonds. Each programme was targeted towards infrastructure financing in India. The basic assumption in defining these efforts is that despite increasing globalisation people still like to 'think local'. Studies of investment by non-resident Indians indicate that 'emotional ties with India' ranks as the single highest motivating factor spurring these diasporic capital flows. Israel and India have raised over $20 billion each through issuing diaspora bonds.[10] Any future diaspora policy for Ireland must give strong consideration to the issuance of a diaspora bond.

Culture: Our Catalyst for Connection

The importance of Irish culture in promoting Ireland, including Irish business, abroad was a prominent theme of the Farmleigh Forum. Since September 2009, there has been considerable public discourse about this outcome. In December 2009, the Minister for Foreign Affairs approved funding of €2.3 million towards the construction of a New York Irish Arts Centre in Manhattan. In March 2010, the government, together with Culture Ireland, announced the appointment of Gabriel Byrne, the Irish actor, as Ireland's new cultural ambassador. In January 2011, he announced a new Culture Ireland initiative, 'Imagine Ireland', which is aimed at promoting Irish culture in the US. In 2011, over 1,000 Irish artists and producers will stage cultural events across 40 states. Leading Irish businessman Dermot Desmond has developed a plan to establish a new centre or university for the performing arts in Ireland. The power of Irish culture must not be underestimated when formulating strategies for engagement by our diaspora. Culture is one of the main catalysts to engage members of the diaspora. Accordingly, despite a paucity of government revenue, Ireland must continue to promote and invest in its culture in order to reap greater dividends in the future.

Plugged In but Shipping Out: The Next Generation

The phenomenon of social networking online (often cited as a product of a new generation of internet technologies or web 2.0) has become the natural practice of almost every millennial (those born in the 1970s–1990s), regardless of nationality. The Irish diaspora are highly active participants in this space;[11] and represent a particular opportunity within this widely connected and tech-savvy Net Generation. Ireland's recent domestic turbulence has produced an outflow of growing numbers of this generation, with most recent estimates exceeding 90,000 emigrant students or early career professionals by December 2011.[12]

This latest wave of emigrants are in the process of anchoring themselves to the local and professional networks they will contribute to in the medium to long term. Consequently, there is a real opportunity for policy-makers to promote collaboration with these young professionals. In 2010, the American Ireland Funds (AIF) developed a strategy to connect members of the organisation's Young Leaders programme, a group numbering several thousand in over a dozen cities in Asia, the US and Europe. It brought together over 300 key influencers within this demographic to attend an international conference of young leaders in Ireland. This networking programme is a good first step. However, it remains to be seen whether the government will succeed in developing a working agenda for similar initiatives that will see real benefits for the Irish economy. As with other initiatives, a concrete set of milestones would enable Irish public representatives and citizens to judge more accurately whether funds invested in diaspora programmes are being spent wisely or whether adaptation is required.

Two non-governmental leaders in the field of engaging the Irish diaspora in this regard are The Ireland Funds and the Irish Technology Leadership Group (ITLG). The Ireland Funds is a worldwide philanthropic body which hosts over 100 events annually in 39 cities around the world. These events are attended by more than 40,000 people – most of whom are members of the Irish diaspora. The revenue raised from these events, which to date amounts to over US$300 million, are then distributed by the Funds to charities in both Northern Ireland and the Republic of Ireland. In December 2010, the Funds announced the launch of its 'Promising Ireland Campaign', a fundraising initiative with a goal of raising $100 million among its global network on four continents by

2013. In addition to promoting diaspora philanthropy, The Ireland Funds also works to engage the Irish diaspora more generally. Each year it holds a conference in Ireland where nearly 300 members of the Funds from across the world come together to strengthen diaspora initiatives and visit projects and initiatives throughout the country. The Ireland Funds has worked assiduously to gain the support of key US leaders, including receiving high-level backing from US Secretary of State Hillary Clinton.

The ITLG is a signpost for the future of diaspora relations and the development of the Irish economy. Established in October 2007, the ITLG is an independent organisation comprised of senior technology leaders in Silicon Valley of Irish extraction. Through the newly opened Irish Innovation Centre (IIC) in San Jose, the group facilitates partnerships with experienced entrepreneurs, technology leaders and venture capitalists to provide comprehensive support for promising Irish companies. Committed to ensuring that Ireland remains a strategic area of investment and opportunity for US technology companies, ITLG collaborates closely with both Enterprise Ireland and the Industrial Development Agency (IDA Ireland).

A Comprehensive Diaspora Policy for Ireland

Irish diaspora policy is currently being driven by many non-governmental initiatives. Over the coming generation, the government should finally take the lead in engaging Ireland's diaspora. A critical element for the future success of an Irish diaspora policy will be prioritisation. Initiatives must also be targeted, with specific objectives, measurable outcomes and full accountability. Implementing a successful national strategy for engaging the diaspora takes time, preparation, patience and proper execution. While many countries have sought to emulate the success of India and Israel, not all have succeeded. Any strategy must be carefully tailored to Ireland's strengths.

There are a multitude of reasons that can lead to the failure of diaspora strategies and it is important that we are aware of these and learn from such mistakes to ensure that we do not repeat them in any future Irish diaspora policy. Firstly, as previously noted, diaspora initiatives are relatively simple to initiate but difficult to maintain unless tangible results materialise. Examples of initiatives which are now considered not to carry much significance include South African Network of Skills Abroad (SANSA), Digital Diaspora Network for Africa, which is currently inactive, and Red Caldas in Colombia. There tends to be no shortage of interest and conferences on diaspora issues, but without specific 'takeaways', or projects, the initial enthusiasm dissipates and runs out of steam. There is a tendency to announce initiatives with great fanfare but without carefully mapping out their implementation. It is time to stop paying lip-service to the importance of our diaspora and actually draft a policy that harmonises current and future initiatives.

There is a significant opportunity for a more joined-up approach among government agencies which in the past have not coordinated fully or have even worked in isolation from each other. For example, in the Department of Foreign Affairs, the 'Promoting Ireland Abroad Division' includes the Bilateral Economic Relations Section, which deals with Ireland's bilateral economic and trade relations with countries throughout the world. Arguably, this division has the same mandate as IDA Ireland and Enterprise Ireland. All of these agencies undertake independent promotion of Ireland as a country for investment. In sum, there is a need for greater coordination and collaboration in marketing Ireland overseas. An improved division of labour is required that clearly delineates lead responsibility for each element of Ireland's brand mix, be it investment, trade, tourism, culture, entertainment, sport or philanthropy, and maps the interaction between the various agencies. To continue with the status quo will result in mixed messages and mixed results. A more systematic, strategic approach supervised by the Department of An Taoiseach would offer one way of ensuring that duplication of effort and missed opportunities can be avoided.

To expect the Taoiseach to micro-manage the coordination of Ireland's diaspora relations would be naïve and unrealistic. However, responsibility for diaspora relations should be clearly given to a minister of state in the Department of An Taoiseach. This Minister's principal responsibility would be to ensure that the Department of Foreign Affairs, Enterprise Ireland and IDA Ireland are working coherently towards a comprehensive engagement of the diaspora. Israel is a leader in utilising such a ministerial position to best effect: regularly convening with academics, think tanks and the private sector, the Ministry for Information and Diaspora Relations has actively sought innovative ways to connect with the Israeli diaspora, recognising the importance of a two-way flow of intellectual, social, cultural and financial capital. Ireland does not require a separate department for diaspora relations; but it does need a responsible government minister holding the diaspora portfolio to coordinate a 'whole of government' approach. If Ireland is to effectively leverage the might of its diaspora, such a dedicated and permanent resource within government is critical. Placing such a portfolio in the Department of An Taoiseach would also grant the responsible minister the authority to cut through interdepartmental rivalry or lack of cooperation as required.

Segmentation of the Diaspora: Forty Shades of Green

A frequent error in the formulation of diaspora strategies is the wrong-headed assumption that a diaspora is a fairly homogenous and tightly knit group. Although individuals may be, statistically, 'members of a diaspora', this does not mean they have a sense of belonging. In fact, the network tends to be diffuse and diverse, with a range of economic, social and ethnic characteristics. Such variety requires differentiated strategies that recognise not only differences between those living in Ireland and those living elsewhere, but also along four other dimensions. Policy must recognise, for example, that those born and educated in Ireland and who live overseas are very different members of the diaspora to those who are third-generation Irish and were born and raised in their country of residence. Secondly, even among those of Irish descent born and raised elsewhere, it is necessary to distinguish among members of the diaspora based on their own life experiences: descendants of Irish farmers still working in agriculture in Uruguay are very different to urban Irish-Americans.

Thirdly, a comprehensive diaspora strategy must also include those who migrated to Ireland and have since re-located elsewhere. There are several hundred thousand 'new Irish', predominantly from Central and Eastern Europe, who spent some time here before moving on or moving home. Many of these people hold an affinity for Ireland after living and working in the country and they too must be considered part of Ireland's diaspora. There are also increasing numbers of international students who graduate from Irish universities each year, yet there is little effort made to continue to connect these future leaders with Ireland after the termination of their studies. This must be reversed through the specific formulation of a policy to retain a connection with these graduates in the future through Irish embassies abroad and diaspora networks, and this would complement existing work undertaken by various universities' alumni offices.

Active segmentation of our Irish diaspora and affinity diaspora members would result in a more focused and strategic approach towards engaging the right people of the diaspora with the right purpose. It should be noted that active segmentation can also work in terms of geographical clusters from within Ireland. Some diaspora policies could increasingly become more province- or county-based. While such an approach may not be hugely relevant in terms of a national governmental diaspora policy, it should be noted that there are many active groups within Ireland connecting with a specific segment of the diaspora that is relevant to them. For example, the Derry Donegal Diaspora Project connects with people around the world from these specific areas. Collaboration and exchange of information between these specific diaspora groups within Ireland and the government is extremely important for the purposes of consistency and to explore whether this 'localised' diaspora approach is more effective in certain incidences.

The Need For A Global Diaspora Policy: Ireland and the BRIC

Irish diaspora policy and emphasis continues to be primarily seen through the prism of relations with diaspora members in the US. This dependency is unsurprising when one considers that Ireland receives more US investment than Russia and China combined, 80 times as much as Greece, and 23 times as much as Portugal.[13] However, emerging global multipolarity is not being catered for in current diaspora policy. Ireland is not developing a diaspora strategy that reaches out to long-standing diaspora members in emerging markets, such as in Latin America, and the 'professional flight' that has seen skilled graduates re-locate to other EU member states and to emerging market economies.

According to the Higher Education Authority, almost 10 per cent of 2009 university graduates are now working abroad.[14] Many of this younger generation of the Irish diaspora will have established firm roots in these countries by 2025 and the government must plan and implement a diaspora policy which has a more global focus than is currently the case. For example, 115 Irish companies are currently doing business in China – three times more compared to 2003. China is now Ireland's seventh largest trading partner and bilateral trade with China is now worth over €6.5 billion annually.[15] If neglect of a growing diaspora in emerging markets such as those in Brazil, Russia, India and China (BRIC) continues, the potential for a large segment of this next generation of Irish emigrants to build economic and social ties with their home country will remain unfulfilled.

In 2010, Irish emigration rates were the highest in the EU.[16] A younger generation of emigrants is becoming increasingly equipped with foreign language skills and a level of education which enables them to secure employment in non-English-speaking EU member states. However, to date, Irish government initiatives towards this new European professional diaspora varies considerably. Some embassies and government agencies are known for proactively engaging with the European diaspora, while others do the bare minimum. Personal initiative is not sufficient however, and better guidance and training should be offered to embassies on how to constructively reach out to the diaspora. One constructive measure would be for the Department of Foreign Affairs to adapt a country-specific diaspora strategy for key EU member states.

Seeking Out the Key Influencers

As well as reaching out generally to the diaspora, it is also vital that Ireland strategically identifies 'key influencers' among this large community. The government must ensure that it has a representative through embassies, consulates or honorary consulates in each country where there is a sizeable Irish diaspora community so that key influencers can be identified and placed within the Global Irish Network. For the sheer size of its diaspora, it is difficult to explain why Ireland has only one-quarter the number of honorary consuls engaged by similar sized EU member states (but with much smaller diasporas) such as Denmark and Finland (see Chapter 10 in this volume). The success of many diaspora programmes has been the input of key influencers, who are often a closely connected few who may be positioned to influence or encourage senior decision makers within policy circles. This is the 'mile wide – inch deep' versus 'inch wide – mile deep' conundrum to any diaspora policy in which a balance must be struck.[17]

Israel, with its innovative and growing information technology sector, provides an excellent example of how to successfully identify and partner with a key influencer among the diaspora through its relationship with Dov Frohman, a talented Israeli scientist who had invented and developed the erasable programmable memory chip (EPROM), and was contracted to the Intel Corporation in the US. Frohman was offered the opportunity to return home to Israel to take up a research and teaching position at the Hebrew University of Jerusalem. To avoid losing his expertise, Intel established its first integrated circuit design centre outside the US, in Haifa, and asked Frohman to lead it. Frohman later played a critical role in Israel becoming a leading centre of worldwide integrated circuit design and manufacturing.

Chile is another example of a country which has sought out its key diaspora members to contribute to the country's economic development. Founded in 2005, ChileGlobal is an international network of Chilean business owners and top-level executives or people with an affinity to Chile who are living abroad and who have an interest in contributing to Chile's economic development. The goal is to help incorporate Chile into the knowledge economy, leveraging the international experience of its members, creating a mechanism of business opportunity attraction, technology transfer and know-how. ChileGlobal harnesses the expertise of more than 80 members, in North America (75 per cent), Europe and Latin America. Members are influential, with an active role in their industries and a strong affinity to Chile. ChileGlobal members contribute with expertise, knowledge and time by supporting businesses, leveraging contacts and expertise, and promoting entrepreneurship in key sectors such as information and communication technology, finance and services, business management, biotech, food, telecoms, marketing and health. Its programme includes internships, mentorships and support for public policy in innovation. It remains to be seen whether the GIN will emulate the success of ChileGlobal. However, its innovative success lends itself to careful analysis by Irish policy-makers.

Other instructive examples of farsighted, and readily achievable, diaspora policies include a database established by the government of Taiwan to track skilled migrants and match them with job opportunities in Taiwan. Similarly, the Jamaican Diaspora Institute has announced that it is compiling a diaspora skills database which will allow for the development of a more dynamic relationship with the Jamaican diaspora across the world. Irish diplomatic missions and overseas agencies already compile such lists. Nevertheless, the challenge is to ensure that it is more widely accessible for policy-makers and private sector investors. Ireland too has its own examples of how to partner key influencers, including with Dan Tully (Merrill Lynch), Kip Condron (AXA), Pat Toole (IBM), John Ryan (Macrovision) and Charles Cawley (MBNA). Ireland should learn from and mainstream the lessons from these positive experiences into government policy.

The Key to a Successful Relationship: Give and Take

Ireland's own current needs are well defined, and an important starting point for any diaspora strategy will be to examine the most appropriate ways in which we can leverage the power of the Irish diaspora to address our current and future challenges. In October 2010, the then Minister for Foreign Affairs, Micheál Martin, observed that an 'enhancement of this relationship will be a valuable asset in Ireland's economic recovery, in particular in providing a competitive edge in certain key markets.'[18] However, perhaps as a product of its sheer volume or the historic remittance of diaspora funds back to those in Ireland's less favourable economy, the domestic attitude is a knee-jerk 'What can the diaspora do for us?', rather than a coherent two-way and mutually rewarding engagement.

Ireland is the only country in the EU, and one of only 50 countries around the world, that does not allow citizens living abroad to vote in general elections, and there has been little focus on introducing a wider representational role for the overseas Irish. Successive efforts to secure voting rights for Irish-born citizens abroad never materialised and the Irish diaspora remain unrepresented in the Seanad[19] (although Irish graduates of Trinity College Dublin and the colleges of the National University of Ireland overseas are entitled to vote for their respective candidates for the university Seanad seats). While there are a plethora of issues surrounding the right-to-vote option, namely 'no representation without taxation', countries such as Australia, France, New Zealand, the US and the UK (in contrast to Ireland) do allow votes from abroad. This is one way to encourage identification between diasporas and homelands, even if turnout is often low. It is an important civic right in an era of globalisation, migration and technological advances. Furthermore, if the entrepreneurial talent available overseas is as capable as is widely suggested, a way could be found to bring some of this talent into the political system, even into the Cabinet.

The Israeli Taglit-Birthright initiative is one of the most successful diaspora programmes in the world and was launched out of a concern about the continuation of Jewish culture and heritage. This programme brings young Jews aged 18–26 to spend ten days in Israel. Research has shown that ten days in Israel is more effective in instilling Jewish pride and heritage than five years in a Jewish school. In 2009, 22,000 people travelled to Israel on this programme. The trip leaves a lasting impact at an impressionable age. In 2009, the Cohen Center for Modern Jewish Studies at Brandeis University published *Generation Birthright Israel*, a research study attesting to the profound and long-term impact on alumni of the Taglit-Birthright Israel experience. The study, which focuses on the early rounds of the ten-year-old project, documents participants' strengthened connections to Israel, their greater sense of belonging to the Jewish people, and their increased interest in building Jewish families.[20] Seventy-five per cent of the attendees come from the US.[21] Other countries, such as India, Armenia and Poland, have started similar programmes. Ireland should investigate adopting a programme that enables young members of the diaspora to travel to Ireland in order to develop links with the country.

Many countries, in developing their diaspora strategies, have included a mechanism for formal recognition. While it may be considered unnecessary, an act of recognition or expression of appreciation is a mechanism through which we can pay tribute to the contributions of the diaspora. It will, in turn, potentially increase engagement, raise awareness and generate substantial good will. An obvious mechanism is through the creation of a formal civic honours system, like the Order of Canada, the Legion d'Honneur in France or the Order of Australia. The Office of the President could create its own system through which acts of civil service might be recognised. Additionally, Section 12 of the Irish Nationality and Citizenship Act 1956 allows the President, on advice of the government, to '... grant Irish citizenship as a token of honour to a person, or the child or grandchild of a person who, in the opinion of the government, has done signal honour or rendered distinguished service to the nation'. Examples of individuals who have received this honour are sparing, but include Tip O'Neill, Jean Kennedy Smith, Jack Charlton and Alfred Chester Beatty.

In 2005, President Mary McAleese, speaking about the Irish diaspora in New York, recognised that,

> In every sphere of life in their adopted countries they made, and continue to make, a hugely significant contribution, which has garnered friends and respect for Ireland all around the world. No matter how difficult the circumstances, they always found space in their lives to help one another, to create a better future for the next generation of young emigrants and to send help back home. We celebrate their achievements and take pride in them.[22]

A salutation of such achievements must be demonstrated through an annual formal honours ceremony for members of the Irish diaspora by the granting of honorary Irish citizenship or a newly constituted civic award.

A successful awards system for Ireland to follow is the Pravasi Bharatiya Samman Awards, which are an expression of honour by the government of India to members of the Indian diaspora. They have been organised by the Ministry of Overseas Indian Affairs every year since 2003. Pravasi Bharatiya Samman awards are reserved exclusively for non-resident Indians and persons of Indian origin. The awards are conferred on those overseas Indians who have made an outstanding contribution towards fostering better understanding abroad of India and its civilisation; for persons who have extended their support to India's causes and concerns; and for those who made the country proud by exceptional performance in their field of merit. It would not be difficult for Ireland to introduce a similar annual awards system for diaspora members as an improved alternative to the ad-hoc President's Award system that is currently in place.

It must be remembered that while there are a great number of high-level influencers within the Irish diaspora who can contribute to Ireland's economic recovery and future stability, there are also vulnerable and forgotten members of our Irish diaspora, particularly older persons living in isolation, poverty and deprivation without the support of family and friends. Any future Irish diaspora policy must also provide for these members of the 'Forgotten Irish' – most of whom would have made provision for Ireland throughout their lives through substantial remittances. The Department of Foreign Affairs-led Emigrant Support Programme, with an annual budget of just under €15 million, should be more closely linked with diaspora networks such as The Ireland Funds, which in 2007 launched a philanthropic campaign entitled 'The Forgotten Irish', principally directed at those migrants who went to Britain in the second half of the twentieth century.

Conclusion: A New Contract with the Diaspora

Given the staggering number of people around the world who are Irish, of Irish descent, have an Irish affiliation or are simply 'friends of Ireland', a comprehensive diaspora strategy must ensure that each diverse layer of the diaspora feels connected and engaged. There is no one-size-fits-all policy, rather a range of tailored, carefully researched and systematically implemented policies must be introduced to ensure that each segment of the diaspora recognises the fundamental opportunity it possesses to shape Ireland's future.

So what role should the government play in future diaspora engagement? The optimum situation would be for government to act as a nexus, creating the conditions conducive for differentiated diaspora organisations to exist, working in partnership with both private sector and civil society initiatives and above all being on the constant lookout for key influencers. It has a pivotal role to play in giving its imprimatur and support, making clear to diaspora members that they are valued by involving them as participants in meetings and policy-making fora.

This chapter has outlined four different strategic priorities for government over the coming generation in the area of engaging Ireland's diaspora. Firstly, it is important to recognise the 'forty shades of green', namely that there are many different types of Irish across the world. Secondly, the re-emergence of emigration and the changing nature of global politics and economics mean that a future-proof diaspora strategy will have to cater for Irish-born twenty-somethings in Shanghai and Singapore as well as Irish-American retirees in Boston. Thirdly, engaging key influencers, the

Irish Dov Frohmans, will remain a priority for Ireland's economic success. Finally, the strategy must recognise that the diaspora is not something to be tapped – there must be some meaningful reward for the global Irish getting involved 'back home'.

The arguments presented in this chapter are founded upon the belief that a meaningful two-way relationship with Ireland's diaspora will bring significant benefits to the country as it seeks to rebuild itself over the coming generation. Historically, Ireland's engagement with its diaspora has been largely one of receiving significant remittances from its community of emigrants abroad. The 2009 forum at Farmleigh may just signify the start of a new contract between the country and its diaspora. Government policy also needs to reflect that while the US-based diaspora is crucial, there are many other countries with long-standing and new diaspora communities that have been comparatively ignored.

Ireland's diaspora constitutes an immense source of 'soft power', an investment in which, if resourced properly, will provide an exponential dividend. This revitalised relationship should be built on strong foundations. Realising this potential will require a common strategy implemented across government, led by the Department of An Taoiseach. It is time to get organised.

10

Strategic, Coherent and Constructive: Three Pillars for a New Irish Foreign Policy

Ed Burke

Goodbye Ireland, Hello Moldova: Lessons from Sweden

Since the earliest days of its membership of the United Nations (UN), Ireland's leaders have had a tendency to blush with delight when Irish foreign policy is compared to that of the Nordic countries, especially Sweden. However, if Irish diplomats prided themselves on being with Sweden, it came as a rude awakening in 2010 when Sweden's Ministry for Foreign Affairs coldly announced that it no longer saw the need to maintain its diplomats in Ireland and promptly shut its embassy after 65 years. By contrast, maintaining embassies in Kosovo and Moldova was considered vital due to the importance of these countries to European security.

Where Ireland clings to caution in its foreign policy, Sweden exudes daring. The Swedish Minister for Foreign Affairs, Carl Bildt, has made no secret that he views neutrality as an out-moded concept in the post-Cold War era and has not hesitated to support the North Atlantic Treaty Organisation (NATO)-led war in Afghanistan. Bildt has been similarly unabashed in stating repeatedly that only through the EU's Common Foreign and Security Policy (CFSP) can Sweden defend its interests in a multipolar world. Virtually every foreign policy commitment drafted by Sweden is articulated in terms of what Europe can do on the world stage.[1] It is Europe, therefore, that is the singular conduit of Sweden's international aspirations.

The imperative to Sweden, as to Ireland, is clear: Divisions within Europe have exacerbated decline abroad. The retreat into national sovereignty that characterised Europe's response to the financial crisis exposed a weakness in governance that nearly brought about the collapse of the Eurozone. Fiascos such as the climate negotiations at Copenhagen in 2009 or the clambering of EU member states to acquire, uninvited, seats at G20 summits underline the barely disguised contempt in which US, Chinese and Indian diplomats hold Europe for speaking out of two corners of its mouth, on the one hand delegating negotiating power on trade to the European Commission and then usurping that mandate based on domestic political point-scoring in respective member states.[2]

Economic statistics speak clearly of a shift in influence away from Ireland and Europe: China is predicted to become the world's largest economy in 2032, over 20 per cent larger than the US by 2050, while almost 60 per cent of G20 economic growth in the next 40 years will come from Brazil, China, India, Russia and Mexico. The combined gross domestic product (GDP) at purchasing power parity (PPP) per capita of the largest four EU member state economies (Germany, the UK, France and Italy) will sink to just half that of India in less than 40 years, while Asia now already outstrips Europe in terms of defence spending.[3] Ireland has no unique diaspora or cultural advantage with any of these 'emerging powers' such as it currently enjoys with the US. Alone, Ireland's political influence in the world will count for next to nothing. A strong, coherent Europe is therefore inherently in Ireland's interests. However, to achieve such an aim will require a major shift in how Ireland conducts its foreign policy.

Ireland's membership of the EU has been the most important international commitment of the state since its foundation. Moreover, it has profound consequences for conventional 'Westphalian'[4] concepts of foreign policy, converting our relations with other European countries into a hybrid of foreign and domestic policy. Yet despite the clear incentive of a small state seeking sanctuary and opportunity within a larger alliance, Ireland has been largely a reactive member of the EU, obsessed with seeking tactical advantage rather than sharing strategic vision within Europe. It is indeed remarkable that Ireland has for so long been perceived, almost uncritically, as the 'star pupil' of the EU, considering its myriad objections to EU reforms and deeper integration with regard to taxation, justice and home affairs, agriculture and defence. The Irish tendency to say 'non' in Brussels has not been counterbalanced by putting forth large policy initiatives aimed at making Europe more cohesive and secure. Brigid Laffan and Jane O'Mahony have diplomatically observed that 'Big ideas on the future of the EU tend not to emanate from Irish shores.'[5]

Irish officials are often unsure whether they can take a position on certain issues due to a lack of coordination mechanisms and initiative in Dublin, instead adopting a 'checklist' approach, identifying the 'five or six problematic areas' for Ireland in a given proposal and then working through ways of addressing these concerns in tandem with the relevant department in Dublin. In sum, Ireland is predominantly a taker rather than a shaper of policy in Europe. Excellent at tactical negotiation, as personified through the masterful steering through of the Constitutional Treaty by former Taoiseach Bertie Ahern in 2004, Ireland is less adept at policy formulation.

In 2011, Irish diplomatic firepower will be dwarfed by the establishment of the European Union's own diplomatic corps, the European External Action Service, which will employ approximately 7,000 personnel in 136 countries. Ireland needs to have a wider, more strategic view on Europe that reflects the deepening impact of the EU upon Irish governance and opportunities for greater collective influence abroad. The impetus of the Lisbon Treaty and the economic crisis require a fundamental and comprehensive re-think of how Ireland projects its interests.

Ireland did not produce a White Paper on Foreign Policy until 1996, and has not revisited it since. However, the major cornerstones of Irish diplomacy have remained relatively static in the last half century, being concerned with Northern Ireland and relations with the UK, the EU, promoting Irish economic interests abroad and diaspora relations – particularly in the US – and contributing to the UN and associated multilateral organisations.[6] Irish diplomacy is likely to undergo an unprecedented, unfamiliar and thoroughly uncomfortable audit following the recent financial crisis. For the Irish citizen, however, such a rigorous analysis of Irish tools of diplomatic influence is a welcome opportunity to shape a leaner and more results-orientated foreign policy. Here, this chapter will be confined to an exploration of Irish diplomacy in, and through, Europe, and Ireland's contribution towards international peace and security. As with the other chapters in this book, it will begin by describing how we got where we are today before detailing how Irish foreign policy needs to be reorientated around a strategic, coherent and constructive approach. Throughout the chapter comparative reference will be made to the Nordic countries, not because these countries offer an infallible guide on how to conduct diplomacy, but rather to underline the point that if Ireland truly wishes to exert disproportionate influence in the world, it must have the essential tools with which to do so. Whatever about the merits and failings of the foreign policies of Norway, Denmark or Finland, as formulated by their respective political leaders, these similarly sized countries' foreign and defence ministries are well-resourced to deliver influence in the world.

'Faith of our Fathers': Inheriting, and Persevering with, an Outdated Diplomacy

The formative years of Irish foreign policy occurred during the early years of Ireland's UN membership, particularly 1957–1961, when Ireland, led by a committed Minster for Foreign Affairs, Frank Aiken, promoted policies related to nuclear non-proliferation, decolonisation and UN peacekeeping. Lofty goals of 'world peace and nuclear disarmament' became cornerstones of Irish foreign policy, despite the obvious fact that Ireland in truth had little capacity to influence either if more powerful member states were uninterested. The month or so which Ireland's Minister for Foreign Affairs would spend at the UN General Assembly each year became the highlight of the diplomatic calendar. Less altruistic goals, such as membership of the European Economic Community (EEC), were of little interest to Aiken, a reflection of a trend whereby Irish 'interests' in terms of setting realistic and results-orientated goals for the conduct of our relations with other states were rarely addressed in a strategic manner. The term 'Irish foreign policy' was normally seen through the prism of Ireland's membership of the UN.[7]

'Between Iraq and Israel': Ireland's Commitment to the UN and International Development

Ireland has been a useful, if not indispensable, facilitator for the UN Secretary-General over more than half a century. Ireland has made a significant contribution to peacekeeping over more than five decades, consistently deploying a high proportion of the Irish Defence Forces overseas (6 per cent in 2007) on UN or EU operations.[8] An Irish commitment to disarmament dates back to Éamon de Valera's term as Acting President of the Assembly of the League of Nations in 1932. Ireland was one of the co-sponsors of the Nuclear Non-Proliferation Treaty (NPT), which came into force in 1970 and has since played an active role in the Nuclear Suppliers' Group (NSG), which regulates global trade in nuclear energy. In 2008, Ireland was one of the 'last men standing', together with Austria, in objecting to the normalisation of commerce in nuclear energy following India's clandestine nuclear armament programme, which sparked a similar proliferation by Pakistan. 'On principle' and out of loyalty to the future viability of the NPT, Irish diplomats initially held out against pressure from the Bush administration in the US to waive a ban on nuclear commerce with India.[9] Finally, together with Austria, Ireland caved. The consequences for the NPT are still unclear but signing up to the treaty now seems to offer scant reward. Ireland's capitulation in the face of intense arm-twisting from other, larger members of the NSG is perhaps understandable, but it is nevertheless a stain on a once proud commitment to nuclear disarmament.

The convention on cluster munitions hosted by Ireland in Dublin in 2008 provided a more demonstrable, and partially successful, example of Ireland's commitment to disarmament. Despite US opposition, Irish diplomats lobbied tactfully, and ultimately successfully, to get the UK to sign up to a convention banning the use of cluster munitions, together with 70 other states. Unfortunately, the world's most significant producers of cluster munitions – China, India, Israel, Pakistan, Russia and the US – to date have not signed up to the convention. However, like the NPT, Ireland has provided a valuable opportunity for disarmament even if the world's most powerful countries remain deaf to such concerns.

The newly constituted and poorly resourced Conflict Resolution Unit in the Department of Foreign Affairs has relatively weak relations with the Department of Defence and to date has played no role in any Irish overseas peace support operation. Ireland's selection of Timor-Leste as the first country to which it dispatched a Conflict Resolution Special Envoy was late, coming two years after the comprehensive defeat of a rebellious faction of the country's tiny military, but welcome in terms of allocating resources to a country riven with complex divisions. Ireland's budget for conflict resolution in Timor-Leste is small, barely €1 million per annum, with much of this being outsourced to non-governmental mediation organisations such as the Centre for Humanitarian Dialogue. Such a piecemeal approach to conflict resolution compares unfavourably with the serious resources committed by countries such as Norway and Switzerland.[10]

In the UN, as in the EU, Irish diplomats deploy the tired mantra of a small country 'punching above its weight'. This may be true in that the UN Secretariat and other member states have frequently looked to Ireland as a small English-speaking country without colonial baggage to act as a mediator or persuader with regard to a certain course of action, but such rhetoric of assured over-achievement has arguably bred complacency. For example, Ireland's most recent Security Council term (2001–2002) was relatively undistinguished. One UN Secretariat official who served as a senior adviser to the Secretary-General during this period described Ireland's contribution as 'unremarkable, neither proactive nor negative in any conspicuous way'.[11] This was despite the enormous opportunity Ireland had to lead on the world stage in the immediate period following the 11 September 2001 attacks on New York and Washington when Ireland's ambassador chaired the UN Security Council. In the period that preceded the greatest threat to the UN's relevance and legitimacy in recent times – the Iraq war – Irish diplomats were increasingly muted despite then Minister for Foreign Affairs Brian Cowen's earlier assurances that the Irish position mirrored that of France. Instead, arrangements were quietly made to extend refuelling facilities to the US military at Shannon airport.[12]

Ireland has shown an uncanny ability to become unfamiliar with the 'elephant in the room' when it is expedient or just simply uninterested. Then Minister for Foreign Affairs Micheál Martin was able to give an address in the UN General Assembly in 2010 without mentioning the word 'Afghanistan' once. Ireland's ability to opt out of a serious commitment to the UN-mandated stabilisation effort in Afghanistan points to an exceptionalism derived from the mists of US sentiment. This favoured treatment of Ireland, born of an influential diaspora movement, has ensured that Ireland can persevere with an outmoded policy of neutrality and continue to 'free ride' behind the efforts of others to keep Europe secure. The US has consistently asked Ireland for very little. It forgave Irish neutrality in World War II, providing Ireland with the twelfth highest Marshall Aid allocation. In Afghanistan, the US again expected very little in terms of Irish support. However, such a privileged position has much more to do with domestic US politics rather than a triumph of Irish diplomacy.

In 2008, Irish Overseas Development Assistance (ODA) reached a high-water mark of €920 million. This was subsequently reduced to €722 million as the pinch of economic recession began to tell on Ireland's ODA Budget.[13] Of this, almost 70 per cent of Irish Aid funding (Irish Aid is the Irish government's overseas development agency, operating as a division of the Department of Foreign Affairs) is allocated bi-laterally, primarily in nine partner countries (seven in sub-Saharan Africa: Ethiopia, Lesotho, Malawi, Mozambique, Tanzania, Uganda and Zambia, and two in south-east Asia: Timor-Leste and Vietnam). Ireland has prioritised hunger and food insecurity in its policies and strategies, arguing that failure to address the global hunger crisis impedes progress across all the Millennium Development Goals (MDGs). A focus on agricultural productivity and hunger reduction, education and enhancing local governance capacity are the mainstays of Irish aid programmes in its nine priority countries. Ireland has been praised by an Organisation for Economic

Co-Operation and Development – Development Assistance Committee (OECD-DAC) peer review as 'a leading player in implementing international aid effectiveness principles'.[14] However, the National Recovery Plan announced by the government in late 2010 outlining almost €200 million of cuts in the Department of Foreign Affairs Budget from 2011 to 2014, primarily from the ODA Budget, means that Ireland will inevitably miss its UN commitment to spend 0.7 per cent of gross national income (GNI) on ODA by 2012.

'Selling', rather than 'Giving', Irish Sovereignty to the EU

When former Taoiseach Jack Lynch was asked in 1973 to sum up what membership of the EEC meant for Ireland he responded with one word: 'opportunity'. The limitations of sovereign isolation were learned in earnest during a barren period that saw an economic war with the UK, rejection of the Commonwealth and the introduction of disastrous economic policies of nationalisation and protectionism. Taoisigh Sean Lemass and Jack Lynch had seen the bitter harvest of those years and showed enough vision not to repeat past mistakes. Ironically for those republicans who continue to oppose membership, Ireland's participation in the EEC/EU ended Ireland's economic dependency upon the UK. In 1973, 54 per cent of Irish exports went to the UK, and only 21 per cent to the rest of Europe. The Single European Act signed in 1986 was critical towards increasing Irish trade with other European countries and by 2007 this trend had been reversed, with only 18 per cent of exports going to the UK, compared with 45 per cent to the rest of the EU. During a twenty-year period, from 1973 to 1993, Ireland received over €17 billion in structural and cohesion funding and European taxpayers have been instrumental in keeping Irish agriculture viable. Since 1973, Irish farmers have received more than €41 billion from the Common Agricultural Policy (CAP), payments which particularly favoured large producers (20 per cent of farmers received 80 per cent of funds in 2000). By 2002, CAP still accounted for almost 45 per cent of the EU's Budget,[15] despite only 5 per cent of the European workforce being employed in agriculture. Some respite to the EU Budget came from the introduction of the Single Payment Scheme, which sought to decouple the linkage between support payments and production, while also incentivising sound environmental practices.[16] The EU also began to act in concert on the world stage, for example defending Irish and other member state reservations over the reform of agricultural subsidies in the World Trade Organisation and other multilateral fora.[17]

A remarkable achievement of Irish diplomacy in Brussels is that, despite having one of the highest GDPs per capita in the EU, Ireland never became a net contributor to the EU Budget in almost 40 years of membership. This is not something to be proud of. Long-standing frustrations in Germany over the unwillingness of other relatively wealthy countries such as Ireland to pull its weight in providing similar funds for new, poorer member states were in evidence during the 2010 negotiations to provide an EU loan to stabilise Ireland's public finances. German taxpayers' fatigue over footing so much of Europe's bills for so long contributed to the punitive interest rates set as a condition of EU support to Ireland at the end of 2010.[18] During recent years of prosperity, Ireland could well have afforded a major injection into EU structural funds or to the EU humanitarian aid budget for example. However, avoiding such a commitment does point to a certain Irish dexterity or acumen in negotiating the corridors of power in Brussels.

Despite the myriad economic benefits offered by membership of the EU, Ireland's political commitment to a more integrated Europe has been highly questionable. Ireland effectively sold bits of its sovereignty in return for European coin or, as Brigid Laffan and Jane O'Mahony put it, 'Successive governments agreed to further economic and political integration in return for monetary benefits.'[19] For years, Irish ministers and diplomats have prided themselves in going to Brussels and wringing concessions and carrots from the EU. Such an attitude of bravura in raiding Brussels for major concessions while conceding little has narrowed the focus in the public mindset to 'what can Ireland get from Europe without giving anything in return', away from the far more important rationale of 'why Ireland needs to be a constructive player in a stronger Europe'.

Irish diplomats for years concealed the state's cautious conservatism with regard to European integration by assiduously avoiding being to the fore of shooting down proposals, while discreetly encouraging the role of other, often larger, member states in loudly objecting to same. Despite Ireland's tepid commitment to integration, European leaders loudly trumpeted Ireland as the success story of Europe. EU Structural Funds had worked; Ireland was reborn. This message was critical to support for the momentous growth of the EU eastwards.[20]

Ireland's days as European 'Wunderkind' are firmly at an end. European leaders are not only furious at Ireland for ignoring warnings from the EU in the decade preceding Ireland's economic collapse, but also resented being lectured to by Irish leaders who castigated previous attempts to set budgetary rules. European Central Bank Governor Jean-Claude Trichet was particularly irritated that Ireland showed such fiscal recklessness during a period in the mid-noughties[21] when Irish public spending grew by 12 per cent per annum at the same time as Finance Ministers Charlie McCreevy and, later, Brian Cowen, adopted a 'slash and burn' approach to tax rates and state revenues.[22]

Although Germany, like Ireland in 2001, broke its commitments made under the Lisbon Growth and Stability Pact, such a disregard for rules is a trait not shared by Gerhard Schröder's successor, Angela Merkel. The sending of Charlie McCreevy to Brussels by the Irish government also rankled with European Commission insiders, many of whom viewed him as a maverick rather than a capable pair of hands to deal with internal market affairs. Before leaving the Commission in late 2009, McCreevy launched a personal attack upon French President Nicolas Sarkozy for promoting French interests within the Commission, drawing vitriol from Paris at a particularly sensitive time for Ireland in its relations with the EU.[23] The rejection of the Lisbon Treaty in 2008 also battered Ireland's reputation in Brussels, where other member state governments could not fathom how a country that had received so much from the EU could be so ambivalent towards its future.

Strategic, Coherent and Constructive: What Ireland's Foreign Policy Needs

Irish foreign policy needs to be re-constituted. Firstly, Ireland needs to be more strategic in its international relations, slaying some 'sacred cows' that negatively impact on its relations with other states and logically explaining why. Secondly, a 'whole of government' approach to foreign policy is required to ensure coherence between the Department of Foreign Affairs and other instruments of government that set and conduct our foreign policy, most particularly with respect to the EU. Thirdly, Irish foreign policy must be constructive as well as realistic, anchored to building a stronger EU, clearly and rationally pointing out why Irish interests in much of the world will be better served by a more European approach, not least in relation to trade and security. Ireland is perceived on many issues to be reactive and occasionally a 'spoiler' of initiatives aimed at improving EU cooperation. It is time to get off the fence and fully commit to supporting a stronger EU in the world.

Strategic

Problems with Irish foreign policy are a reflection of the broader failings of the Irish political system. The wide-ranging reforms to Irish governance outlined elsewhere in this book are also crucial to a more strategic, analytical foreign policy that yields better results for Ireland's external interests. The Department of Foreign Affairs currently lacks a sufficiently resourced policy unit that can provide on-going medium- to long-term strategic analysis to the Minister for Foreign Affairs. This is not down to a desire of Irish diplomats to ignore strategy. Rather, it is a direct consequence of a lack of priority given by Irish public representatives to the long-term development of Irish foreign policy.

Is Anybody Listening? Engaging the Oireachtas

Few, if any, members of the Oireachtas, beyond those representatives appointed to the Departments of An Taoiseach and Foreign Affairs, have a significant role in the shaping of Irish foreign policy; parliamentary oversight in Ireland with regard to government foreign policy is regarded as among of the worst in the EU.[24] This is particularly damaging considering that as a result of the Raymond Crotty vs. An Taoiseach[25] Supreme Court ruling in 1987, Irish citizens are now directly consulted through referenda on whether to assent to technical and complex changes to the EU, for example. Having an informed, public debate on foreign policy is therefore almost uniquely important if the Irish electorate are to make an informed choice at the ballot box on Ireland's international commitments. It is also crucially important that Oireachtas committees are invested with tangible powers, such as denying a minister a negotiating mandate on a certain issue, in order to boost public faith and interest in Oireachtas debates on European and international issues. One proposal that would enhance public confidence in the capacity of the Oireachtas to oversee such issues would be for the Joint Committees on European Affairs and Foreign Affairs to appoint a TD or Senator to act as a rapporteur on specific issues such as agriculture, development assistance or justice and home affairs, producing annual reports on developments and opportunities for Irish policy.[26] Political parties could also gain significant leverage over foreign policy by selecting talented Irish citizens as candidates for election who are also members of the diaspora of a country strategically important to Irish interests.

Internally, the Department of Foreign Affairs also needs to become more open to external scrutiny. Whereas other foreign ministries welcome open or 'Chatham House Rule' discussions with foreign policy analysts, Irish diplomats are notoriously closed. Norway's Ministry for Foreign Affairs, for example, annually invites external consultants to conduct extensive audits of its contribution to conflict resolution and overseas development, publishing the occasionally less-than-flattering results on its website.[27] Such an approach enables a learning culture within the Ministry and a sense of transparency and awareness with regard to the expenditure of funds. Ireland lacks a single think tank that can undertake a constructive analysis of Irish foreign policy; the small and under-resourced Institute of International and European Affairs (IIEA) is so close to the Department of Foreign Affairs as to make it almost indistinguishable.[28]

Re-Wiring Iveagh House

Within the Department of Foreign Affairs an overly zealous institutional caution exists that clings to an almost exclusively 'generalist' approach to diplomacy and frowns upon thematic and regional experts, limiting the quality of strategic analysis. Given the difficulties of expanding an over-stretched diplomatic service, Ireland should instead increasingly take the opportunity to employ experts and officials seconded from other departments on short-term contracts to advise on specific areas of foreign policy. Irish diplomatic recruitment is still essentially based on the civil service principles of the UK's *Northcote–Trevelyan Report*, commissioned in 1854. It is now completely outdated, limiting new ideas and expertise being infused into Irish foreign policy by non-career civil servants. For example, the Finnish Ministry of Foreign Affairs is a leader in recruiting specialist experts for a set period of time to serve in the Ministry, in embassies or on EU Common Security and Defence Policy (CSDP) missions. In 2008, the Finnish government employed such external experts to establish a highly regarded civilian Crisis Management Centre that manages its overseas civilian contribution to international security.[29]

Training for existing diplomats is also severely limited compared to some other European foreign ministries. Extensive language training (such as is offered by the UK Foreign and Commonwealth Office for example in Mandarin or Arabic) is rarely permitted and not encouraged. The Department of Foreign Affairs also needs to be much bolder in substantially expanding Ireland's network of honorary consulates. Similar-sized countries, such as Denmark and Finland, have much smaller diaspora populations compared to the 70 million people of Irish descent in the world, yet both countries' foreign ministries maintain approximately four times the number of honorary consulates as Ireland does globally. The Department of Foreign Affairs should be much more proactive in locating those 'key influencers' of the diaspora described in Chapter 9 of this book and adding them to Ireland's diplomatic network.

The Department of Foreign Affairs has recently adopted a regional approach to Ireland's relations with emerging market countries: Ireland's Asia Strategy has had some significant successes in increasing trade opportunities in China and south-East Asia but, due to a stretched departmental budget, it has probably gone as far as it can go in terms of opening new embassies and recruiting additional diplomats.[30] Ireland also recently unveiled a Gulf Strategy to follow that of Asia, very belatedly opening an embassy in the United Arab Emirates (UAE). However, with approximately five diplomats in two locations (Riyadh and Abu Dhabi) with responsibility for six countries (Bahrain, Kuwait, Oman, Qatar, Saudi Arabia and the UAE), Ireland's resources on the ground are self-evidently thin. Meanwhile, since the Economic Division within the Department of Foreign Affairs was re-designed to deal with EU affairs, the number of Department of Foreign Affairs diplomats dealing specifically with Irish economic affairs has been extremely limited.

The Promoting Ireland Abroad Division (PIAD) has convened valuable investment fairs in Ireland and abroad but its scope is limited due to insufficient numbers of personnel. The Department of Foreign Affairs has shown a welcome desire to further boost Ireland's economic relations with the US,[31] opening a new consulate in Atlanta (with plans for another in Houston) and producing a series of well-thought-out strategy papers. To its credit, the Department of Foreign Affairs has also in recent years put much thought and effort into developing a model to co-locate Irish government agencies abroad: 'Ireland House', comprising the Department of Foreign Affairs, the Industrial Development Agency (IDA Ireland), Enterprise Ireland, Bord Bia and Tourism Ireland. Such a model has been introduced to great effect in Madrid and Tokyo in terms of improving intergovernmental coherence and should be replicated in other locations.[32]

Ireland should consolidate its diplomatic resources in those parts of the world most vital to Irish political and economic interests. A recent increase in Irish diplomats in Brussels is therefore crucial and should be followed by a similar amelioration of Irish diplomats and trade representatives in the US, taken from embassies in countries less vital to national economic recovery. Sending the same number of diplomats to Bucharest as to New Delhi is of questionable logic. The government should consider fully integrating agencies such as IDA Ireland and Enterprise Ireland under the Department of Foreign Affairs to avoid duplication of effort. The Department of Foreign Affairs should assume a clearly delineated leading role as the government department responsible for 'international trade', simultaneously creating an 'economic diplomacy' career path similar to other European diplomatic services, to which personnel currently serving in the Departments of Finance and Enterprise, Trade and Innovation, and the IDA Ireland and Enterprise Ireland agencies could also be eligible to apply. Many of Ireland's overseas missions are predominantly trade promotion orientated, yet diplomats receive only rudimentary preparation for such duties and ambassadors have little authority to coordinate the activities of overseas government agencies. Such an approach would go some way towards addressing the ad hoc relationship that currently exists between the Department of Foreign Affairs and Ireland's investment and trade agencies, as well as freeing up additional diplomatic resources.

The government could also appoint specific trade ambassadors in the future, seeking counsel and representation from such global business titans as Peter Sutherland. Furthermore, there is also an opportunity to appoint ambassadors to lead on specific thematic issues such as conflict resolution and disarmament, global hunger, trade reform or climate change, including talented representatives from outside the conventional diplomatic pool who could also manage their own cross-cutting budget line (persons with extensive UN service such as the former Head of the UN Relief and Works Agency (UNRWA) in Gaza, John Ging, come to mind). Importantly, the government needs to repeatedly emphasise the value of Irish diplomacy to a somewhat sceptical public. As Table 10.1 makes clear, Irish diplomatic resources are well below those of similarly sized countries such as Denmark and Finland. A new government should also ensure that the Department of Foreign Affairs does not have to repeat populist, cost-cutting, but ultimately self-damaging measures such as cancelling or significantly scaling down key networking and marketing events, including St Patrick's Day receptions.

Ireland's response to the establishment of the European External Action Service – the new diplomatic service of the European Union – has been surprisingly sedate. In early 2010, the Secretary General of the Department of Foreign Affairs, David Cooney, observed that the European External Action Service, one of the most ambitious and perceptible consequences of the Lisbon Treaty, would not have a significant impact on Ireland's own conduct of its foreign policy.[33] Ireland has also been one of the most conservative of member states in insisting that only generalist career diplomats within existing member state foreign services, as opposed to contracted experts, are recruited to the European External Action Service.[34] The Department of Foreign Affairs does not appear to have a clear strategy on how to respond to the enormous opportunity presented by the European External Action Service.

Table 10.1: Ireland's Diplomatic and Aid Resources (2009 unless stated otherwise)

Country	Population (in Millions)	GNI Per Capita (US$)	Overseas Diplomatic and Trade Missions	Honorary Consulates	Department of Foreign Affairs Personnel	Overseas Development Assistance (ODA) (US$ Millions), 2008	ODA as a Percentage of GNI, 2008
Ireland	4.450	48,420	75	90	1,577	1.327	0.59
Denmark	5.529	54,420	113	450	2,700	2.803	0.82
Finland	5.228	43,910	99	400	1,831	1.165	0.44

Source: Data taken from the Department of Foreign Affairs, Houses of the Oireachtas, OECD-DAC, the UN, the Ministry of Foreign Affairs of the Kingdom of Denmark and the Ministry of Foreign Affairs of the Republic of Finland.

In engaging with the European External Action Service, Ireland should emphatically not swallow whole Sweden's example of a 'new model foreign policy'. Political information from member state capitals is critical to levering advantage during negotiations in Brussels, where even the smallest member state can derail Irish interests and the abrupt unilateral closure of embassies in other EU member states is easily one of the most expeditious ways for a country to 'lose friends and alienate people'. Although Sweden has correctly diagnosed that the old ways of diplomacy are no longer viable, it has over-reached itself. Ireland should not act so rashly, but neither should it stand still. Ireland should not hedge its bets completely on the European External Action Service: its development is too brittle to begin prematurely closing embassies. However, in certain cases the physical co-location of the Irish Embassy within the EU Delegation should clearly be closely examined, beginning with Irish Aid priority countries like Mozambique. Ireland should also look at the option of attaching Irish officials to EU delegations in countries with significant market potential. Could, for example, Enterprise Ireland or IDA Ireland officials be co-located with an EU delegation, expanding Ireland's reach to many countries where it currently has no diplomatic, trade or aid presence? The Oireachtas has been slow to pose such questions, and neither has the Department of Foreign Affairs been particularly forthcoming in providing answers.

Coherent

In recent years, partially in response to the shock first-time rejections of the Nice and Lisbon Treaties, the government has introduced coordination mechanisms to ensure a more coherent approach to Irish policy-making in Europe. However, with the exceptional crisis aside, government ministers are by-and-large left to 'get on with it' in Brussels, receiving far less input from the Department of An Taoiseach and their Cabinet colleagues on the minutiae of EU policy developments than they would on domestic legislation. Unlike many other EU member states, the Irish government does not issue 'guidance notes' on substantive policy issues. The Department of An Taoiseach remains understaffed in terms of human resources and expertise to coordinate a more comprehensive strategic approach to Europe. On questions of Ireland's international security commitments, interdepartmental cooperation remains woefully deficient, way behind the 'comprehensive approach' championed by Ireland's Nordic partners.[35]

Organising for Influence in Europe

Irish policy-making in Europe is centred on the 'holy trinity' of the Departments of An Taoiseach, Foreign Affairs and Finance. The Department of Foreign Affairs is undoubtedly the government department with the best 'panoramic view' of Irish policy in Europe, channelling information from and back to Dublin through its Permanent Representation to the EU in Brussels, as well as through its network of embassies in respective member states. The EU Division leads in most areas in terms of monitoring developments within the EU for the Department of Foreign Affairs, although the Political Division takes precedence on external European policy such as the Common Foreign and Security Policy (CFSP) and Ireland's commitment to the EU's Common Security and Defence Policy (CSDP).

The capacity of individual departments to make their own policy flounders on the rock of the Department of Finance, if such a policy has repercussions for the national Budget. Unlike the Department of Foreign Affairs, which acts more as a facilitator for other government departments, the Department of Finance plays a robust role in vetting all EU proposals that affect the Irish Exchequer. The Department of Finance, together with the Central Bank, also plays a critical role in Europe though the Economic and Financial Council (ECOFIN), meetings of Finance Ministers of the Eurozone (the Eurogroup) and the European Central Bank, as well as representing Ireland in the preparation of the EU Budget. A range of departments send personnel to the Irish Permanent Representation in Brussels. In recent years, the Department of Foreign Affairs has both advocated and delivered upon a significantly better resourced and well-run Permanent Representation to the EU in Brussels.

Given the ever increasing importance of Brussels to Irish domestic policy, the Department of An Taoiseach has played a more prominent role in formulating Ireland's European policy in recent years. The Minister of State for Europe in the Department of An Taoiseach has become the central coordinating authority on cross-departmental matters. In 2002, a standing Interdepartmental Coordinating Committee on EU Affairs was created to move towards a 'whole of government' approach to Europe. This committee of senior officials fed into the Cabinet EU Sub-Committee chaired by an Taoiseach, both welcome developments in terms of harmonising Irish policy in the EU.[36] Ireland has come a long way in streamlining its relations in the EU.

Despite these existing mechanisms for coordinating Irish policy, engagement from the Department of An Taoiseach remains ad hoc, usually associated with immediate crisis-solving rather than the long-term development of Irish strategic interests in Europe. One of the key reasons why Ireland has a poor reputation in terms of implementing EU directives is that many government departments that are affected by these have not received adequate information from the lead department that has negotiated on Ireland's behalf in Brussels.[37] Briefing material and position papers for a Council of Ministers or Council of Permanent Representatives meeting are seldom widely distributed by the responsible lead department. Even within the lead department, information can be 'stovepiped', being prepared by one section without consultation with other affected units and being sent straight to the relevant minister. The Departments of Foreign Affairs, Agriculture and Justice generally do circulate regular reports on EU negotiations within their departments but this is by no means practised or enforced throughout government.[38] One remedy to a lack of coordination would be to appoint sections within the Department of An Taoiseach focused on specific areas of European policy to lead cross-departmental committees. Another would be to introduce a 'Friday meeting' co-chaired by the Head of the European and International Affairs Division at the Department of An Taoiseach and the Irish Permanent Representative to the EU for key officials involved in setting their respective departments' contribution to Irish–EU policy.

A Comprehensive Approach to International Security

Ireland's role in security sector reform is small in scale, with the exception of approximately twenty personnel (Garda and civilian) deployed on CSDP missions at any given time. The Department of Foreign Affairs has rightly won praise for establishing a rapid response corps of Irish volunteers whom the government may second to intergovernmental organisations during a crisis, but few of these individuals have experience or training in serving alongside the Irish Defence Forces on a possible UN or EU overseas deployment. Overall, however, the Department of Foreign Affairs should be applauded for taking a more proactive approach to civilian crisis management, drafting a much needed strategic concept in early 2011, in contrast to the relative lack of enthusiasm of the Department of Justice and Garda headquarters for overseas deployments.

Ireland now has a growing number of opportunities within the EU to harmonise its security policy with other member states. The establishment of a Common Security and Defence Policy (CSDP), rationalisation of defence 'burden-sharing' under the European Defence Agency, establishment of fora such as the Political and Security Committee, the Committee for Civilian Aspects of Crisis Management (CIVCOM) and the Military Committee are significant and unprecedented challenges for Irish defence policy. Moreover, after the bitter experience of serving in ineffective UN peacekeeping missions during the 1990s (including as part of the chaotic UN Operation in Somalia II (UNOSOM II) in 1993 and 1994), Ireland, like other European countries, has an increasing preference to serve under European rather than UN command.[39] Ireland has played an important role in providing leading personnel to nascent CSDP missions: Assistant Garda Commissioner Kevin Carty was selected to lead the EU Police Mission in Bosnia (EUPM) in 2006 and, in 2008, Major General Pat Nash was nominated as Force Commander for the EUFOR Mission deployed to Chad and the Central African Republic (EUFOR Tchad/RCA), to which Ireland also provided 400 troops. However, if Ireland is to play a more significant role in EU deployments, there is an urgent requirement to rethink the instruments of government which support the CSDP.

Ireland likes to be compared to Nordic countries on defence policy, but compares badly in terms of resourcing its military and civilian commitment to conflict management (see Table 10.2). Ireland has virtually no military air capacity in terms of deploying or supplying troops overseas and to provide crucial in-theatre support. Ireland is therefore frequently reliant upon others coming to its assistance or making last minute ad hoc and expensive leasing arrangements with private firms – a dependence which resulted in an embarrassing delay in the arrival of Irish EUFOR troops in Chad in 2008. An amelioration of the Air Corps Budget to enable a minimum level of expeditionary capability is long overdue. In the case of Chad, the Department of Defence made 'an expensive error' of €3 million in belatedly leasing Russian helicopters that were unable to carry EUFOR personnel, resulting in Irish troops being without adequate air transportation for four months.[40] There is a difference between a rational pooling of resources with other EU member states, desirable as that is, and having no capacity at all in terms of very basic military capabilities.

The fallout from the economic crisis creates an opportunity to comprehensively assess all of Ireland's defence assets. Irish resources should primarily be focused on enabling rapid overseas deployments, fighting 'small wars' in complex environments and prioritising naval protection of Irish waters. However, to advocate savings of over €237 million to a Defence Budget of just over €900 million (including pensions costs), as recommended by the budgetary review body, an Bord Snip Nua, is grossly irresponsible. Ireland already has one of the lowest defence spending rates of national GDP, which was almost halved from 1997 to 2007.[41] Sizeable cuts to the Defence Budget risks consigning the Irish military to near incapable irrelevance.

Table 10.2: Ireland's Defence Commitments in 2008 in Comparision to Denmark and Finland

Country	Population (in Millions)	GNI Per Capita (US$)	Military Personnel	Troops Deployed Overseas	Defence Spending as a Percentage of GDP	Number of Civilian Personnel Committed to CSDP Missions (Percentage of Total)	Percentage Share of the UN Regular Budget
Ireland	4.450	48,420	10,350	659	0.53	16 (0.8%)	0.445
Denmark	5.529	54,420	21,000	1,300	1.3	77 (4.1%)	0.739
Finland	5.228	43,910	32,029	700	1.3	104 (5.4%)	0.569

Source: Data from NATO, the European Defence Agency, the World Bank and D. Korski and R. Gowan, *Can the EU Rebuild Failing States? A Review of Europe's Civilian Capacities* (Brussels: European Council on Foreign Relations, 2009).

A small corps of trained reserve civilian 'stabilisation advisers', such as those deployed by Denmark or Norway alongside the military, equipped with a small budget for Quick Impact Projects[42] and with a background in development assistance and/or conflict analysis, would make a significant contribution towards improving Ireland's capacity to respond to complex threat environments in intra-state conflicts. However, such a step would require the strengthening of the International Security Policy Section in the Department of Foreign Affairs. The Defence Forces should also be encouraged to develop more doctrine and contingency plans drawn from experiences in such conflicts as Lebanon, Timor-Leste, Kosovo and Chad, as well as thinking more concretely as to how it should cooperate with Irish and international civilian agencies. In 2010, in recognition of Ireland's UN service, the Irish Ambassador to the UN was invited to take on the role of co-facilitator of a major review of the UN's peace-building architecture. Ireland should start at home, thoroughly and honestly evaluating its own mechanisms to support international crisis management as well as those of the UN. The government must also decide whether it is resolutely committed to international conflict resolution as a priority of Irish foreign policy. If the answer is yes, then the Conflict Resolution Unit in the Department of Foreign Affairs must be resourced accordingly.

A first step towards improving Ireland's military and civilian crisis management capabilities would be for the Oireachtas to commission a report on improving intergovernmental cooperation in relation to overseas deployments. The current Oireachtas committee system is inadequate, with defence being lumped together in a joint committee with justice and women's rights. It is about time that Ireland finally has a parliamentary committee solely dedicated to defence matters that can produce strategic policy documents on countering threats to Irish and international security.

The concept of employing a 'comprehensive approach' to Irish overseas stabilisation operations – military, diplomatic and development aid – has never been effectively realised. There is little oversight and interest from the Department of An Taoiseach in ensuring 'unity of effort' or in operationalising a fund that can be used specifically for civil–military operations during Irish overseas military deployments. Relations between the Department of Defence and the relevant parts of the Department of Foreign Affairs remain ad hoc at best. Although a small amount of aid money was made available for civil–military projects in Chad and Lebanon and a political adviser was dispatched with the Irish contingent for at least some part of the EUFOR-TChad/RCA operation, such gestures are insufficient. The Defence Forces suffered from a chronic lack of political advice and pre-deployment intelligence prior to being sent to Chad and Irish Aid were generally uninterested in providing significant funding for what was a critical country of interest in terms of Ireland's international security commitments. At the time of the Irish deployment, the *Financial Times'* Europe correspondent observed how other EU member states saw the French-dominated EUFOR TChad/RCA Operation as 'a prop for French foreign policy in a former African colony' and had no desire to jump into such a 'maelstrom' that 'pits a French-supported ruler – dictator, some would say – against a rebel movement that doesn't want an EU military presence there.'[43] An unprepared Ireland was fortunate to escape so lightly.

It is glaringly obvious that Irish Aid has been run on a shoestring budget in terms of personnel. Despite being responsible for a budget of close to €1 billion, in 2008 Irish Aid had less than 40 full-time representatives deployed worldwide to provide day-to-day management of programme implementation.[44] The wisdom of deploying non-specialist Irish diplomats (third secretaries) to help oversee aid programmes in countries such as Malawi, in addition to sending expensive ambassadors to establish even more costly embassies in countries with no strategic interest to Ireland, is highly questionable, if not simply inefficient. Instead, the government should send a small Irish Aid team with support from an Irish embassy in a nearby country more relevant to Irish political and economic interests.

Ireland also has a limited capacity for long-term aid planning and research, a situation exacerbated by the haemorrhaging of experienced personnel due to the decentralisation of Irish Aid to Limerick.[45] Planning is vital to aid coherence and meeting international expectations. Consequently, this component of Irish Aid should be resourced as a priority. Until recently, there was a pronounced lack of coordination structures to facilitate Irish Aid cooperation with other departments (such as the Departments of Agriculture and Environment) in terms of strategic development of Irish Aid projects. Former Minister for Foreign Affairs Micheál Martin deserves recognition for creating an interdepartmental Committee on Development in 2007, which has seen a greatly enhanced dialogue between departments on Ireland's development priorities. Nevertheless, dialogue is meaningless unless clear political direction is given to guarantee cooperation. Currently, government departments such as Justice are reluctant to contribute resources to support Irish overseas security or aid commitments.

Constructive

In October 2010, then Taoiseach Brian Cowen, in a speech at the annual Fianna Fáil commemoration of Wolfe Tone at Bodenstown, defiantly, and ultimately futilely, rejected calls for an international financial bailout of Ireland's public finances, solemnly invoking Ireland's patriot dead:

> While we may differ on how to achieve our goals, I know that the Opposition leaders will agree with Tone when he said that we are better off conducting our own affairs than being subject to others' control.[46]

A week prior to Ireland appealing for a bailout from the EU and the International Monetary Fund, amidst rumours of a Brussels-led occupation, Finance Minister Brian Lenihan was forced to deny in the Dáil that there were any 'Commission officials in my department on a permanent or any other basis. They do not have offices or regular spaces in my department. That does not exist.'[47] What is surprising in all these remarks is not the appeal to honour dead Irishmen, a political weapon blunted from hyperbolic overuse even in twenty-first-century Ireland, but rather the narrow definition of the EU as 'other'. Despite a recognition by some within Ireland's body politic that Westphalian concepts of statehood are outmoded, that 'in an interdependent world sovereignty and self-determination are relative, not absolute concepts', the prospect of the European Commission, in which Ireland has pooled but not absolute sovereignty, calling the shots was enough to raise a primordial fear for self-preservation among even the most avowed Europhile. Europe was still decidedly a 'foreign' place.[48]

Hyperbole has been even more in evidence in terms of the prospect of Ireland playing a constructive role in relation to European security. Ireland has been very reluctant to sign up to any European defence pact that offers military assurances to another EU state if attacked. In originally opposing Ireland's membership of the Partnership for Peace, then Opposition leader Bertie Ahern practically accused the Fine Gael-led government of treachery: 'Will we have British troops back in the Curragh?'[49] Given such an absence of rational discussion on defence policy, it is unsurprising that the Irish electorate proved to be so ill-informed during the recent Lisbon referenda (33 per cent of Irish voters believed that the Lisbon Treaty would lead to conscription to an 'EU Armed Forces').[50] Past governments have failed to inform and failed to lead. Now, more than ever, Irish public representatives need to be honest about why Ireland is willing to pool its sovereignty and increase its commitment to a more integrated and secure Europe.

The Haunting Spectre of European Tax Harmonisation

Ireland has successfully opposed an extension of qualified majority voting to areas of taxation. In doing so, Ireland has been able to hide behind the position of the UK, alongside other smaller states such as Cyprus, Estonia and Malta. Given its veto powers over issues related to taxation, Ireland will maintain control over its corporate tax rate indefinitely. However, Irish diplomats will need to guard against some member states moving towards 'enhanced cooperation' on tax, which could leave Ireland isolated in the Eurozone.

Ireland should show that it has learned the lessons of its financial meltdown and appreciate that our poor policy decisions nearly shattered international confidence in the Eurozone. Rules have to be set and only broken in the most exceptional of circumstances with the consent of all other parties. Following the 2011 general election, the new Irish government should therefore announce an independent inquiry into the causes of Ireland's financial crisis and specifically task it with coming up with proposals for European mechanisms to resist such a scenario in the future. This does not imply ceding lower corporate tax rates, but rather welcoming deeper European integration in order to better regulate the European financial sector.

'Uncommon Law': Justice and Home Affairs

Irish reservations over further integration of justice and home affairs are seldom debated and are shrouded in a complexity that turns off all but the most wonkish or legalistic of the Irish electorate. Opposition tends to be led by those legal scholars and practitioners, such as former Minister for Justice Michael McDowell, who fear an erosion of the Irish common law system. Ireland's attitude has been described as one of 'extreme caution' and Ireland is one of the most conservative of European member states in opposing calls for a European public prosecutor, taking a hard line during the Constitutional Treaty negotiations in 2003–2004 over legal jurisdiction.[51] Ireland has also exhibited a marked hesitation with regard to the harmonisation of immigration, asylum and civil cooperation. This has frustrated countries such as Spain and Poland that bear the brunt of illegal migration to the EU and desire greater assistance from other EU member states to protect Europe's borders.

Although Ireland contributes to the EU police agency, Europol, it risks being left behind as the Schengen countries[52] move towards even greater security, border and intelligence cooperation. Ireland's position is a difficult one, as Ireland must be careful to protect its Common Travel Area with the UK in order to avoid negative consequences for North–South political and economic cooperation. However, Ireland has never lobbied the UK particularly strongly on Schengen, preferring to use it as a cloak with which to opt out from deeper justice and home affairs cooperation in other areas. Ireland, like the UK, has been denied access to valuable data from the Schengen countries on applicants who have been refused visas, an action which prompted the UK to take a case to the European Court of Justice, which it subsequently lost.[53] Instead of continuing to entrench Ireland's reputation as an unconstructive naysayer, the government should commission a study that would offer some insight into opportunities for the EU to develop a compromise between the common law system and the more 'principles-based' legal systems of the majority of EU member states, as well as clearly advocating the merits of closer policing cooperation. This could help avoid the type of legal wrangling seen with regard to differing interpretations of the European arrest warrant, for example.

Ireland also needs to address the chronic lack of resources dedicated towards liaising with other EU member states to prevent crime and save the state millions of euro in lost revenue due to smuggling activities. As of mid-2010, there were only five Irish Garda liaison officers posted overseas in countries with strong links to criminal syndicates in Ireland, in addition to a paltry two in Europol and one serving at Interpol. There is no Garda liaison presence in key central and eastern European smuggling transit counties, including the Baltic states, Poland, Bulgaria and Romania. Currently, Ireland has only one Garda in London working as a criminal liaison officer.[54] Considering its Common Travel Area with the UK and their mutual interest in preventing arms, cigarette and drugs smuggling to Northern Ireland, Ireland should develop a more integrated partnership with the UK abroad in response to the increasing globalisation of crime.

'Dig-Outs for Ireland': Giving Up the CAP Addiction

The days when Irish economic activity was synonymous with agriculture are long gone. It is, however, clearly still important; agriculture and associated agri-food businesses make up almost 10 per cent of the workforce and 8 per cent of annual GDP.[55] Ireland is highly protectionist with regard to its agricultural sector, remaining implacable in the face of pleas from many of its European partners to accept a more liberal market structure. Ireland's uncompromising stance in Europe in rejecting Trade

Commissioner Peter Mandelson's reforms, which would have partially opened up European markets to the developing world, brings into question the sincerity of Ireland's aid commitments. Due to the initiative of other member states, CAP has thankfully undergone successive reforms in recent years that have eased the burden on both the European taxpayer and the developing world. Ireland's CAP conservatism is linked to assiduous lobbying by a slick farming lobby that spends half its annual budget on public relations campaigns in Brussels.

Irish diplomats will face a major challenge in 'fighting to stand still' with regard to CAP given the demand for a redistribution of CAP funds towards those new member states with a greater reliance upon agriculture. The eradication of CAP is not a panacea to boost developing world trade with Europe. However, a more flexible and nuanced Irish approach to international trade negotiations would be welcome in terms of freeing up mutually beneficial opportunities for trade and investment between the developed and developing worlds. Ultimately, Ireland should support the phased elimination of CAP, while simultaneously allocating EU funds for diversification and taking care to avoid the fallout from an overly abrupt market liberalisation in the developing world. Neither should Irish agriculture stand still. Rather it should follow the example of producers such as New Zealand and adapt, ending protectionism by seeking out new markets in a world increasingly short of food.[56]

Ending Neutrality: Getting the Hurler off the Ditch

Major Irish overseas military deployments are predicated upon the 'triple lock' system, whereby the operation must have a UN mandate and be approved by the Cabinet and the Dáil. This system can be unwieldy in that it may hinder operations carried out on behalf of the EU and the Organisation for Security and Cooperation in Europe (OSCE) that do not have a UN mandate. For example, Irish military personnel were unable to serve in the EU-led mission to Macedonia (Operation Concordia), which had not received a specific UN mandate.

Questions of neutrality have dogged Irish participation in the NATO-led Partnership for Peace, which allows non-members to access NATO resources in preparing for or undertaking overseas deployments, and the EU Nordic Battlegroup, a standby force that should, theoretically, be able to deploy within a matter of hours anywhere in the world. However, it is far from certain as to whether such a 'rapid deployment' would be truly expeditious if the Dáil was in recess or slow to conclude a debate in the Oireachtas that would provide the proper sanction. Similarly, in the case of a natural disaster, without a specific UN mandate it is not clear whether Irish troops have to opt out from providing security and facilitating the delivery of humanitarian assistance.

Ireland's current deployment of seven troops as part of the International Security Assistance Force (ISAF) in Afghanistan clearly illustrates the folly of current Irish defence policy. Ireland has taken sides in a red-hot counter-insurgency operation and its flag (by alphabetical coincidence) is one of the most prominent in ISAF headquarters in Kabul (being beside the main entrance). Yet, Ireland has only contributed to the ISAF under a technicality which allows the Taoiseach to deploy twelve Irish soldiers or fewer on an overseas mission without going through the triple lock system. This contribution to an international coalition has clearly undermined any claims to neutrality, yet conversely (due to its miniscule size alone) it has done little to help the Afghan government or Ireland's NATO allies. As so often in its defence policy, Ireland has fallen between two stools – half-in and half-out.

Lengthy debates over Irish neutrality are largely meaningless as a consequence of the 1993 Defence (Amendment) Act, which permitted Irish troops to take sides in 'peace enforcement' operations sanctioned by the UN Security Council. Irish politicians have been timid, if not simply uninterested, in putting arguments for a re-positioning of Irish defence policy to the electorate, seeing little gain to be made of it in terms of domestic politics, unwilling to explain why permitting Russia and China (as permanent members of the Security Council) to veto Irish military overseas deployments no longer makes sense. Finland and Sweden, who lead the EU Nordic Battlegroup, have effectively abandoned neutrality and consequently are not restricted in taking rapid decisions to enable the overseas deployment of their troops in an emergency. Neutrality is largely an obsolete concept; the world is uninterested in whether Ireland is neutral or not. For example, it is difficult to find evidence to demonstrate that Norway's membership of NATO has affected its standing as a much-lauded member of the UN, leading international peace mediator and contributor to crisis management. Moreover, Ireland is not exempt from the security threats that have accompanied globalisation, including cyber-terrorism and Islamic extremism. Even if neutrality is defined by some political leaders in Ireland as simply meaning an aversion to military alliances, Ireland's commitment to the EU's Common Security and Defence Policy renders such a definition obsolete. In late 2010 and early 2011, Irish Defence Forces personnel once again travelled to Scandinavia to train and equip to stand up as part of the EU's Nordic Battlegroup (other members include Sweden, Finland and Estonia). Although Irish and European political leaders have been masters of evasion on the subject in the past, the EU is now a military as well as a political and economic alliance. A new government needs to explain why this is a good thing and why EU peace support operations compliment rather than detract from Ireland's commitment to international security. The time has come to question whether, as the Department of Foreign Affairs claims, Irish neutrality is truly a 'resource' and not a hindrance.[57] Neutrality once served a purpose in securing the state. No longer.

Since the ratification of the Lisbon Treaty, Ireland has done enormous damage to its reputation as a small but distinguished contributor to the EU's CSDP by constantly objecting to measures designed to move towards Permanent Structured Cooperation in Defence (PSCD) and the deepening of the capacity of the European Defence Agency. Ireland's vocal position against developing systematic defence 'burden sharing' among member states has clearly frustrated larger EU countries, especially as Ireland is one Europe's smallest defence contributors in terms of GDP per capita. It is inherently in the interests of a cash-strapped Ireland to argue for a common EU defence budget as proposed by the French Minister for Defence in 2009. Most of Europe's €200 billion worth of military equipment is wasted on duplicating outdated equipment and maintaining Cold-War-era land forces that cannot deploy outside Europe.[58] However, the Department of Defence is remarkably guarded, if not closed, in terms of its dealings with other departments and its civilian officials lack training and expertise on more technical aspects of defence policy, damaging perceptions of Ireland in Brussels.[59]

Finally, as a means of mitigating the damage caused to the NPT in recent times by the clandestine nuclear arms proliferation activities undertaken by India, Iran and Pakistan, among others, Ireland would do well to proactively support a call by Dr Mohammed El Baradei, former director of the International Atomic Energy Agency (IAEA), to establish a multilateral nuclear energy bank that would enable countries to access nuclear energy technology for domestic power generation purposes under a carefully supervised international regime. This would be a first step towards removing an easy grievance or excuse used by would-be proliferators in the course of developing a nuclear arms capability.

A New Irish Foreign Policy

The blunt advice offered by President Barack Obama's former Chief of Staff Rahm Emanuel not to let 'a serious crisis go to waste' is also applicable to a resurgent Ireland in the world. The world has changed drastically since the end of the Cold War – the global population has grown by almost one-third in less than twenty years and globalisation has ushered in a multipolar era. The opportunities of interconnectedness have also made us even more vulnerable to the shifting tectonics of economic trends in far-away countries as well as to attacks by global terrorist and criminal networks. Ireland needs to respond more strategically to these events. To maintain the status quo is to be left behind. Most importantly, Ireland should seek greater advantage and shelter in the world through the EU.

If Ireland is to regain respect in Europe, it will have to be seen to give as well as take, and moreover to demonstrate its long-term constructive opinion on what a more effective, integrated and secure EU in the world will concretely look like. As former President of the European Parliament Pat Cox memorably observed, Ireland still needs 'a vision for Europe that is more sophisticated than milking a cow'.[60] Rather than resisting the further development of a more integrated EU foreign and trade policy, Ireland should determinedly support it.

Ireland should ally itself with those countries that wish to see a more consistent approach to Europe's external relations. Ireland will never have a seat at the G20 nor will it wield significant influence on the UN Security Council until such a time as Europe can act collectively in its interests. It is inherently in Ireland's interests to look forward to the day when an Irish diplomat sits at one of the permanent representative seats at the UN Security Council, obviously not as a representative of Ireland, but as a European ambassador representing the EU as part of a much-needed reform of the UN Security Council that consolidates the UK and French veto-wielding seats into one EU representation. Ireland should simultaneously maximise the use of its own diplomatic resources, com-plimenting the existing pool of career diplomats with an injection of experts on limited contracts, expanding the number of honorary consuls and 'special representatives', while also being at the forefront of the devel-opment of a new European diplomacy.

Despite inherent difficulties, Ireland should be a proactive contributor to the lengthy and complex process of constructing a European CFSP. In the short term, Ireland should also focus on the easier task of making EU policy on economic, trade and monetary policy more coherent, agree-ing measures to avoid the near-fractious disaster of Ireland's own public finances collapse and the precarious position in which that placed the Eurozone. Ireland should also strongly make the case for European coun-tries to stop under-cutting each other in critical global capitals such as Beijing, Riyadh and New Delhi, where the EU as a foreign policy actor is largely ignored or even ridiculed, but instead embrace a truly functional European trade and investment strategy in each location.

A more multipolar world fixed around countries with which Ireland does not have a comparable advantage relative to its relations with Europe and the US spells increasing irrelevance for Ireland on the world stage. In responding to this challenge, Ireland fundamentally has but one option – embed the state within Europe, sharing sovereignty in order to exert sufficient strength in a multipolar world. The number one interest of Irish foreign policy then is a stronger Europe and it is to that end we should primarily leverage our influence and potential.

11

Conclusion

Ronan Lyons and Ed Burke

Goodbye to All That: Ireland as It Should Be

'Ireland is the old sow that eats her farrow.' This caustic observation by Stephen Dedalus in James Joyce's *A Portrait of the Artist as a Young Man* remains one of the most biting insults ever coined to describe Ireland. The image of Ireland as an irrational animal whose nature condemns it to destroy its young sums up the depths of despair felt by generations of young Irish people in the twentieth century at the lack of economic opportunity and social space in which to develop, or even stay, in their own country. It is easy in these uncertain times to resurrect grim comparisons with the past. It is indeed a national disgrace that, as of early 2011, one in four young people is unemployed, with the majority of those considering emigrating by the end of the year.

However, the Ireland of the 2010s is not the Ireland of the 1950s or the Ireland of the 1980s. Those days are gone. Ireland will not go backwards. It has too much talent, too many ideas and too many possibilities. This is not to underestimate the challenges; Ireland has much to do this decade to put its house in order. The biggest mistake we could make, however, is to focus narrowly on limited short-term objectives, such as getting our deficit back to some target level by 2015, without looking at the bigger picture. This would be to miss the opportunity presented to the country in its current crisis.

We believe that Ireland must be a country where new ideas count. Vested interests must be set aside in favour of efficiency and accountability; the beleaguered and short-changed taxpayers who have unfailingly paid their dues to the state, before suffering the ignominy of seeing their country bankrupted – including by a bank, Anglo Irish, they had barely heard of and certainly never invested in – must come before the sectoral interests of the few who have played such a disproportionate role in Irish politics. The consultative process of policy-making must not be the preserve of the elite and it emphatically should not be the exclusive preserve of older generations. As outlined in the preceding chapters, Ireland needs to reorganise and decentralise its decision making, capitalising on opportunities for innovative government rendered by the information age.

As this book makes clear, Ireland's decision-making system labours under a public service model designed in the nineteenth century, in which hierarchy and inflexibility still trump performance and innovation. As late as 2010, the majority of the Oireachtas could probably recall when Éamon de Valera was Taoiseach and John Charles McQuaid Archbishop of Dublin. It is unsurprising, then, that Ireland's institutions do not reflect those who came of age at the end of the twentieth and beginning of the twenty-first century. Not only are a younger, educated and mobile generation put off by the stagnant political and public institutions of state, but the few independent think tanks and non-governmental organisations that deal with public policy have long been underfunded and largely ignored by policy-makers.

However, those born since 1970 should not simply wait for this situation to right itself. John Mayer has a song called 'Waiting for the World to Change', in which he sings: 'Now we see everything that's going wrong | With the world and those who lead it | We just feel like we don't have the means | To rise above and beat it'.

This cannot be the attitude of Ireland's younger generation. They must instead actively contribute, by advocating, listening to and voting for ideas, and helping to comprehensively reform Irish governance.

This book is the beginning of an attempt to do just that. It does not have all the ideas. There are a great number of young Irish people with insights and ideas for the future; only ten are featured here and we do not claim to speak for all young Irish people. As mentioned, this book is but a sample, showing how a group from the generation of Irish men and women born in the 1970s and 1980s can think differently and constructively. We have not dealt with all the issues; policy discussions on health, civil society, justice and crime we leave to others better placed to help Ireland reinvent itself in those areas. We hope that with this book the conversation is only beginning.

The mistakes made in recent years and the challenges of reforming our public institutions should not obscure Ireland's strengths and its progress. Education and prosperity for this generation of under-40s were hard-won by previous generations, most decisively since the 1950s, when Ireland turned away from economic and cultural isolationism. A new generation is being tested, but we are better placed than any before to meet that test. It's time to get started.

Endnotes

Chapter 2

1. *Irish Times*, 'Department Denies Call to Sack Economist', 20 July 2010.
2. These documents are available on <www.thestory.ie> [accessed 13 January 2011].
3. There were sixteen documents released but only two of these related to the arguments for or against the measure taken within the Department.
4. See, for instance, 'Just Why a Scrappage Scheme Might Help Car Sales', *Irish Independent*, 28 January 2009, or 'Scrappage Plan Could Raise €100m', *Irish Times*, 7 October 2009.
5. See <http://www.irishtimes.com/indepth/renewing-the-republic/> [accessed 13 January 2011].
6. M. Gallagher, 'Does Ireland Need a New Electoral System?', in C. McGrath and E. O'Malley (eds.), *Irish Political Studies: Key Contributions* (London: Routledge, [1987], 2007); David Farrell's paper to the 2010 MacGill Summer School, 'Irish Electoral Reform: Three Myths and a Proposal', available from: <http://politicalreformireland.files.wordpress.com/2010/07/irish_electoral_reform-2.pdf> [accessed 13 January 2011].
7. M. Gallagher, 'The Oireachtas: President and Parliament' in J. Coakley and M. Gallagher (eds.), *Politics in the Republic of Ireland*, fifth edition (London: Routledge, 2010).
8. M. Gallagher, 'Parliamentary Parties and the Party Whips' in M. MacCarthaigh and M. Manning (eds.), *The Oireachtas* (Dublin: Insitute of Public Administration, 2011).
9. There is limited research on how government operates, so we don't really know, and can only rely on what ministers and civil servants say. For a preliminary discussion of government see E. O'Malley and S. Martin, 'The

Government and the Taoiseach' in Coakley and Gallagher, *Politics in the Republic of Ireland*.

10. Ombudsman's Office, *Lost at Sea Scheme: Special Report* (Dublin: The Stationary Office, 2009).

Chapter 3

1. For a (promotional) discussion of the use of online networking tools in the public sector, see IBM, *Five Million People Around the Water-Cooler: How the UK Public Sector can Harness the Power of Social Networking* (IBM, 2008), available from: <https://www-304.ibm.com/easyaccess/publicuk/gclcontent/gcl_xmlid/135297> [accessed 10 December 2010].

2. *OECD Public Management Reviews – Ireland: Towards an Integrated Public Service* (OECD, 2008).

3. See <http://ec.europa.eu/information_society/eeurope/i2010/docs/bench marking/egov_benchmark_2007.pdf> [accessed 10 December 2010].

4. OECD, *Ireland: Towards an Integrated Public Service*, pp. 26–27.

5. See, for example, the reaction by the Civil, Public and Services Union (CPSU) in 2005 to a decision by the Department of Communication to withhold payments due under Sustaining Progress, 'Communication Breakdown', *Aontas* (April/May 2005), p. 13, available from: <http://www.cpsu.ie/images/ContentBuilder/Aontas_May.pdf> [accessed 10 December 2010].

6. Goldsmith Fitzgerald, *Civil Service Commission Staff Retention Survey* (Dublin: Goldsmith Fitzgerald, 1999).

7. Public Sector Pensions Commission, *Reforming Public Sector Pensions: Solutions to a Growing Challenge* (London: Public Sector Pensions Commission, July 2010), available from: <http://www.public-sector-pensions-commission. org.uk/wp-content/themes/pspc/images/Public-Sector-Pensions-Commission-Report.pdf> [accessed 10 December 2010].

8. G. Boyle, R. McElligott and J. O'Leary, 'Public–Private Wage Differentials in Ireland, 1994–2001' (National University of Ireland, Maynooth, 2004), available from: <http://eprints.nuim.ie/147/1/N142_10_04.pdf> [accessed 10 December 2010].

9. Deutsche Bank Research, *Germany 2020: New Challenges for a Land on Expedition* (DB Research, 3 October 2007), available from: <http://www.dbresearch.com/PROD/DBR_INTERNET_EN-PROD/PROD00000000002 10852.pdf> [accessed 10 December 2010].

10. Figures for expenditure and revenue-raising by local government as a proportion of the total come from the OECD National Accounts and Revenue Statistics databases.

11. J.M. Keynes, *The General Theory of Employment, Interest and Money* (London: Macmillan, 1936), p. v (Preface).

Chapter 4

Michael Courtney would like to thank Ronan Lyons, Ed Burke and, in no particular order, Professor Alan Barrett, Erica Dobbs, Monica Sapielak and the Centre for Cultural Practice, Ruairi McKiernan, Artur Banaszkiewicz and the Polish Embassy in Ireland, Q. Abdul, Fidele Mutwarasibo, the Immigrant Council of Ireland, Des Delaney, Professor James Wickham, Ahmet Dursan, the Turkish Embassy in Ireland, Ozlem Akkaya, Dr Hakan Aksoy, Elena Bresolin and the Latin America Solidarity Centre for their advice, assistance and cooperation in completing this chapter.

The opinions expressed by interviewees and survey respondents are their own personal opinions and not the opinions of their affiliated organisations, diplomatic missions or governments.

1. M. Hilliard, 'Union Leader Condones Attacks on Black Drivers', *Sunday Tribune*, 5 April 2009, available from: <http://www.tribune.ie/news/homenews/article/2009/apr/05/union-leader-condones-attacks-on-black-drivers/> [accessed 6 December 2010].

2. Central Statistics Office, *Census 2006: Volume 5 – Ethnic or Cultural Background (including the Irish Traveller Community)* (Dublin: The Stationary Office, 2007).

3. See Chapter 9 for a full description of policy in relation to Ireland's international diaspora.

4. F. Caffrey, 'The List: The World's Best Places to Be an Immigrant', *Foreign Affairs*, 11 February 2008, available from: <http://www.foreignpolicy.com/articles/2008/02/10/the_list_the_worlds_best_places_to_be_an_immigrant> [accessed 6 December 2010].

5. F. Heckmann and D. Schnapper (eds.), *The Integration of Immigrants in European Societies: National Differences and Trends of Convergence* (Stuttgart: Luscious & Luscious, 2007).

6. H. Entzinger and R. Biezeveld, *Benchmarking in Immigrant Integration*, available from: <http://en.scientificcommons.org/17691097> [accessed 6 December 2010].

7. 'French Parliament Passes Burka Ban', *Irish Times*, 13 July 2010, available from: <http://www.irishtimes.com/newspaper/breaking/2010/0713/breaking45.html> [accessed 6 December 2010].

8. E. Sciolino, 'Britain Grapples with Role for Islamic Justice', *New York Times*, 18 October 2008, available from: <http://www.nytimes.com/2008/11/19/world/europe/19shariah.html?_r=1&ref=sharia_islamic_law> [accessed 6 December 2010].

9. I. Hauck, 'Immigrant Integration in Canada: Policy Objectives, Program Delivery and Challenges', *Integration Branch, Citizenship and Immigration Canada*, 16 May 2001, available from: <http://atwork.settlement.org/downloads/atwork/Immigrant_Integration_in_Canada_discussion_paper_Hauck_May01.pdf> [accessed 6 December 2010].

10. Office of the Minister for Integration, 'Migration Nation: Statement on Integration Strategy and Diversity Management' (1 May 2008), available from: <http://www.integration.ie/website/omi/omiwebv6.nsf/page/AXBN-7SQDF91044205-en/$File/Migration%20Nation.pdf> [accessed 6 December 2010].

11. B. Fanning, J. Shaw, J.A. O'Connell and M. Williams, 'Irish Political Parties, Immigration and Integration in 2007', research report on behalf of the Migration and Citizenship Research Initiative, University College Dublin

(25 April 2007), available from: <http://www.ucd.ie/mcri/Political%20 Parties,%20Immigration%20and%20Integration.pdf> [accessed 11 January 2011].

12. R.K. Carty, *Party and Parish Pump: Electoral Politics in Ireland* (Waterloo, ON: Wilfrid Laurier University Press, 1981).

13. G. McElroy and M. Marsh, 'Candidate Gender and Voter Choice: Analysis from a Multi-Member Preferential Voting System', *Political Research Quarterly OnlineFirst* (15 May 2009), pp. 1–12, available from: <http://www. tcd.ie/ines/files/McElroy_and_Marsh_PRQ.pdf> [accessed 11 January 2011]. This study found that Irish voters do not discriminate against female candidates even when there is an opportunity to vote for another candidate from the same party, lending further support to the conclusion that party and constituency work are the dominant determinants of vote choice in Ireland.

14. B. Fanning and F. Mutwarasibo, 'Nationals/Non-Nationals: Immigration, Citizenship and Politics in the Republic of Ireland', *Ethnic and Racial Studies*, Vol. 30, No. 3 (2007), pp. 439–460.

15. B. Fanning, N. O'Boyle and J. Shaw, 'New Irish Politics: Political Parties and Immigrants in 2009', research paper (20 April 2009), available from: <http://www.ucd.ie/mcri/resources/new_irish_politics_report_final.pdf> [accessed 11 January 2011].

16. B. Fanning and N. O'Boyle, 'Immigrant Political Participation in the Republic of Ireland: Socio-Political Capital and Motivational Stakes', working paper series WP09/12, University College Dublin (November 2009), available from: <http://www.ucd.ie/t4cms/wp12_immigrant_political_participation_fanning_o'boyle.pdf> [accessed 6 December 2010].

17. M. O'Regan, 'The Newsmakers: Where Are They Now?', *Irish Times*, 2 August 2010, available from: <http://www.irishtimes.com/newspaper/ireland/2010/0802/1224276043259.html> [accessed 6 December 2010].

18. J. Niessen, T. Huddleston and L. Citron, *Migrant Integration Policy Index* (Brussels: British Council and Migration Policy Group, 2007).

19. *Irish Times*, 'Migrant Workers Need Protection', 8 April 2005, provides a brief summary of the exploitation of migrant workers by Gama Construction and Irish Ferries.

20. J. Marshall, 'Freedom of Religious Expression and Gender Equality: *Sahin v Turkey*', *Modern Law Review*, Vol. 69, No. 3 (May 2006), pp. 459–461.

21. D. Delaney and F. Cavatorta, 'The Exclusion of Denizens within the Irish Social and Political Opportunity Structure: The Cosmopolitan Case of Muslims in the Republic of Ireland' (2010), available from: <http://www. ecprnet.eu/databases/conferences/papers/635.pdf> [accessed 6 December 2010]; *Irish Times*, 'No Directive on Hijabs in Classroom to Be Issued', 9 September 2008.

22. *Irish Times*, 'No Directive on Hijabs in Classroom to Be Issued'.

23. *Irish Times*, 'Bill to Accommodate Sharia Law', 4 February 2010.

24. For a more detailed discussion on the operation of *Sharia* law in Muslim countries see <http://www.cfr.org/publication/8034/islam.html> [accessed 13 January 2011].

25. See <http://www.siptu.ie/PressRoom/NewsReleases/> and <http://www. siptu.ie/hotels/InformationforUnionMembers/> [accessed 13 January 2011].

26. Gaelic Athletic Association, *GAA Inclusion and Integration Strategy 2009–2015* (30 September 2008), available from: <http://www.gaa.ie/content/documents/publications/inclusion_and_integration/GAA_Inclusion_Integration_Strategy_100110225137.pdf> [accessed 6 December 2010]; Football Association of Ireland, 'FAI Unites against Racism' (18 October 2006), available from: <http://www.fai.ie/index.php?option=com_content&view=article&id=1295&catid=80:archive&Itemid=355> [accessed 11 January 2011].

27. Survey conducted by author.

Chapter 5

1. Demographic estimates from the Central Statistics Office (CSO), Population and Migration Estimates, 2010.

2. Of 31 developed economies covered in the *OECD Economic Outlook* (Paris: OECD, September 2010), output rose in 13 between 2007 and 2010 and only in 11 countries did output fall by more than 2 per cent. Ireland's fall in GDP is estimated by the OECD at 11 per cent.

3. Sources: Employment and export statistics: CSO. E-commerce and motor-way statistics: Eurostat.

4. See O. Blanchard, Comments on P. Honohan and B. Walsh, 'Catching Up With the Leaders: The Irish Hare', *Brookings Papers on Economic Activity*, Vol. 1 (2002), pp. 58–67.

5. Source: IBM Global Investment Locations Database, *Annual Report 2008*.

6. R. Thom, 'The Influence of Sterling on Irish Interest Rates', *Economic and Social Review*, Vol. 26, No.4(1995), pp. 403–416.

7. See, for example, *Straits Times*, 'Iceland to Adopt Euro?', 30 November 2008, available from: <http://www.straitstimes.com/Breaking+News/Money/Story/STIStory_308577.html> [accessed 3 December 2010] and *The Guardian*, 'Opposition to Euro Wanes in Sweden and Denmark', 27 November 2008, available from: <http://www.guardian.co.uk/business/2008/nov/27/euro-currencies-sweden-denmark> [accessed 3 December 2010].

8. The real interest rate is the nominal interest rate minus the inflation rate. If the nominal interest rate is 4% and there is an inflation of 5%, the real interest rate will be negative (4-5= -1%). With deflation, a low nominal interest rate can be high in real terms. For example, a nominal interest rate of 4% in a deflationary environment where the price level drops 5% gives a real interest rate of 4-(-5) = 9%.

9. All figures come from the OECD Stat.extracts service, *11. Government Expenditure by Function* (Stats.OECD, extracted 3 December 2010), available from: <http://stats.oecd.org/Index.aspx?DataSetCode=SNA_TABLE11>, with the exception of wages data, which come from the CSO.

10. All figures from *Taxing Wages* (OECD, 11 May 2010), available from: <http://www.oecd.org/document/34/0,3343,en_2649_34533_44993442_1_1_1_1,00.html> [accessed 3 December 2010].

11. A 2006 Bank of Ireland *Wealth of the Nation* report found that almost three-quarters (72 per cent) of all Irish wealth was held in property.

12. R. Kitchin, J. Gleeson, K. Keaveney and C. O'Callaghan, 'A Haunted Landscape: Housing and Ghost Estates in Post-Celtic Tiger Ireland', NUI Maynooth, NIRSA working paper series no. 59 (2010).

13. European Mortgage Federation, *Hypostat 2007*, available from: <http://www. hypo.org/Content/default.asp?pageId=524> [accessed 4 February 2011].

14. K. Regling and M. Watson, *A Preliminary Report on the Sources of Ireland's Banking Crisis* (Dublin: Commission of Investigation into the Banking Sector in Ireland, 31 May 2010), available from: <http://www.bankingin-quiry.gov.ie/Preliminary%20Report%20into%20Ireland's%20Banking%20 Crisis%2031%20May%202010.pdf> [accessed 3 December 2010].

15. See, for example, F. Ruane and R. Lyons, 'Wage Determination in the Irish Economy'; and J. O'Leary, 'Benchmarking the Benchmarkers', both in *ESRI Quarterly Economic Commentary* (Winter 2002).

16. W. Münchau, 'Berlin Weaves a Deficit Hair-Shirt for Us All', *Financial Times*, 21 June 2010.

17. See F.G. Barry, 'Fiscal Policy in a Small Open Economy with Unemployment and Capital Accumulation', *Scandinavian Journal of Economics*, Vol. 87, No. 3 (September 1985), pp. 474–486.

18. *Der Spiegel*, 'EU Commission Plans Closer Oversight of National Budgets', 12 May 2010, available from: <http://www.spiegel.de/international/ europe/0,1518,694583,00.html> [accessed 3 December 2010].

19. Ernst & Young, *Quarterly Economic Forecast* (April 2010).

20. European Commission, *Communication from the Commission to the European Parliament, the European Council, the Council, the European Central Bank, the Economic and Social Council and the Committee of the Regions: Reinforcing Economic Policy Coordination* (Brussels: European Commission, 12 May 2010), COM(2010) 250 Final, pp. 6–7.

21. Many of the current objections to public service charges are due to concerns about double taxation, suggesting some awareness of the relationship between services, general taxation and prices.

22. E. Clark, *Eco-Economy Update Series* (Washington, DC: Earth Policy Institute, 2007).

23. In that sense, a stamp duty was essentially a tax on moving home and thus reduced labour mobility and more than likely increased congestion costs.

24. R. Miller, *'Digital Universe' Nears a Zettabyte* (Data Center Knowledge, 4 May 2010), available from: <http://www.datacenterknowledge.com/ archives/2010/05/04/digital-universe-nears-a-zettabyte/> [accessed 3 December 2010].

25. See G. Van Der Veen, 'Changing Statistics Netherlands: Driving Forces for Changing Dutch Statistics', paper presented at the Seminar on the Evolution of National Statistical Systems Commemorative Event for the Sixtieth Anniversary of the United Nations Statistical Commission, New York, 23 February 2007.

Chapter 6

1. T. Mun, *England's Treasure by Forraign Trade* (New York: MacMillan and Co., 1895), p. 119 [reprint from the original 1664 book].

2. World Economic Forum, *Global Competitiveness Report* (Geneva: WEF, 2010); Institute for Management Development, *World Competitiveness Yearbook* (2010), available from: <https://www.worldcompetitiveness.com/OnLine/App/Index.htm> [accessed 18 January 2011].

3. M.E. Porter, C. Ketels and M. Delgado, 'The Microeconomic Foundations of Prosperity: Findings from the Business Competitiveness Index', in *Global Competitiveness Report 2006–2007* (Geneva: World Economic Forum, 2006).

4. National Competitiveness Council, *Annual Competitiveness Report: Benchmarking Ireland's Performance 2010* (Dublin: NCC, 2010), p. 10.

5. National Competitiveness Council, *Ireland's Productivity Performance 2006* (Dublin: NCC, 2006).

6. *Ibid.*

7. *Ibid.*

8. National Competitiveness Council, *Annual Competitiveness Report 2010* (Dublin: NCC, 2006).

9. *Ibid.*

10. Porter, Ketels and Delgado, 'The Microeconomic Foundations of Prosperity', p. 53.

11. The WEF competitiveness framework is based on eleven components: institutions, infrastructure, macroeconomic environment, health and primary education, higher education and training, goods market efficiency, labour market efficiency, financial market development, technological readiness, market size, and business sophistication and innovation.

12. National Competitiveness Council, *Annual Competitiveness Report 2010*.

13. *Ibid.*

14. National Competitiveness Council, *Statement on Education and Training* (Dublin: NCC, 2009).

15. Department of Education and Science, *Report of the Project Maths Implementation Support Group* (June 2010), available from: <http://www.iua.ie/media-and-events/press-releases/releases/2007/documents/ReportoftheProjectMathsImplementationSupportGroup9June2010.pdf> [accessed 19 January 2011].

16. National Competitiveness Council, *Statement on Education and Training*. Though still unacceptably high at 11.5 per cent in 2007, the proportion of early school leavers compares favourably to 15 per cent in 2000 and an EU-15 average of 16.9 per cent in 2007.

17. *Ibid.*

18. C. Hidalgo and R. Hausmann, 'The Building Blocks of Economic Complexity', Center for International Development working paper no. 186 (September 2009).

19. National Competitiveness Council, *Costs of Doing Business in Ireland 2010 Volume 1* (Dublin: NCC, 2010).

20. Bill and Melinda Gates Foundation, *Working with Teachers to Develop Fair and Reliable Measures of Effective Teaching (MET)* (June 2010), available from: <http://www.gatesfoundation.org/highschools/Documents/met-framing-paper.pdf> [accessed 11 January 2011]. The goal of the MET project is to improve the quality of information about teaching effectiveness available to education professionals within states and districts.

21. R. Gordon, T. Kane and D. Staiger, 'Identifying Effective Teachers Using Performance on the Job', The Brookings Institute discussion paper 2006-01 (2006). According to this research for the US, certification of teachers bears little relationship to teacher effectiveness (measured by impacts on student achievement). Further research would be necessary to ascertain whether this is also the case in Ireland.

22. Department of Education and Science, *Report of the Project Maths Implementation Support Group* (Dublin: Department of Education and Science, June 2010).

23. C. Conneely, J. Lawlor and B. Tangney, 'Towards a Pragmatic Model for Group-Based, Technology-Mediated, Project-Orientated Learning: An Overview of the B2C Model' in N.D. Lytras et al. (eds.), *Tech-Education: Communications in Computer and Information Science*, Vol. 73 (2010), pp. 602–609.

24. W. Korte and T. Hüsing, *Benchmarking Access and Use of ICT in European Schools* (Empirica, November 2006), available from: <http://www.empirica.com/publikationen/documents/No08-2006_learnInd.pdf> [accessed 19 January 2011].

25. Organisation for Economic Co-Operation and Development, *Technology Use and Educational Performance in PISA 2006* (Paris: OECD, March 2010).

26. J. Ryan, *The Next Leap: Competitive Ireland in the Digital Age* (Dublin: IIEA, 2008).

27. See <http://www.tcd.ie/funding-priorities/priority/participation/bridge.php> for further details [accessed 11 January 2011].

28. World Bank, World Development Indicators Online Database 2011, available from: <http://data.worldbank.org/data-catalog/world-development-indicators> [accessed 19 January 2011].

29. V. Gray, T. Kelly and M. Minges, *Broadband Korea: Internet Case Study* (International Telecommunication Union, March 2003), available from: <http://www.itu.int/ITU-D/ict/cs/korea/material/CS_KOR.pdf> [accessed 19 January 2011].

30. According to figures from the OECD, Ireland lags behind leading countries in terms of upgrading the broadband network to fibre optics. In Ireland, less than 1 per cent of connections are over fibre, compared to 51 per cent in Japan, 46 per cent in South Korea and 21 per cent in Sweden. See Table 6.2.

31. These three sectors were highlighted by a 2008 report by the IIEA called *The Next Leap: Competitive Advantage in the Digital Era* and proposals in the area of digital media and cloud computing won the Your County, Your Call competition in 2010.

32. M. Porter, 'Building the Microeconomic Foundations of Prosperity: Findings from the Business Competitiveness Index', in X. Sala-i-Martin (ed.), *The Global Competitiveness Report 2003–2004* (New York: Oxford University Press, 2004).

33. Ryan, *The Next Leap*.

34. Eurostat, *Economy and Finance Indicators* (2010), available from: <http://epp.eurostat.ec.europa.eu/portal/page/portal/eurostat/home/> [accessed 11 January 2011].

35. National Competitiveness Council, *Costs of Doing Business in Ireland 2010*.

36. *Ibid*.

37. Department of the Taoiseach, *Towards 2016: Ten-Year Framework Social Partnership Agreement, 2006–2015* (Dublin: The Stationary Office, 2006).

Chapter 7

1. *New York Times*, 'Oil Prices Pass Record Set in '80s but then Recede', 3 March 2008.
2. Sustainable Energy Authority of Ireland, *Energy in Ireland 1990–2008* (Dublin: SEAI, 2009).
3. *Financial Times*, 'Oil Shock "Likely" within Decade, Warns Huhne', 23 July 2010.
4. S. Solomon, D. Qin, M. Manning, Z. Chen, M. Marquis, K.B. Averyt, M.Tignor and H.L. Miller (eds.), *Climate Change 2007: The Physical Science Basis*, contribution of Working Group I to the *Fourth Assessment Report* of the Intergovernmental Panel on Climate Change (Cambridge and New York: Cambridge University Press, 2007), p. 5 and p. 10.
5. *The Guardian*, 'World Feeling the Heat as 17 Countries Experience Record Temperatures', 12 August 2010.
6. See, for example, H.D. Pritchard, R.J. Arthern, D.G. Vaughan and L.A. Edwards, 'Extensive Dynamic Thinning on the Margins of the Greenland and Antarctic Ice Sheets', *Nature*, Vol. 461 (15 October 2009), pp. 971–975; or W.T. Pfeffer, J.T. Harper and S. O'Neel, 'Kinematic Constraints on Glacier Contributions to 21st-Century Sea-Level Rise', *Science*, Vol. 321 (5 September 2008), pp. 1340–1343.
7. Department of Industry, Commerce and Energy, *Energy-Ireland: Discussion Document on Some Current Energy Problems and Options* (Dublin: The Stationary Office, 1978), p. 43.
8. *Ibid.*
9. Danish Energy Agency, *Energy Statistics 2009* (Copenhagen: DEA, 2010), available from: <http://www.ens.dk/en-US/Info/FactsAndFigures/Energy_statistics_and_indicators/Annual%20Statistics/Documents/Energi%20Statistics%202009.pdf> [accessed 20 December 2010].
10. Department of Industry, Commerce and Energy, *Energy-Ireland*, p. 80.
11. *Ibid.*
12. O. Coughlan, 'Irish Climate-Change Policy from Kyoto to the Carbon Tax: A Two-Level Game Analysis of the Interplay of Knowledge and Power', *Irish Studies in International Affairs*, Vol. 18 (2007), pp. 131–153.
13. Government of Ireland, *Limitation and Reduction of CO$_2$ and Other Greenhouse Gases in Ireland*, report prepared by Environmental Resources Management in association with Byrne Ó Clérigh and the Economic and Social Research Institute for the Department of Public Enterprise and the Department of the Environment (Dublin: The Stationary Office, 1998).
14. *Ibid.*
15. European Environmental Agency, *The Contribution of Good Environmental Regulation to Competitiveness* (Copenhagen: EEA, 2005).
16. M.S. Andersen, T. Barker, E. Christie, P. Ekins, J.F. Gerald, J. Jilkova, S. Junankar, M. Landesmann, H. Pollitt, R. Salmons, S. Scott and S. Speck

(eds.), *Competitiveness Effects of Environmental Tax Reforms* (Aarhus: National Environmental Research Institute, 2007).

17. R. Kitchin, J. Gleeson, K. Keaveney, and C. O'Callaghan, 'A Haunted Landscape: Housing and Ghost Estates in Ireland' (Maynooth: The National Institute for Regional and Spatial Analysis (NIRSA), 2010), pp. 37–46.

18. *Irish Times*, 'European Environment Agency Cites Dublin as a Worst-Case Scenario of Urban Planning', 4 October 2006.

19. J.P. Clinch and J. Healy, 'Domestic Energy Efficiency in Ireland: Correcting Market Failure', *Energy Policy*, Vol. 28, No. 1 (2000), pp. 1–8.

20. Department of the Environment, Heritage and Local Government, *Carbon Budget Statement 2010* (11 December 2009), Appendix 1, p. 28, available from: <http://www.environ.ie/en/Publications/Environment/Atmosphere/PublicationsDocuments/FileDownLoad,21822,en.pdf> [accessed 12 December 2010].

21. European Automobile Manufacturers' Association, 'New Vehicle Registrations by Country' (2008), available from: <http://www.acea.be/index.php/news/news_detail/new_vehicle_registrations_by_country/> [accessed 10 November 2010].

22. Sustainable Energy Authority of Ireland, *Transport Energy Usage in Ireland* (2010), available from: <http://www.seai.ie/Power_of_One/Getting_Around/HCIYC/Transport_Energy_Usage/> [accessed 15 September 2010].

23. Carbon dioxide equivalent (CO_2-eq) is the measurement used for greenhouse gases. All greenhouse gases (methane, nitrous oxide and carbon dioxide) have different warming potentials per tonne, and CO_2-eq converts them all into the warming potential of CO_2 (e.g. 1 tonne methane = 21 tonne CO_2-eq).

24. Environmental Protection Agency, *Ireland's Greenhouse Gas Emissions Projections 2010–2020* (28 April 2010), available from: <http://www.epa.ie/downloads/pubs/air/airemissions/EPA_GHG_Emission_Projections_2010.pdf> [accessed 16 October 2010].

25. Department of Agriculture, Fisheries and Food, *Food Harvest 2020: A Vision for Irish Agri-Food and Fisheries* (Dublin: The Stationary Office, July 2010).

26. *Ibid.*, p. 23.

27. J. Curtin, J. Donoghue and M. Dowling (eds.), *From Farm to Fork: A Sustainability Enhancement Programme for Irish Agriculture* (Dublin: IIEA, 2009).

28. B. Motherway and N. Walker, *Ireland's Low Carbon Opportunity* (Dublin: SEAI, 2009).

29. J. Curtin, *Jobs, Growth and Reduced Energy Costs: Greenprint for a National Energy Efficiency Retrofit Programme* (Dublin: IIEA, 2009).

30. See also Chapter 3 for a discussion on the potential of local authority bonds and the importance of a property tax.

31. Baseload plants are the production facilities used to meet some or all of a given region's continuous energy demand and produce energy at a constant rate, usually at a low cost relative to other production facilities available to the system.

32. Eirgrid, *Grid 25: A Strategy for the Development of Ireland's Electricity Grid for a Sustainable and Competitive Future* (Dublin: Eirgrid, 2008).

33. Department of Energy, Communications and Natural Resources, *Delivering a Sustainable Energy Future for Ireland*, Energy White Paper (Dublin: DCENR, 2007), available from: <http://www.dcenr.gov.ie/NR/rdonlyres/54C78A1E-4E96-4E28-A77A-3226220DF2FC/27356/EnergyWhitePaper12 March2007.pdf> [accessed 20 December 2010].

34. The impact of decentralisation – or, more accurately, administrative reloca-tion – on the performance of Ireland's public service is discussed in more detail in Chapter 3.

35. Danish Commission on Climate Change Policy, *Green Energy: The Road to a Danish Energy System without Fossil Fuels* (Copenhagen: DCCCP, 2010).

Chapter 8

1. J. Powell, *Great Hatred, Little Room: Making Peace in Northern Ireland* (London: The Bodley Head, 2008), p. 106.

2. K. Hannon, 'Tiocfaidh Ár Mercs, He Said Crossing the Border', *Irish Examiner*, 14 December 1999, available from: <http://archives.tcm.ie/irishexaminer/1999/12/14/i_text.htm> [accessed 30 July 2010].

3. J. Todd, 'Northern Ireland: From Multiphased Conflict to Multilevelled Settlement', *Nationalism and Ethnic Politics*, Vol. 15, No. 3 (2009), pp. 336–354.

4. *Ibid.*, p. 336.

5. J. Coakley and L. O'Dowd (eds.), *Crossing the Border: New Relationships between Northern Ireland and the Republic of Ireland* (Dublin: Irish Academic Press, 2007), p. 10.

6. T. Garvin, *Judging Lemass: The Measure of the Man* (Dublin: Royal Irish Academy, 2009), pp. 3–4.

7. J. McGarry and B. O'Leary, *The Northern Ireland Conflict: Consociational Engagements* (Oxford: Oxford University Press, 2004).

8. D. De Breadún, *The Far Side of Revenge: Making Peace in Northern Ireland* (Cork: The Collins Press, 2008), p. 208.

9. J. Tonge, *The New Northern Irish Politics?* (Basingstoke: Palgrave Macmillan, 2005), p. 166.

10. Coakley and O'Dowd, *Crossing the Border*, p. 39.

11. Maryfield: building which housed Irish civil servants in Belfast and gave the Irish government a role in Northern Ireland, agreed under the Anglo Irish Agreement.

12. T. Blair, *A Journey* (London: Hutchinson, 2010).

13. G. Walker, 'The British–Irish Council', in R. Wilford (ed.), *Aspects of the Belfast Agreement* (New York: Oxford University Press, 2001).

14. British Council Ireland, *Through Irish Eyes: Irish Attitudes towards the UK* (London: British Council Ireland, 2004).

15. J. Darby and R. MacGinty (eds.), *Contemporary Peacemaking: Conflict, Violence and Peace Processes* (Basingstoke and New York: Palgrave and Macmillan, 2003).

16. Community Relations Council, *Towards Sustainable Security: Interface Barriers and the Legacy of Segregation in Belfast* (Belfast: CRC, 2008).

17. J. Hughes, A. Campbell, M. Hewstone and E. Cairns, 'Segregation in Northern Ireland: Implications for Community Relations Policy', *Policy Studies*, Vol. 28, No. 1 (2007), pp. 33–53.

18. R.D. Osborne, 'Education and the Labour Market', in R.D. Osborne and I. Shuttleworth (eds.), *Fair Employment in Northern Ireland: A Generation On* (Belfast: Blackstaff Press, 2004), p. 72.

19. Deloitte, *Research into the Financial Cost of the Northern Ireland Divide* (Belfast: Deloitte, 2007).

20. E. Tannam, 'Public Policy: The EU and the Good Friday Agreement', in Coakley and O'Dowd, *Crossing the Border*, p. 115.

21. Andy Pollak, speaking on cross-border issues at the Joint Committee of the Implementation of the Good Friday Agreement (19 November 2009), available online: <http://debates.oireachtas.ie/DDebate.aspx?F= GFJ20091119. xml&Node=H2&Page=3> [accessed 30 July 2010].

22. Central Statistics Office, *Ireland, North and South: A Statistical Profile* (2008), available from: <http://www.cso.ie/releasespublications/ documents/other_releases/northsouth2008/labourmarket.pdf> [accessed 30 July 2010].

23. GVA is the value of goods and services produced in an area, industry or sector of an economy.

24. Oxford Economics and Economic Research Institute of Northern Ireland, *Cutting Carefully: How Repairing UK Finances Will Impact NI*, a report for NICVA (2010), available from: <http://www.nicva.org/sites/default/ files/Oxford%20Economics%20Report%20-%20impact%20on%20NI%20 July%202010.pdf> [accessed 30 July 2010].

25. The border region bodies: the North-West Regional Cross-Border Group, the East Border Region (EBR), the Border, Midland and Western (BMW) Regional Assembly, the Border Region Authority, the Irish Central Border Area Network, the European Regions Network for the Application of Communications Technology (ERNACT), and the EU Committee on the Regions.

26. The report is formally known as *A New Beginning: Policing in Northern Ireland*. It was carried out by the Independent Commission on Policing for Northern Ireland, and was chaired by the British Conservative politician Chris Patten. It investigated and recommended very detailed changes on policing in Northern Ireland, which had major practical and symbolic significance, such as changing the name of the Royal Ulster Constabulary, the establishment of the Police Ombudsman and 50:50 Catholic–Protestant recruitment to the new Police Service of Northern Ireland.

27. International Monitoring Commission, *The Twenty-Third Report of the International Monitoring Commission* (Belfast: IMC, 2010).

28. Europol, *TE-SAT 2010 EU Terrorism and Situation Trend Report* (2010), available from: <http://www.consilium.europa.eu/uedocs/cmsUpload/ TE-SAT%202010.pdf> [accessed 30 July 2010].

29. Separatist here means dissident republicans, and is measured and adjusted for population size.

30. R. Dudley Edwards, *Aftermath: The Omagh Bombing and the Families' Pursuit of Justice* (London: Harvill Secker Random House, 2009), p. 95.

31. D. McAleese, 'Matt Baggott: I Don't Have a Problem with the Viewpoint of Dissidents ... I Have a Problem When Bullies Get Too Much Space', *Belfast Telegraph*, 1 December 2010.

32. G. Moriarty, 'McAleese Attends PSNI Graduation', *Irish Times*, 23 July 2010, available from: <http://www.irishtimes.com/newspaper/breaking/2010/0723/breaking40.html> [accessed 30 July 2010].

33. H. McDonald, 'Real IRA Target Banks: "They Branded Banks as Criminals"', *The Guardian*, 14 September 2010, available from: <http://www.guardian.co.uk/uk/audio/2010/sep/14/real-ira-northern-ireland-banks> [accessed 14 September 2010].

34. Consultative Group on the Past, *Report of the Consultative Group on the Past* (Belfast: CGP, 2009), available from: <http://www.irishtimes.com/focus/2009/troubles/index.pdf> [accessed 30 July 2010].

Chapter 9

1. M. Wolf, 'Will the Nation State Survive Globalisation?', *Foreign Affairs*, Vol. 80, No. 1 (November/December 2001), pp. 178–190.

2. K. Aikins, A. Sands and N. White, *A Comparative Review of International Diaspora Strategies: The Global Irish Making a Difference Together* (The Ireland Funds, September 2009), available from: <http://www.irlfunds.org/news/ffund/diaspora.asp> [accessed 10 October 2010].

3. The word 'diaspora' comes from the Greek *dia* meaning 'through' or 'over' and *speiro* meaning 'dispersal' or 'to sow'. Diaspora traditionally referred to a very specific situation: the exile of the Jews from the Holy Land and their dispersal throughout the globe. The word is now used to refer to the overseas population of many countries.

4. Aikins, Sands and White, *A Comparative Review of International Diaspora Strategies*.

5. J. Hunt, 'Lessons in How to Go Big from Silicon Valley Success', *Irish Times*, 26 November 2010.

6. T.M. Nielsen and L. Riddle, 'Why Diasporas Invest in the Homeland: A Conceptual Model of Motivation', working paper series, George Washington University, Washington DC (1 July 2007).

7. J.P. Dolan, *The Irish-Americans: A History* (London: Bloomsbury, 2008).

8. Department of Foreign Affairs, *The Global Irish Economic Forum: One Year On* (Dublin: DFA, October 2010), p. 4.

9. The government is working to establish a programme to facilitate up to 500 Irish graduate placements abroad; the initial focus will be in Asia. In May 2010, the government announced funding of €135,000 towards a new Farmleigh Fellowship Programme, which provides 25 Irish participants the opportunity to work in Asia for four months, and to participate in a joint M.Sc. degree in Asian Business Management from University College Cork and Nanyang Business School in Singapore.

10. S. Ketkar and D. Ratha, 'Diaspora Bonds as a New Vehicle for Developing Countries', paper presented at the Privatisation of Development Finance Assistance Symposium, New York, 4 December 2009.

11. See C. Arthur, 'You Want an Interactive Map of Where Facebook Is Used? Happy to Help' (*Guardian.co.uk*, 22 July 2010), available from: <http://www.guardian.co.uk/technology/blog/2010/jul/22/facebook-countries-population-use> [accessed 7 January 2011].

12. S. Connolly, 'Once More our Biggest Export Is our People', *Irish Examiner*, 3 December 2010.

13. *Business and Leadership*, 'US Investment in Ireland Is Greater than in China and Russia', 8 November 2010, available from: <http://www.business andleadership.com/economy/item/26532-us-investment-greater-in-ir> [accessed 11 December 2010].

14. *Irish Examiner*, 'Brain Drain: 100 Graduates Flee a Week to Find Work', 25 August 2010, available from: <http://www.irishexaminer.ie/ireland/brain-drain-100-graduates-a-week-flee-to-find-work-128833.html> [accessed 14 January 2011].

15. C. Coonan, 'EU Calls on China to Open Up Trade', *Irish Times*, 3 September 2010.

16. F. Audley, 'Ireland's Emigration Figure the Highest in the EU', *Irish Post*, 5 August 2010.

17. T. Debass and M. Ardovino, 'Diaspora Direct Investment (DDI): The Untapped Resource for Development', USAID working paper (Washington DC: USAID, 19 May 2009), available from: <http://pdf.usaid.gov/pdf_docs/PNADO983.pdf> [accessed 7 January 2011].

18. Department of Foreign Affairs, *The Global Irish Economic Forum: One Year On*, p. 3.

19. The question of voting rights for Irish citizens living abroad was most recently considered in 2002, by the All-Party Committee on the Constitution. In relation to emigrant participation in political life, the Committee concluded that the right to vote in Oireachtas elections should remain confined to citizens ordinarily resident in the state. However, the renewed Fianna Fáil–Green Party *Programme for Government*, agreed in October 2009, mandates that recommendations should be made on the feasibility of extending the franchise for presidential elections to the Irish abroad.

20. L. Saxe, B. Phillips, T. Sasson et al., *Generation Birthright Israel: The Impact of an Israel Experience on Jewish Identity and Choices* (Waltham, MA: Maurice & Marilyn Cohen Center for Jewish Studies, Brandeis University, October 2009).

21. See the website of Taglit-Birthright Israel at <www.birthrightisrael.com>.

22. Remarks by President McAleese at the ÉAN Emigrant Advice Network Annual International Conference, All Hallows College, Dublin, 30 November 2005.

Chapter 10

The author would like to thank Daniel Keohane, Hugo Brady and Ben Tonra for their generous insights in commenting on earlier versions of this draft. However, the views contained in this chapter are those of the author alone.

1. Ministry of Foreign Affairs of the Kingdom of Sweden, *Statement of Government Policy in the Parliamentary Debate on Foreign Affairs 2010* (Stockholm: Ministry of Foreign Affairs of Sweden, 2010).

2. T. Garton Ash, 'The View from Beijing Tells You Why We Need a European Foreign Policy', *The Guardian*, 10 November 2010.

3. U. Dadush and B. Stancil, 'The G20 in 2050', *International Economic Bulletin* (Washington DC: Carnegie Endowment for International Peace, 2009).

4. The Peace of Westphalia, signed in 1648, is considered to have ushered in a new international order that ended the Wars of Religion in Europe and which, above all, emphasised the non-interference of states in the domestic affairs of other sovereign states. See <http://www.schillerinstitute.org/strategic/treaty_of_westphalia.html>.

5. B. Laffan and J. O'Mahony, *Ireland and the European Union* (London: Palgrave and Macmillan, 2008), p. 52.

6. Department of Foreign Affairs, *Statement of Strategy: 2008–2010* (Dublin: DFA, 2007), p. 7.

7. Laffan and O'Mahony, *Ireland and the European Union*, p. 179.

8. D. Keohane, *Making Sense of the European Security and Defence Policy: Ireland and the Lisbon Treaty* (Dublin: IIEA, 2009).

9. I. Bagehi, 'Austria, Ireland against NSG Waiver for India', *Times of India*, 6 September 2008.

10. For example, the Swiss Ministry of Foreign Affairs' conflict resolution budget amounted to just under €15 million for 2007 alone, while Norway provided funding of €5.1 million alone in the same year to four non-governmental Norwegian international conflict resolution institutes. See Ministry of Foreign Affairs of the Federal Republic of Switzerland, *Peace and Human Rights in Switzerland's Foreign Policy* (2007), available from: <http://www.eda.admin.ch/etc/medialib/downloads/edazen/doc/publi.Par.0261.File.tmp/EDA%20Bericht%2007%20e%20V.pdf> [accessed 16 January 2011]; and the Ministry of Foreign Affairs of the Kingdom of Norway, *Evaluation of the Norwegian Research and Development Activities in Conflict and Peace-Building* (2008), available from: <http://www.norad.no/en/Tools+and+publications/Publications/Publication+Page?key=109834> [accessed 16 January 2011].

11. Interview by the author with a former senior UN Secretariat official, Madrid, 29 October 2010.

12. E. Connolly and J. Doyle, 'The Place of the United Nations in Contemporary Irish Foreign Policy', in M. Kennedy and D. MacMahon (eds.), *Obligations and Responsibilities: Ireland and the United Nations, 1955–2005* (Dublin: Institute of Public Administration and Department of Foreign Affairs, 2005), pp. 362–383.

13. H. O'Neill, 'Ireland's Foreign Aid in 2008', *Irish Studies in International Affairs*, Vol. 20 (2009), pp. 194–222.

14. Organisation for Economic Co-Operation and Development – Development Assistance Committee, *Peer Review: Ireland* (2009), p. 19, available from: <http://www.oecd.org/dataoecd/50/1/42704390.pdf>[accessed 7 December 2010].

15. Sub-Committee on Ireland's Future in the European Union, *Ireland's Future in the European Union: Challenges, Issues and Options* (Dublin: Houses of the Oireachtas, November 2008), p. 22.

16. Data on CAP and Irish agricultural and trade policy is taken from N. Rees, B. Quinn and B. Connaughton, *Europeanisation and New Patterns of*

Governance in Ireland (Manchester: Manchester University Press, 2009), pp. 145–167.

17. C. Davis, 'A Conflict of Institutions? The EU and GATT/WTO Dispute Adjudication', paper for the Department of Politics, Princeton University (12 March 2007), available from: <http://www.princeton.edu/~cldavis/files/euwto.pdf> [accessed 15 January 2011].

18. S. Taylor, 'A New German Language', *European Voice*, 27 May 2010.

19. Laffan and O'Mahony, *Ireland and the European Union*, p. 32.

20. Speech by the Minister for Foreign Affairs of the Federal Republic of Germany, Joschka Fischer, Dublin, 30 April 2001, see *Irish Times*, available from: <http://www.irishtimes.com/newspaper/special/2001/fischer/index.htm> [accessed 18 January 2011].

21. B. Keenan, 'Ministers Didn't Listen to Europe in 2001, They Have to Listen Now', *Irish Independent*, 28 October 2010.

22. *Ibid.* See also Chapter 5 in this volume.

23. A. Willis, 'Irish Commissioner Critical of Sarkozy', *EU Observer*, 20 December 2009.

24. Rees, Quinn and Connaughton, *Europeanisation and New Patterns of Governance in Ireland*, p. 77.

25. Courts Service of Ireland, *Crotty vs. An Taoiseach* (1987), available from: <http://www.courts.ie/supremecourt/sclibrary3.nsf/(WebFiles)/BD8 14893E95839F78025765E003BC6AA/$FILE/Crotty%20v%20An%20 Taoiseach_1987.rtf> [accessed 16 January 2011].

26. Oireachtas reform is discussed in greater detail in Chapter 2.

27. See, for example, Ministry of Foreign Affairs of the Kingdom of Norway, *Evaluation of the Norwegian Research and Development Activities in Conflict and Peace-Building*.

28. D. O'Brien, *Ireland, Europe and the World: Writings on a New Century* (Dublin: Gill and Macmillian, 2009), p. 113.

29. D. Korski and R. Gowan, *Can the EU Rebuild Failing States? A Review of Europe's Civilian Capacities* (Brussels: European Council on Foreign Relations, 2009).

30. M. Hennigan, *Irish Trade Statistics: Policymakers Opt for Spain and Delusion rather than Confront Challenging Facts* (Finfacts, 12 August 2007), available from: <http://www.finfacts.ie/irishfinancenews/article_1010787.shtml> [accessed 17 January 2011].

31. Although it has less than 1 per cent of the EU's population, Ireland attracted 25 per cent of all new US investment to the EU between 1995 and 2005; Sub-Committee on Ireland's Future in the European Union, *Ireland's Future in the European Union*, p. 20.

32. B. Laffan quoted in J. Burns, 'The Fat that Needs Trimming from Ireland's Diplomatic Belly', *Sunday Times*, 14 March 2010.

33. Secretary General of the Department of Foreign Affairs' Testimony before the Oireachtas Public Accounts Committee, Houses of the Oireachtas, 21 January 2010, available from: <http://debates.oireachtas.ie/ACC/2010/01/21/00003.asp> [accessed 15 December 2010].

34. This reflects a broader trend of rigidity within the Irish public service that is developed in Chapter 3.

35. J. Mustonen, F. Stepputat, G. Grönberg, K. Friis and S. Rehman, *Nordic Approaches to Whole-of-Government: In Afghanistan and Beyond* (Oslo: Norwegian Institute of International Affairs, 2010).

36. Rees, Quinn and Connaughton, *Europeanisation and New Patterns of Governance in Ireland*, p. 71.

37. A. Cahill, 'Ireland Facing Court Action over EU Rules Failure', *Irish Examiner*, 26 June 2010.

38. Laffan and O'Mahony, *Ireland and the European Union*, p. 72.

39. It is noticeable, for example, that Ireland, one of only two European countries to contribute contingents to the original UN peacekeeping mission to the Congo in the 1960s (ONUC), has not contributed to its successor (MONUC), currently the UN's largest peacekeeping commitment. See also a statement by then Minister for Defence, Sean Barrett, on Ireland's decision not to deploy a further commitment to UNOSOM II, Houses of the Oireachtas, *Dail Debates* (1995), available from: <http://debates.oireachtas.ie/dail/1995/10/19/00004.asp> [accessed 17 January 2010].

40. J. McEnro, 'Department Defends €3m Blunder on Chad Helicopters', *Irish Examiner*, 13 November 2009; and C. Lally, 'Officer's Book on Irish Mission in Chad Gives Frank Account of Events', *Irish Times*, 30 September 2010.

41. Keohane, *Making Sense of the European Security and Defence Policy*.

42. See UK Department for International Development (DFID), *Quick Impact Projects: A Handbook for the Military* (2006), available from: <http://webarchive.nationalarchives.gov.uk/+/http://www.dfid.gov.uk/pubs/files/qip/booklet.pdf> [accessed 17 January 2011].

43. T. Barber, 'Hanging by a Thread in Chad', *Financial Times*, 13 February 2010.

44. Helen O'Neill, 'Ireland's Foreign Aid in 2008', p. 201.

45. Decentralisation is discussed in more detail in Chapter 3.

46. An Taoiseach, Brian Cowen, quoted in M. Minihan and M. O'Regan, 'Opposition to Be Briefed on State's Financial Position', *Irish Times*, 18 October 2010.

47. M. O'Halloran, 'Minister Denies EU Officials Are Based in his Department', *Irish Times*, 11 November 2010.

48. Minister of State, Martin Mansergh TD, 'Was It for This? The State of the Nation', letter to the *Irish Times*, 20 November 2010.

49. Bertie Ahern, leader of the Opposition, speech in Dáil Eireann, 28 March 1996, quoted in Laffan and O'Mahony, *Ireland and the European Union*, p. 190.

50. See Millward Brown/IMC, *Post-Lisbon Treaty Referendum Research Findings* (Dublin: Department of Foreign Affairs, September 2008), available from: <http://www.dfa.ie/uploads/documents/Publications/Post%20Lisbon%20Treaty%20Referendum%20Research%20Findings/post%20lisbon%20treaty%20referendum%20research%20findings_sept08.pdf> [accessed 27 November 2010].

51. A. Dur and G. Mateo, 'The Irish EU Presidency and the Constitutional Treaty: Neutrality, Skills and Effective Mediation', *Irish Political Studies*, Vol. 23, No. 1 (2008), pp. 107–122.

52. Countries which have signed up to the Schengen Agreement, effectively ending border restrictions between co-signatories, include members of the

EU (excluding Bulgaria, Cyprus, Ireland, Romania and the UK) and Iceland, Norway and Switzerland. Bulgaria, Cyprus, Liechtenstein and Romania are currently involved in accession talks.

53. H. Brady, *Britain's Schengen Dilemma* (London: Centre for European Reform, 2009).

54. Houses of the Oireachtas, 'Written Answers by the Minister for Justice, Equality and Law Reform' (8 July 2010), available from: <http://www. kildarestreet.com/wrans/?id=2010-07-08.2067.0> [accessed 5 January 2011].

55. Teagasc, *Ireland and the Agri-Food Business* (2010), available from: <http:// www.teagasc.ie/agrifood/> [accessed 17 January 2011].

56. For an account on ending agricultural subsidies in New Zealand, see a report by the Institute for Economic Affairs, R.W.M. Johnson, *New Zealand's Agricultural Reforms and their International Implications* (2000), available from: <http://www.staff.ncl.ac.uk/david.harvey/AEF873/ NZReformsJohnson.pdf> [accessed 17 January 2011].

57. Department of Foreign Affairs, *Statement of Strategy: 2008–2010*, p. 13.

58. N. Whitney, *Re-Energising Europe's Security and Defence Policy* (London: European Council for Foreign Relations, 2009).

59. Correspondence between the author and an EU official, 7 December 2010.

60. Laffan and O' Mahony, *Ireland in the European Union*, p. 32.

References

Official Reports, Policy Papers and Working Papers

Aikins, K., Sands, A. and White, N., *A Comparative Review of International Diaspora Strategies: The Global Irish Making a Difference Together* (The Ireland Funds, September 2009), available from: <http://www.irlfunds.org/news/ffund/diaspora.asp> [accessed 10 October 2010].

Andersen, M.S., Barker, T., Christie, E., Ekins, P., Gerald, J.F., Jilkova, J., Junankar, S., Landesmann, M., Pollitt, H., Salmons, R., Scott, S. and Speck, S. (eds.), *Competitiveness Effects of Environmental Tax Reforms* (Aarhus: National Environmental Research Institute, 2007).

Bank of Ireland, *Wealth of the Nation* (Dublin: Bank of Ireland, 2006).

Bill and Melinda Gates Foundation, *Working with Teachers to Develop Fair and Reliable Measures of Effective Teaching (MET)* (June 2010), available from: <http://www.gatesfoundation.org/highschools/Documents/met-framing-paper.pdf> [Accessed 11 January 2011].

Boyle, G., McElligott, R. and O'Leary, J., 'Public–Private Wage Differentials in Ireland, 1994–2001' (NUI Maynooth, 2004), available from: <http://eprints.nuim.ie/147/1/N142_10_04.pdf> [accessed 10 December 2010].

Brady, H., *Britain's Schengen Dilemma* (London: Centre for European Reform, 2009).

British Council Ireland, *Through Irish Eyes: Irish Attitudes towards the UK* (London: British Council Ireland, 2004).

Brown, M., *Post-Lisbon Treaty Referendum Research Findings* (Dublin: DFA, September 2008), available from: <http://www.dfa.ie/uploads/documents/Publications/Post%20Lisbon%20Treaty%20Referendum%20Research%20Findings/post%20lisbon%20treaty%20referendum%20research%20findings_sept08.pdf> [accessed 27 November 2010].

Central Statistics Office, *Census 2006: Volume 5 – Ethnic or Cultural Background (including the Irish Traveler Community)* (Dublin: The Stationary Office, 2007).

Central Statistics Office, *Ireland, North and South: A Statistical Profile* (2008), available from: <http://www.cso.ie/releasespublications/documents/other_releases/northsouth2008/labourmarket.pdf> [accessed 30 July 2010].

Clark, E., *Eco-Economy Update Series*, (Washington, DC: Earth Policy Institute, 2007).

Community Relations Council, *Towards Sustainable Security: Interface Barriers and the Legacy of Segregation in Belfast* (Belfast: CRC, 2008).

Consultative Group on the Past, *Report of the Consultative Group on the Past* (Belfast: CGP, 2009), available from: <http://www.irishtimes.com/focus/2009/troubles/index.pdf> [accessed 30 July 2010].

Courts Service of Ireland, *Crotty vs. an Taoiseach* (1987), available from: <http://www.courts.ie/supremecourt/sclibrary3.nsf/(WebFiles)/BD814893E95839F78025765E003BC6AA/$FILE/Crotty%20v%20An%20Taoiseach_1987.rtf> [accessed 16 January 2011].

Curtin, J., *Jobs, Growth and Reduced Energy Costs: Greenprint for a National Energy Efficiency Retrofit Programme* (Dublin: IIEA, 2009).

Curtin, J., Donoghue, J. and Dowling, M. (eds.), *From Farm to Fork: A Sustainability Enhancement Programme for Irish Agriculture* (Dublin: IIEA, 2009).

Dadush, U. and Stancil, B., 'The G20 in 2050', *International Economic Bulletin* (Washington DC: Carnegie Endowment for International Peace, 2009).

Danish Commission on Climate Change Policy, *Green Energy: The Road to a Danish Energy System without Fossil Fuels* (Copenhagen: DCCCP, 2010).

Danish Energy Agency, *Energy Statistics 2009* (Copenhagen: DEA, 2010), available from: <http://www.ens.dk/enUS/Info/FactsAndFigures/Energy_statistics_and_indicators/Annual%20Statistics/Documents/Energi%20Statistics%202009.pdf> [accessed 20 December 2010].

Davis, C., 'A Conflict of Institutions? The EU and GATT/WTO Dispute Adjudication', paper for the Department of Politics, Princeton University (12 March 2007), available from: <http://www.princeton.edu/~cldavis/files/euwto.pdf> [accessed 15 January 2011].

Debass, T. and Ardovino, M., 'Diaspora Direct Investment (DDI): The Untapped Resource for Development', USAID working paper (Washington DC: USAID, 19 May 2009), available from: <http://pdf.usaid.gov/pdf_docs/PNADO983.pdf> [accessed 7 January 2011].

Delaney, D. and Cavatorta, F., 'The Exclusion of Denizens within the Irish Social and Political Opportunity Structure: The Cosmopolitan Case of Muslims in the Republic of Ireland' (2010), available from: <http://www.ecprnet.eu/databases/conferences/papers/635.pdf> [accessed 6 December 2010].

Department of Agriculture, Fisheries and Food, *Food Harvest 2020: A Vision for Irish Agri-Food and Fisheries* (Dublin: The Stationary Office, July 2010).

Department of Education and Science, *Report of the Project Maths Implementation Support Group* (June 2010), available from: <http://www.iua.ie/media-and-events/press-releases/releases/2007/documents/ReportoftheProjectMathsImplementationSupportGroup9June2010.pdf> [accessed 19 January 2011].

Department of Energy, Communications and Natural Resources, *Delivering a Sustainable Energy Future for Ireland*, Energy White Paper (Dublin: DCENR, 2007), available from: <http://www.dcenr.gov.ie/NR/rdonlyres/54C78A1E-4E96-4E28-A77A-3226220DF2FC/27356/EnergyWhitePaper12March2007.pdf> [accessed 20 December 2010].

Department of Environment, Heritage and Local Government, *Carbon Budget Statement 2010* (11 December 2009, available from: <http://www.environ.ie/en/Publications/Environment/Atmosphere/PublicationsDocuments/FileDownLoad,21822,en.pdf> [12 December 2010].

Department of Foreign Affairs, *Statement of Strategy: 2008–2010* (Dublin: DFA, 2007).

Department of Foreign Affairs, *The Global Irish Economic Forum: One Year On* (Dublin: DFA, October 2010).

Department of Industry, Commerce and Energy, *Energy-Ireland: Discussion Document on Some Current Energy Problems and Options* (Dublin: The Stationary Office, 1978).

Department of the Taoiseach, *Towards 2016: Ten-Year Framework Social Partnership Agreement, 2006–2015* (Dublin: The Stationary Office, 2006).

Deutsche Bank Research, *Germany 2020: New Challenges for a Land on Expedition* (DB Research, 3 October 2007), available from: <http://www.dbresearch.com/PROD/DBR_INTERNET_EN-ROD/PROD0000000000210852.pdf> [accessed 10 December 2010].

Eirgrid, *Grid 25: A Strategy for the Development of Ireland's Electricity Grid for a Sustainable and Competitive Future* (Dublin: Eirgrid, 2008).

Environmental Protection Agency, *Ireland's Greenhouse Gas Emissions Projections 2010–2020* (28 April 2010), available from: <http://www.epa.ie/downloads/pubs/air/airemissions/EPA_GHG_Emission_Projections_2010.pdf> [accessed 16 October 2010].

Ernst & Young, *Quarterly Economic Forecast* (April 2010).

European Commission, *Communication from the Commission to the European Parliament, the European Council, the Council, the European Central Bank, the Economic and Social Council and the Committee of the Regions: Reinforcing Economic Policy Coordination* (Brussels: European Commission, 12 May 2010).

European Environmental Agency, *The Contribution of Good Environmental Regulation to Competitiveness* (Copenhagen: EEA, 2005).

Europol, *TE-SAT 2010 EU Terrorism and Situation Trend Report* (2010), available from: <http://www.consilium.europa.eu/uedocs/cmsUpload/TE-SAT%202010.pdf> [accessed 30 July 2010].

Fanning, B. and O'Boyle, N., 'Immigrant Political Participation in the Republic of Ireland: Socio-Political Capital and Motivational Stakes', working paper series WP09/12, University College Dublin (November 2009), available from: <http://www.ucd.ie/t4cms/wp12_immigrant_political_participation_fanning_o'boyle.pdf> [accessed 6 December 2010].

Fanning, B., O'Boyle, N. and Shaw, J. 'New Irish Politics: Political Parties and Immigrants in 2009', research paper (20 April 2009), available from: <http://www.ucd.ie/mcri/resources/new_irish_politics_report_final.pdf> [accessed 11 January 2011].

Fanning, B., Shaw, J., O'Connell, J.A. and Williams, M., 'Irish Political Parties, Immigration and Integration in 2007', research report on behalf of the Migration and Citizenship Research Initiative, University College Dublin (25 April 2007), available from: <http://www.ucd.ie/mcri/Political%20Parties,%20Immigration%20and%20Integration.pdf> [accessed 11 January 2011].

Farrell, D., 'Irish Electoral Reform: Three Myths and a Proposal', paper presented at the 2010 MacGill Summer School, available from: <http://political-reformireland.files.wordpress.com/2010/07/irish_electoral_reform-2.pdf> [accessed 13 January 2011].

Goldsmith Fitzgerald, *Civil Service Commission Staff Retention Survey* (Dublin: Goldsmith Fitzgerald, 1999).

Gordon, R., Kane, T. and Staiger, D., 'Identifying Effective Teachers Using Performance on the Job', The Brookings Institute discussion paper 2006-01 (2006).

Government of Ireland, *Limitation and Reduction of CO_2 and Other Greenhouse Gases in Ireland*, report prepared by Environmental Resources Management in association with Byrne Ó Clérigh and the Economic and Social Research Institute for the Department of Public Enterprise and the Department of the Environment (Dublin: The Stationary Office, 1998).

Gray, V., Kelly, T. and Minges, M., *Broadband Korea: Internet Case Study* (International Telecommunication Union, March 2003), available from: <http://www.itu.int/ITU-D/ict/cs/korea/material/CS_KOR.pdf> [accessed 19 January 2011].

Hauck, I., 'Immigrant Integration in Canada: Policy Objectives, Program Delivery and Challenges', *Integration Branch, Citizenship and Immigration Canada*, 16 May 2001, available from: <http://atwork.settlement.org/downloads/atwork/Immigrant_Integration_in_Canada_discussion_paper_Hauck_May01.pdf> [accessed 6 December 2010].

Hidalgo, C. and Hausmann, R., 'The Building Blocks of Economic Complexity', Center for International Development working paper no. 186 (September 2009).

Houses of the Oireachtas, 'Written Answers by the Minister for Justice, Equality and Law Reform' (8 July 2010), available from: <http://www.kildarestreet.com/wrans/?id=2010-07-08.2067.0> [accessed 5 January 2011].

IBM, *Five Million People Around the Water-Cooler: How the UK Public Sector can Harness the Power of Social Networking* (IBM, 2008), available from: <https://www-304.ibm.com/easyaccess/publicuk/gclcontent/gcl_xmlid/135297> [accessed 10 December 2010].

IBM Global Investment Locations Database, *Annual Report 2008*.

Institute for Economic Affairs, *New Zealand's Agricultural Reforms and their International Implications* (2000), available from: <http://www.staff.ncl.ac.uk/david.harvey/AEF873/NZReformsJohnson.pdf> [accessed 17 January 2011].

Institute for Management Development, *World Competitiveness Yearbook* (2010), available from: <https://www.worldcompetitiveness.com/OnLine/App/Index.htm> [accessed 18 January 2011].

International Monitoring Commission, *The Twenty-Third Report of the International Monitoring Commission* (Belfast: IMC, 2010).

Keohane, D., *Making Sense of the European Security and Defence Policy: Ireland and the Lisbon Treaty* (Dublin: IIEA, 2009).

Ketkar, S. and Ratha, D., 'Diaspora Bonds as a New Vehicle for Developing Countries', paper presented at the Privatisation of Development Finance Assistance Symposium, New York, 4 December 2009.

Kitchin, R., Gleeson, J., Keaveney, K. and O'Callaghan, C., 'A Haunted Landscape: Housing and Ghost Estates in Post-Celtic Tiger Ireland', NUI Maynooth, NIRSA working paper series no. 59 (2010).

Korski, D. and Gowan, R., *Can the EU Rebuild Failing States? A Review of Europe's Civilian Capacities* (Brussels: European Council on Foreign Relations, 2009).

Korte, W. and Hüsing, T., *Benchmarking Access and Use of ICT in European Schools* (Empirica, November 2006), available from: <http://www.empirica.com/publikationen/documents/No08-2006_learnInd.pdf> [accessed 19 January 2011].

National Competitiveness Council, *Ireland's Productivity Performance 2006* (Dublin: NCC, 2006).

Ministry of Foreign Affairs of the Federal Republic of Switzerland, *Peace and Human Rights in Switzerland's Foreign Policy* (2007), available from: <http://www.eda.admin.ch/etc/medialib/downloads/edazen/doc/publi.Par.0261.File.tmp/EDA%20Bericht%202007%20e%20V.pdf> [accessed 16 January 2011].

Ministry of Foreign Affairs of the Kingdom of Norway, *Evaluation of the Norwegian Research and Development Activities in Conflict and Peace-Building* (2008), available from: <http://www.norad.no/en/Tools+and+publications/Publications/Publication+Page?key=109834> [accessed 16 January 2011].

Ministry of Foreign Affairs of the Kingdom of Sweden, *Statement of Government Policy in the Parliamentary Debate on Foreign Affairs 2010* (Stockholm: Ministry of Foreign Affairs of Sweden, 2010).

Motherway, M. and Walker, N., *Ireland's Low Carbon Opportunity* (Dublin: SEAI, 2009).

Mustonen, J., Stepputat, F., Grönberg, G., Friis, K. and Rehman, S., *Nordic Approaches to Whole-of-Government: In Afghanistan and Beyond* (Oslo: Norwegian Institute of International Affairs, 2010).

National Competitiveness Council, *Statement on Education and Training* (Dublin: NCC, 2009).

National Competitiveness Council, *Annual Competitiveness Report: Benchmarking Ireland's Performance 2010* (Dublin: NCC, 2010).

National Competitiveness Council, *Costs of Doing Business in Ireland 2010 Volume 1* (Dublin: NCC, 2010).

Nielsen, T.M. and Riddle, L., 'Why Diasporas Invest in the Homeland: A Conceptual Model of Motivation', working paper series, George Washington University, Washington DC (1 July 2007).

Niessen, J., Huddleston, T. and Citron, L., *Migrant Integration Policy Index* (Brussels: British Council and Migration Policy Group, 2007).

Office of the Minister for Integration, 'Migration Nation: Statement on Integration Strategy and Diversity Management' (1 May 2008), available from: <http://www.integration.ie/website/omi/omiwebv6.nsf/page/AXBN-7SQDF91044205-en/$File/Migration%20Nation.pdf> [accessed 6 December 2010].

Ombudsman's Office, *Lost at Sea Scheme: Special Report* (Dublin: The Stationary Office, 2009).

Organisation for Economic Co-Operation and Development, *Technology Use and Educational Performance in PISA 2006* (Paris: OECD, March 2010).

Organisation for Economic Co-Operation and Development, *Taxing Wages* (11 May 2010), available from: <http://www.oecd.org/document/34/0,3343,en_2649_34533_44993442_1_1_1_1,00.html> [accessed 3 December 2010].

Oxford Economics and Economic Research Institute of Northern Ireland, *Cutting Carefully: How Repairing UK Finances Will Impact NI*, a report for NICVA (2010), available from: <http://www.nicva.org/sites/default/files/Oxford%20Economics%20Report%20-%20impact%20on%20NI%20July%202010.pdf> [accessed 30 July 2010].

Porter, M., 'Building the Microeconomic Foundations of Prosperity: Findings from the Business Competitiveness Index', in X. Sala-i-Martin (ed.), *The Global Competitiveness Report 2003–2004* (New York: Oxford University Press, 2004).

Porter, M.E., Ketels, C. and Delgado, M., 'The Microeconomic Foundations of Prosperity: Findings from the Business Competitiveness Index', in *Global Competitiveness Report 2006–2007* (Geneva: World Economic Forum, 2006).

Public Sector Pensions Commission, *Reforming Public Sector Pensions: Solutions to a Growing Challenge* (London: Public Sector Pensions Commission, July 2010), available from: <http://www.public-sector-pensions-commission.org.uk/wp-content/themes/pspc/images/Public-Sector-Pensions-Commission-Report.pdf> [accessed 10 December 2010].

Regling, K. and Watson, M., *A Preliminary Report on the Sources of Ireland's Banking Crisis* (Dublin: Commission of Investigation into the Banking Sector in Ireland, 31 May 2010), available from: <http://www.bankinginquiry.gov.ie/Preliminary%20Report%20into%20Ireland's%20Banking%20Crisis%2031%20May%202010.pdf> [accessed 3 December 2010].

Ryan, J., *The Next Leap: Competitive Ireland in the Digital Age* (Dublin: IIEA, 2008).

Saxe, L., Phillips, B., Sasson, T. et al., *Generation Birthright Israel: The Impact of an Israel Experience on Jewish Identity and Choices* (Waltham, MA: Maurice & Marilyn Cohen Center for Jewish Studies, Brandeis University, October 2009).

Solomon, S., Qin, D., Manning, M., Chen, Z., Marquis, M., Averyt, K.B., Tignor, M. and Miller, H.L. (eds.), *Climate Change 2007: The Physical Science Basis*, contribution of Working Group I to the Fourth Assessment Report of the Intergovernmental Panel on Climate Change (Cambridge and New York: Cambridge University Press, 2007).

Sub-Committee on Ireland's Future in the European Union, *Ireland's Future in the European Union: Challenges, Issues and Options* (Dublin: Houses of the Oireachtas, November 2008).

Sustainable Energy Authority of Ireland, *Energy in Ireland 1990–2008* (Dublin: SEAI, 2009).

Sustainable Energy Authority of Ireland, *Transport Energy Usage in Ireland* (2010), available from: <http://www.seai.ie/Power_of_One/Getting_Around/HCIYC/Transport_Energy_Usage/> [accessed 15 September 2010].

Teagasc, *Ireland and the Agri-Food Business* (2010), available from: <http://www. teagasc.ie/agrifood/> [accessed 17 January 2011].

UK Department for International Development (DFID), *Quick Impact Projects: A Handbook for the Military* (2006), available from: <http://webarchive. nationalarchives.gov.uk/+/http://www.dfid.gov.uk/pubs/files/qip/booklet. pdf> [accessed 17 January 2011].

Van Der Veen, G., 'Changing Statistics Netherlands: Driving Forces for Changing Dutch Statistics', paper presented at the Seminar on the Evolution of National Statistical Systems Commemorative Event for the Sixtieth Anniversary of the United Nations Statistical Commission, New York, 23 February 2007.

Whitney, N., *Re-Energising Europe's Security and Defence Policy* (London: European Council for Foreign Relations, 2009).

World Economic Forum, *Global Competitiveness Report* (Geneva: WEF, 2010).

Books and Book Chapters

Carty, R.K., *Party and Parish Pump: Electoral Politics in Ireland* (Waterloo, ON: Wilfrid Laurier University Press, 1981).

Coakley, J. and O'Dowd, L. (eds.), *Crossing the Border: New Relationships between Northern Ireland and the Republic of Ireland* (Dublin: Irish Academic Press, 2007).

Connolly, E. and Doyle, J., 'The Place of the United Nations in Contemporary Irish Foreign Policy', in M. Kennedy and D. MacMahon (eds.), *Obligations and Responsibilities: Ireland and the United Nations, 1955–2005* (Dublin: Institute of Public Administration and Department of Foreign Affairs, 2005).

Darby, J. and MacGinty, R. (eds.), *Contemporary Peacemaking: Conflict, Violence and Peace Processes* (Basingstoke and New York: Palgrave and Macmillan, 2003).

De Breadún, D., *The Far Side of Revenge: Making Peace in Northern Ireland* (Cork: The Collins Press, 2008).

Dolan, J.P., *The Irish-Americans: A History* (London: Bloomsbury, 2008).

Dudley Edwards, R., *Aftermath: The Omagh Bombing and the Families' Pursuit of Justice* (London: Harvill Secker Random House, 2009).

Gallagher, M., 'Does Ireland Need a New Electoral System?' in C. McGrath and E. O'Malley (eds.), *Irish Political Studies: Key Contributions* (London: Routledge, [1987], 2007).

Gallagher, M., 'The Oireachtas: President and Parliament' in J. Coakley and M. Gallagher (eds.), *Politics in the Republic of Ireland*, fifth edition (London: Routledge, 2010).

Gallagher, M., 'Parliamentary Parties and the Party Whips' in M. MacCarthaigh and M. Manning (eds.), *The Oireachtas* (Dublin: Institute of Public Administration, 2011).

Garvin, T., *Judging Lemass: The Measure of the Man* (Dublin: Royal Irish Academy, 2009).

Heckmann, F. and Schnapper, D. (eds.), *The Integration of Immigrants in European Societies: National Differences and Trends of Convergence* (Stuttgart: Luscious & Luscious, 2007).

Keynes, J.M., *The General Theory of Employment, Interest and Money* (London: Macmillan, 1936).

Laffan, B. and O'Mahony, J., *Ireland and the European Union* (London: Palgrave and Macmillan), 2008.

McGarry, J. and O'Leary, B., *The Northern Ireland Conflict: Consociational Engagements* (Oxford: Oxford University Press, 2004).

Mun, T., *England's Treasure by Forraign Trade* (New York: MacMillan and Co., 1895) [reprint from the original 1664 book].

O'Brien, T., *Ireland, Europe and the World: Writings on a New Century* (Dublin: Gill and Macmillian, 2009).

O'Malley, E. and Martin, S., 'The Government and the Taoiseach' in J. Coakley and M. Gallagher (eds.), *Politics in the Republic of Ireland*, fifth edition (London: Routledge, 2010).

Osborne, R.D., 'Education and the Labour Market', in R.D. Osborne and I. Shuttleworth (eds.), *Fair Employment in Northern Ireland: A Generation On* (Belfast: Blackstaff Press, 2004).

Powell, J., *Great Hatred, Little Room: Making Peace in Northern Ireland* (London: The Bodley Head, 2008).

Rees, N., Quinn, B. and Connaughton, B., *Europeanisation and New Patterns of Governance in Ireland* (Manchester: Manchester University Press, 2009).

Tannam, E., 'Public Policy: The EU and the Good Friday Agreement', in J. Coakley and L. O'Dowd (eds.), *Crossing the Border* (Dublin: Irish Academic Press, 2007).

Tonge, J., *The New Northern Irish Politics?* (Basingstoke: Palgrave Macmillan, 2005).

Walker, G., 'The British–Irish Council', in R. Wilford (ed.), *Aspects of the Belfast Agreement* (New York: Oxford University Press, 2001).

Journal Articles

Barry, F.G., 'Fiscal Policy in a Small Open Economy with Unemployment and Capital Accumulation', *Scandinavian Journal of Economics*, Vol. 87, No. 3 (September 1985), pp. 474–486.

Blanchard, O., 'Catching Up With the Leaders: The Irish Hare', *Brookings Papers on Economic Activity*, Vol. 1 (2002), pp. 58–67.

Clinch, J.P. and Healy, J., 'Domestic Energy Efficiency in Ireland: Correcting Market Failure', *Energy Policy*, Vol. 28, No. 1 (2000), pp. 1–8.

Conneely, C., Lawlor, J. and Tangney, B., 'Towards a Pragmatic Model for Group-Based, Technology-Mediated, Project-Orientated Learning: An Overview of the B2C Model' in N.D. Lytras et al. (eds.), *Tech-Education: Communications in Computer and Information Science*, Vol. 73 (2010), pp. 602–609.

Coughlan, O., 'Irish Climate-Change Policy from Kyoto to the Carbon Tax: A Two-Level Game Analysis of the Interplay of Knowledge and Power', *Irish Studies in International Affairs*, Vol. 18 (2007), pp. 131–153.

Dur, A. and Mateo, G., 'The Irish EU Presidency and the Constitutional Treaty: Neutrality, Skills and Effective Mediation', *Irish Political Studies*, Vol. 23, No. 1 (2008), pp. 107–122.

Fanning, B. and Mutwarasibo, F., 'Nationals/Non-Nationals: Immigration, Citizenship and Politics in the Republic of Ireland', *Ethnic and Racial Studies*, Vol. 30, No. 3 (2007), pp. 439–460.

Hughes, J., Campbell, A., Hewstone, M. and Cairns, E., 'Segregation in Northern Ireland: Implications for Community Relations Policy', *Policy Studies*, Vol. 28, No. 1 (2007), pp. 33–53.

Marshall, J., 'Freedom of Religious Expression and Gender Equality: *Sahin v Turkey*', *Modern Law Review*, Vol. 69, No. 3 (May 2006), pp. 459–461.

McElroy, G. and Marsh, M., 'Candidate Gender and Voter Choice: Analysis from a Multi-Member Preferential Voting System', *Political Research Quarterly Online First* (15 May 2009), pp. 1–12, available from: <http://www.tcd.ie/ines/files/McElroy_and_Marsh_PRQ.pdf> [accessed 11 January 2011].

OECD Public Management Reviews, 'Ireland: Towards an Integrated Public Service' (OECD, 2008).

O'Leary, J., 'Benchmarking the Benchmarkers', *ESRI Quarterly Economic Commentary* (Winter 2002).

O'Neill, H., 'Ireland's Foreign Aid in 2008', *Irish Studies in International Affairs*, Vol. 20 (2009), pp. 194–222.

Pfeffer, W.T., Harper, J.T. and O'Neel, S., 'Kinematic Constraints on Glacier Contributions to 21st-Century Sea-Level Rise', *Science*, Vol. 321 (5 September 2008), pp. 1340–1343.

Pritchard, H.D., Arthern, R.J., Vaughan, D.G. and Edwards, L.A., 'Extensive Dynamic Thinning on the Margins of the Greenland and Antarctic Ice Sheets', *Nature*, Vol. 461 (15 October 2009), pp. 971–975.

Ruane, F. and Lyons, R., 'Wage Determination in the Irish Economy', *ESRI Quarterly Economic Commentary* (Winter 2002).

Thom, R., 'The Influence of Sterling on Irish Interest Rates', *Economic and Social Review*, Vol. 26, No.4 (1995), pp. 403–416.

Todd, J., 'Northern Ireland: From Multiphased Conflict to Multilevelled Settlement', *Nationalism and Ethnic Politics*, Vol. 15, No. 3 (2009), pp. 336–354.

Newspaper and Magazine Articles

Audley, F., 'Ireland's Emigration Figure the Highest in the EU', *Irish Post*, 5 August 2010.

Bagehi, I., 'Austria, Ireland against NSG Waiver for India', *Times of India*, 6 September 2008.

Barber, T., 'Hanging by a Thread in Chad', *Financial Times*, 13 February 2010.

Burns, J., 'The Fat that Needs Trimming from Ireland's Diplomatic Belly', *Sunday Times*, 14 March 2010.

Business and Leadership, 'US Investment in Ireland Is Greater than in China and Russia', 8 November 2010, available from: <http://www.businessandleadership.com/economy/item/26532-us-investment-greater-in-ir> [accessed 11 December 2010].

Caffrey, F. 'The List: The World's Best Places to Be an Immigrant', *Foreign Affairs*, 11 February 2008, available from: <http://www.foreignpolicy.com/

articles/2008/02/10/the_list_the_worlds_best_places_to_be_an_immi-grant> [accessed 6 December 2010].

Cahill, A., 'Ireland Facing Court Action over EU Rules Failure', *Irish Examiner*, 26 June 2010.

Civil, Public and Services Union (CPSU), 'Communication Breakdown', *Aontas* (April/May 2005, p. 13), available from: <http://www.cpsu.ie/images/ContentBuilder/Aontas_May.pdf> [accessed 10 December 2010].

Connolly, S., 'Once More our Biggest Export Is our People', *Irish Examiner*, 3 December 2010.

Coonan, C., 'EU Calls on China to Open Up Trade', *Irish Times*, 3 September 2010.

Financial Times, 'Oil Shock "Likely" within Decade, Warns Huhne', 23 July 2010.

Garton Ash, T., 'The View from Beijing Tells You Why We Need a European Foreign Policy', *The Guardian*, 10 November 2010.

The Guardian, 'Opposition to Euro Wanes in Sweden and Denmark', 27 November 2008, available from: <http://www.guardian.co.uk/business/2008/nov/27/euro-currencies-sweden-denmark> [accessed 3 December 2010].

The Guardian, 'World Feeling the Heat as 17 Countries Experience Record Temperatures', 12 August 2010.

Hannon, K., 'Tiocfaidh Ár Mercs, He Said Crossing the Border', *Irish Examiner*, 14 December 1999, available from: <http://archives.tcm.ie/irishexaminer/1999/12/14/i_text.htm> [accessed 30 July 2010].

Hilliard, M., 'Union Leader Condones Attacks on Black Drivers', *Sunday Tribune*, 5 April 2009, available from: <http://www.tribune.ie/news/homenews/article/2009/apr/05/union-leader-condones-attacks-on-blackdrivers/> [accessed 6 December 2010)].

Hunt, J., 'Lessons in How to Go Big from Silicon Valley Success', *Irish Times*, 26 November 2010.

Irish Examiner, 'Brain Drain: 100 Graduates Flee a Week to Find Work', 25 August 2010, available from: <http://www.irishexaminer.ie/ireland/braindrain-100-graduates-a-week-flee-to-find-work-128833.html> [accessed 14 January 2011].

Irish Independent, 'Just Why a Scrappage Scheme Might Help Car Sales', 28 January 2009.

Irish Times, 'Migrant Workers Need Protection', 8 April 2005.

Irish Times, 'European Environment Agency Cites Dublin as a Worst-Case Scenario of Urban Planning', 4 October 2006.

Irish Times, 'No Directive on Hijabs in Classroom to Be Issued', 9 September 2008.

Irish Times, 'Scrappage Plan Could Raise €100m', 7 October 2009.

Irish Times, 'Renewing the Republic' series (2010), available from: <http://www.irishtimes.com/indepth/renewing-the-republic/>.

Irish Times, 'Bill to Accommodate Sharia Law', 4 February 2010.

Irish Times, 'French Parliament Passes Burka Ban', 13 July 2010, available from: <http://www.irishtimes.com/newspaper/breaking/2010/0713/breaking45.html> [accessed 6 December 2010].

Irish Times, 'Department Denies Call to Sack Economist', 20 July 2010.

Keenan, B., 'Ministers Didn't Listen to Europe in 2001, They Have to Listen Now', *Irish Independent*, 28 October 2010.

Lally, C., 'Officer's Book on Irish Mission in Chad Gives Frank Account of Events', *Irish Times*, 30 September 2010.

Mansergh, M., TD, Minister of State, 'Was It for This? The State of the Nation', letter to the *Irish Times*, 20 November 2010.

McAleese, D., 'Matt Baggott: I Don't Have a Problem with the Viewpoint of Dissidents ... I Have a Problem When Bullies Get Too Much Space', *Belfast Telegraph*, 1 December 2010.

McDonald, H., 'Real IRA Target Banks: "They Branded Banks as Criminals"', *The Guardian*, 14 September 2010, available from: <http://www.guardian.co.uk/uk/audio/2010/sep/14/real-ira-northern-ireland-banks> [accessed 14 September 2010].

McEnro, J., 'Department Defends €3m Blunder on Chad Helicopters', *Irish Examiner*, 13 November 2009.

Minihan, M. and O'Regan, M., 'Opposition to Be Briefed on State's Financial Position', *Irish Times*, 18 October 2010.

Moriarty, G., 'McAleese Attends PSNI Graduation', *Irish Times*, 23 July 2010, available from: <http://www.irishtimes.com/newspaper/breaking/2010/0723/breaking40.html> [accessed 30 July 2010].

Münchau, W., 'Berlin Weaves a Deficit Hair-Shirt for Us All', *Financial Times*, June 21 2010.

New York Times, 'Oil Prices Pass Record Set in '80s but then Recede', 3 March 2008.

O'Halloran, M., 'Minister Denies EU Officials are Based in his Department', *Irish Times*, 11 November 2010.

O'Regan, M., 'The Newsmakers: Where Are They Now?', *Irish Times*, 2 August 2010, available from: <http://www.irishtimes.com/newspaper/ireland/2010/0802/1224276043259.html> [accessed 6 December 2010].

Sciolino, E., *New York Times*, 'Britain Grapples with Role for Islamic Justice', 18 October 2008, available from: <http://www.nytimes.com/2008/11/19/world/europe/19shariah.html?_r=1&ref=sharia_islamic_law> [accessed 6 December 2010].

Der Spiegel, 'EU Commission Plans Closer Oversight of National Budgets', 12 May 2010, available from: <http://www.spiegel.de/international/europe/0,1518,694583,00.html> [accessed 3 December 2010].

Straits Times, 'Iceland to Adopt Euro?', 30 November 2008, available from: <http://www.straitstimes.com/Breaking+News/Money/Story/STIStory_308577.html> [accessed 3 December 2010].

Taylor, S., 'A New German Language', *European Voice*, 27 May 2010.

Willis, A., 'Irish Commissioner Critical of Sarkozy', *EU Observer*, 20 December 2009.

Wolf, M., 'Will the Nation State Survive Globalisation?', *Foreign Affairs*, Vol. 80, No. 1 (November/December 2001), pp. 178–190.

Press Releases and Speeches

Ahern, B. (leader of the Opposition), speech in Dáil Eireann, 28 March 1996, quoted in B. Laffan and J. O'Mahony, *Ireland and the European Union* (London: Palgrave and Macmillan), 2008.

Barrett, S., Minister for Defense, Houses of the Oireachtas, *Dail Debates* (1995), available from: <http://debates.oireachtas.ie/dail/1995/10/19/00004.asp> [accessed 17 January 2010].

European Automobile Manufacturers' Association, 'New Vehicle Registrations by Country' (2008), available from: <http://www.acea.be/index.php/news/news_detail/new_vehicle_registrations_by_country/> [accessed 10 November 2010].

Fischer, J. (Minister for Foreign Affairs of the Federal Republic of Germany), speech given in Dublin, 30 April 2001, see *Irish Times*, available from: <http://www.irishtimes.com/newspaper/special/2001/fischer/index.htm> [accessed 18 January 2011].

Football Association of Ireland, 'FAI Unites against Racism' (18 October 2006), available from: <http://www.fai.ie/index.php?option=com_content&view=article&id=1295&catid=80:archive&Itemid=355> [accessed 11 January 2011].

Gaelic Athletic Association, *GAA Inclusion and Integration Strategy 2009–2015* (30 September 2008), available from: <http://www.gaa.ie/content/documents/publications/inclusion_and_integration/GAA_Inclusion_Integration_Strategy_100110225137.pdf> [accessed 6 December 2010].

Pollak, A., speaking on cross-border issues at the Joint Committee of the Implementation of the Good Friday Agreement (19 November 2009), available online: <http://debates.oireachtas.ie/DDebate.aspx?F=GFJ20091119.xml&Node=H2&Page=3> [accessed 30 July 2010].

Secretary General of the Department of Foreign Affairs' Testimony before the Oireachtas Public Accounts Committee, Houses of the Oireachtas, 21 January 2010, available from: <http://debates.oireachtas.ie/ACC/2010/01/21/00003.asp>, [accessed 15 December 2010].

SIPTU, News Releases, available from: <http://www.siptu.ie/PressRoom/NewsReleases/> [accessed 13 January 2011].

SIPTU, 'Information for Union Members', available from: <http://www.siptu.ie/hotels/InformationforUnionMembers/> [accessed 13 January 2011].

Data Sets and Online Resources

Arthur, C., 'You Want an Interactive Map of Where Facebook Is Used? Happy to Help' (*Guardian.co.uk*, 22 July 2010), available from: <http://www.guardian.co.uk/technology/blog/2010/jul/22/facebook-countries-population-use> [accessed 7 January 2011].

Central Statistics Office, *Population and Migration Estimates*, 2010.

Central Statistics Office, *Employment and Export Statistics*.

Entzinger, H. and Biezeveld, R., *Benchmarking in Immigrant Integration*, available from: <http://en.scientificcommons.org/17691097> [accessed 6 December 2010].

European Mortgage Federation, *Hypostat 2007*, available from: <http://www.hypo.org/Content/default.asp?pageId=524> [accessed 4 February 2011].

Eurostat, *E-Commerce and Motorway Statistics*.

Hennigan, M., 'Irish Trade Statistics: Policymakers Opt for Spain and Delusion rather than Confront Challenging Facts', *Finfacts* (12 August 2007) available from: <http://www.finfacts.ie/irishfinancenews/article_1010787.shtml> [accessed 17 January 2011].

Johnson, T. and Vriens, L., *Islam: Governing under Sharia* (Council on Foreign Relations, 10 November 2010), available from: <http://www.cfr.org/publication/8034/islam.html> [accessed 13 January 2011].

OECD Economic Outlook (Paris: OECD, September 2010).

OECD Statistical Extracts Service, *11. Government Expenditure by Function*, (extracted 3 December 2010), available from: <http://stats.oecd.org/Index. aspx?DataSetCode=SNA_TABLE11>.

OECD National Accounts and Revenue Statistics databases.

Miller, R., *'Digital Universe' Nears a Zettabyte* (Data Center Knowledge, 4 May 2010), available from: <http://www.datacenterknowledge.com/archives/2010 /05/04/digital-universe-nears-a-zettabyte/> [accessed 3 December 2010].

The Schiller Institute, *The Treaty of Westphalia, 1648* (the Peace of Westphalia), available from: <http://www.schillerinstitute.org/strategic/treaty_of_ westphalia.html> [accessed 4 February 2011].

Taglit-Birthright Israel: <www.birthrightisrael.com>.

TCD Bridge2College: <http://www.tcd.ie/funding-priorities/priority/ participation/bridge.php> [accessed 11 January 2011].

World Bank, World Development Indicators Online Database 2011, available from: <http://data.worldbank.org/data-catalog/world-development-indicators> [accessed 19 January 2011].

Index